# Student Workbook to Accompany Miller and Lovler's
# *Foundations of Psychological Testing*

## Sixth Edition

Sara Miller McCune founded SAGE Publishing in 1965 to support the dissemination of usable knowledge and educate a global community. SAGE publishes more than 1000 journals and over 800 new books each year, spanning a wide range of subject areas. Our growing selection of library products includes archives, data, case studies and video. SAGE remains majority owned by our founder and after her lifetime will become owned by a charitable trust that secures the company's continued independence.

Los Angeles | London | New Delhi | Singapore | Washington DC | Melbourne

# Student Workbook to Accompany Miller and Lovler's
# *Foundations of Psychological Testing*

## Practical and Critical Thinking Exercises
### Sixth Edition

### Aimee Rhoads
*Consultant, R2 Organizational Strategies*

### Sara D. Pemble
*University of Phoenix*

### Leslie A. Miller
*Founder and Principal, LanneM TM LLC*

### Robert L. Lovler
*Senior Vice President, Global Human Resources, Wilson Learning Corporation*

Los Angeles | London | New Delhi
Singapore | Washington DC | Melbourne

FOR INFORMATION:

SAGE Publications, Inc.
2455 Teller Road
Thousand Oaks, California 91320
E-mail: order@sagepub.com

SAGE Publications Ltd.
1 Oliver's Yard
55 City Road
London EC1Y 1SP
United Kingdom

SAGE Publications India Pvt. Ltd.
B 1/I 1 Mohan Cooperative Industrial Area
Mathura Road, New Delhi 110 044
India

SAGE Publications Asia-Pacific Pte. Ltd.
18 Cross Street #10-10/11/12
China Square Central
Singapore 048423

Acquisitions Editor: Abbie Rickard
Editorial Assistant: Elizabeth Cruz
Production Editor: Astha Jaiswal
Copy Editor: Lana Todorovic-Arndt
Typesetter: C&M Digitals (P) Ltd.
Proofreader: Eleni Maria Georgiou
Cover Designer: Scott Van Atta
Marketing Manager: Katherine Hepburn

Copyright © 2020 by SAGE Publications, Inc.

All rights reserved. Except as permitted by U.S. copyright law, no part of this work may be reproduced or distributed in any form or by any means, or stored in a database or retrieval system, without permission in writing from the publisher.

All third-party trademarks referenced or depicted herein are included solely for the purpose of illustration and are the property of their respective owners. Reference to these trademarks in no way indicates any relationship with, or endorsement by, the trademark owner.

Printed in the United States of America

ISBN: 9781544359755

This book is printed on acid-free paper.

19 20 21 22 23 10 9 8 7 6 5 4 3 2 1

# Contents

| | | |
|---|---|---|
| **Preface** | | vii |
| Chapter 1. | What Are Psychological Tests? | 1 |
| Chapter 2. | Why Is Psychological Testing Important? | 27 |
| Chapter 3. | What Are the Ethical Responsibilities of Test Publishers, Test Users, and Test Takers? | 53 |
| Chapter 4. | How Do Test Users Interpret Test Scores? | 83 |
| Chapter 5. | What Is Test Reliability/Precision? | 111 |
| Chapter 6. | How Do We Gather Evidence of Validity Based on the Content of a Test? | 141 |
| Chapter 7. | How Do We Gather Evidence of Validity Based on Test–Criterion Relationships? | 167 |
| Chapter 8. | How Do We Gather Evidence of Validity Based on a Test's Relation to Constructs? | 195 |
| Chapter 9. | How Do We Construct and Administer Surveys and Use Survey Data? | 221 |
| Chapter 10. | How Do We Develop a Test? | 251 |
| Chapter 11. | How Do We Assess the Psychometric Quality of a Test? | 279 |
| Chapter 12. | How Are Tests Used in Educational Settings? | 311 |
| Chapter 13. | How Are Tests Used in Clinical and Counseling Settings? | 341 |
| Chapter 14. | How Are Tests Used in Organizational Settings? | 365 |

# Preface

If you are reading the preface of this student workbook, you are likely taking a course related to psychological testing and using the sixth edition of Dr. Miller and Dr. Lovler's textbook, *Foundations of Psychological Testing: A Practical Approach.* Along with the release of the sixth edition is this new and improved student workbook designed to help you more actively engage in the learning process. The workbook contains a variety of learning activities to help you understand and apply information, and make progress toward learning and retaining material related to psychological testing. A thorough understanding of concepts and issues foundational to psychological testing is important for several reasons. First, psychological tests affect many individuals personally, including students such as yourself. Each day, different types of professionals administer psychological tests to many individuals, and the results of these tests are used in ways that significantly affect you and those around you. Second, psychological testing is one of the most common methodological courses required for an undergraduate degree in psychology and for many psychology and counseling master's and PhD degrees. Third, the measurement of literacy, at both the undergraduate and graduate levels, is lacking. Mastering the material in the textbook will not only help you perform well in the course you are taking, but also help set you apart from other students. We believe that the material in Miller and Lovler's textbook, combined with the learning activities in the workbook, will contribute to your understanding of concepts and issues associated with the psychological tests that affect you and those around you.

This workbook contains practical and critical thinking exercises that allow you to demonstrate your understanding of material presented in each chapter of the textbook. The workbook also contains multiple-choice questions and short-answer questions that you can use to self-assess your understanding of material in each chapter of the textbook.

The workbook contains chapters that correspond to the chapters in the textbook. Each chapter follows a consistent structure, resulting in straightforward organization and quick access to key pieces of information. Specifically, each chapter is organized into seven sections.

Every chapter begins with a high-level *overview* of the textbook chapter focus and the purpose of the workbook chapter. The chapter overview is followed by six *practical and critical thinking exercises*. The first five exercises include background information and then a specific set of tasks for you to complete, allowing you to demonstrate your understanding of material presented in each chapter of the textbook. For example, chapters that include statistical concepts contain exercises that require computations and application. The sixth exercise is a *reflection exercise* requiring that you identify "Aha!" or "muddy" moments. What follows the practical and critical thinking exercises are three chapter-level projects. The first two are unique to each chapter, requiring that you integrate multiple concepts from the chapter and then produce some type of deliverable. The third chapter-level project is standard throughout the workbook, and it requires that you create a well-thought-out and professional-looking visual learning aid to enhance student understanding of important concepts from the chapter.

Each chapter ends with multiple-choice and short-answer *practice questions,* along with answer keys for both. We believe the answer keys are a useful feature, giving you a variety of low-stakes practice opportunities accompanied by feedback. This will help you progress toward learning and retaining the material.

We know you will find the exercises in this workbook to be a valuable addition to your textbook, which will contribute to your understanding of the important concepts in psychological testing.

## Reviewer Acknowledgments

Ronald S. Palomares, PhD
Texas Woman's University

Jeffrey Maiden
University of Oklahoma

Alexandra Ilie
Illinois State University

David M. Mendelsohn
California State University, San Bernardino

# 1 What Are Psychological Tests?

## Overview

In Chapter 1 of the textbook, you were introduced to psychological testing. Hopefully, after reading the chapter, you have a clearer understanding of what a psychological test is and a greater appreciation for the widespread use of and importance of psychological testing. While Chapter 1 of the textbook included foundational information about psychological testing, Chapter 1 of the workbook provides you with the opportunity to demonstrate your understanding of material presented in the textbook and apply your learning by completing some practical and critical-thinking exercises linked to specific learning objectives. Chapter 1 of the workbook also allows you to complete chapter-level projects to demonstrate your understanding of multiple topics within the chapter. Chapter 1 of the workbook ends with some multiple-choice and short-answer questions you can use to self-assess your understanding of the material.

# Practical and Critical-Thinking Exercises

## Purpose

This section contains five exercises you can complete to demonstrate your understanding and apply your learning (Exercises 1.1–1.5) and one exercise you can complete to reflect on your learning (Exercise 1.6). The exercises, linked to learning objectives, are displayed below.

**Exercise 1.1 — Why Should You Care About Psychological Testing?**
- **Learning Objective:** Have a greater appreciation for why you should care about psychological testing.

**Exercise 1.2 — Can You Recognize Similarities and Differences Among Psychological Tests?**
- **Learning Objective:** Better understand the similarities and differences among psychological tests.

**Exercise 1.3 — How Does Cheating Affect Basic Assumptions?**
- **Learning Objective:** Reflect on how cheating affects two of the basic assumptions about psychological tests.

**Exercise 1.4 — Can You Classify Psychological Tests?**
- **Learning Objective:** Be able to classify and describe different types of psychological tests.

**Exercise 1.5 — Where Can I Locate Online Information About Psychological Tests?**
- **Learning Objective:** Locate online resources to obtain information about psychological tests.

**Exercise 1.6 — Reflect on Your Learning.**
- **Learning Objective:** Describe key takeaways and confusing concepts from Chapter 1.

# Exercise 1.1: Why Should You Care About Psychological Testing?

**OBJECTIVE**

Have a greater appreciation for why you should care about psychological testing.

**BACKGROUND**

Important decisions are made using psychological test results, and these decisions can affect you and those around you. The consequences of these decisions can be significant. To help you recognize the impact psychological tests may have had in your life, for Exercise 1.1, you will identify some of the psychological tests you've taken in the past and then reflect about the importance of those tests.

**YOUR TASK**

1. **List five psychological tests *you* or *someone you know* completed in the past.** Think about tests you've taken at different times in your life (as a child, teenager, young adult, etc.) as well as in various situations (at school, work, doctor's office, government agency, etc.). Also, reflect about psychological tests taken by your spouse, children, parents, siblings, friends, co-workers, and/or supervisors. If you do not remember the exact name of the test, provide a brief description of the test instead.

2. **Explain why the results of each psychological test were important.** Think about why you took the test and how the test results were used.

| Name or Description of the Test | Reason Why the Test Was Important |
|---|---|
| Test Anxiety Inventory **(EXAMPLE)** | I was experiencing extreme anxiety when taking tests in high school. My parents took me to an educational psychologist who did a thorough assessment. As a part of the assessment, the psychologist administered the Test Anxiety Inventory to me. She used the results to help me identify some coping strategies to help reduce my anxiety when taking tests. I feel much more comfortable taking tests now, while in college. |
| 1 | |
| 2 | |
| 3 | |
| 4 | |
| 5 | |

## Exercise 1.2: Can You Recognize Similarities and Differences Among Psychological Tests?

**OBJECTIVE**

Better understand the similarities and differences among psychological tests.

**BACKGROUND**

Broadly defined, a psychological test is a procedure, an instrument, or a device that measures samples of behaviors to make inferences about human attributes, traits, or characteristics; or predict future outcomes. However, tests can differ in various ways. For example, they can differ in terms of the behavior they require you to perform, the construct they measure or predict, their content, how they are administered and formatted, how they are scored and interpreted, and their psychometric quality. In Exercise 1.2, you will explore the similarities and differences among the five psychological tests you identified in Exercise 1.1.

**YOUR TASK**

1. **List the five psychological tests**. Identify five psychological tests that you or another person that you know has taken.

2. **Conduct research on each of the tests.** To find information about each test, refer to the Locating Information About Tests (Web Box 1.2) from Chapter 1.

3. **Document the information needed to explore some of the similarities and differences between the tests**. For each test, document what behavior(s) the test requires a test taker to perform, the construct the test is designed to measure or predict, and what you learn about the administration and format. To refresh your memory of how tests can be similar and different, review the "What Is a Psychological Test" section in Chapter 1.

| Name of Test | Behavior Performed<br>What observable and measurable *action* must a test taker complete? | Psychological Construct<br>What underlying *attribute, trait, or characteristic* is the test designed to measure, or what is the test designed to predict? | Administration and Format<br>How is the test *administered*, and what is the test's *format*? |
|---|---|---|---|
| The College Board's ACT **(EXAMPLE)** | • Answer a series of multiple-choice items | • Measures what students have learned throughout high school—what is most important for success in postsecondary education<br>• Consists of four tests (English, mathematics, reading, and science) and an optional writing test (essay)<br>• Used to predict college readiness | • Administered by a Test Supervisor in a group setting, within classrooms in paper-and-pencil format, or online format at school testing centers |

| Name of Test | Behavior Performed | Psychological Construct | Administration and Format |
|---|---|---|---|
| 1 | | | |
| 2 | | | |
| 3 | | | |
| 4 | | | |
| 5 | | | |

4. **Write one or two substantive, comparative paragraphs.** Review what you learned about each test and explore the similarities and differences between the tests.

# Exercise 1.3: How Does Cheating Affect Basic Assumptions?

**OBJECTIVE**

Reflect on how cheating affects two of the basic assumptions about psychological tests.

**BACKGROUND**

When using psychological tests, we must make several assumptions. For example, we must expect the psychological test we are using measures what it claims to measure or predict. We must assume an individual's behavior, and therefore test score, will typically remain stable over time. We must also assume that test takers understand the items on the test in the same way and that test takers will report accurately and honestly about themselves and their thoughts and feelings. Last, we must assume that a test taker's score has some error, and this error may be attributable to the test itself, the examiner, the examinee, or the environment. While there are things we can do during test development to increase our confidence in some of these assumptions, sometimes these assumptions are violated. Unfortunately, some test takers cheat on psychological tests, specifically when taking high-stakes tests, which directly affects the assumption that individuals will report accurately and honestly about themselves and their thoughts and feelings. To further understand how cheating affects two of the basic assumptions about psychological tests, for Exercise 1.3, you will explore why cheating occurs, what can be done about cheating, and how cheating affects test outcomes.

**YOUR TASK**

1. **Read the information below.**

    Based on the material presented in Chapter 1 of the textbook, you have learned that formalized high-stakes tests have a long history dating back to the Han Dynasty around 200 to 100 BCE. A discussed facet of testing is the topic of cheating. It seems that when important decisions will be made based on test results, certain individuals will be motivated to cheat. Interestingly, there is evidence that the early Chinese examiners had to deal with cheating, and test examiners had procedures and instructions about how to search test takers for cheating materials and how to proctor examinations. One well-known Chinese garment that some believe may have been used for cheating is housed at the East Asian Library at Princeton University and can be viewed at the link here:

    http://eastasianlib.princeton.edu/robe.htm.

    The garment shown in the images dates back to the late 19th century and contains over 700 well-known essays. However, there is little evidence that such a garment could have been successfully used to cheat. Instead, the garment may have been rented and used for good luck.

    Cheating significantly affects at least two of the basic assumptions about psychological tests that were presented in the textbook: *Individuals will report accurately about themselves,* and *individuals will honestly report their thoughts and feelings.* Cheating obviously violates these assumptions.

2. **Answer the questions below.**

   On what types of tests (achievement, intelligence, personality, and/or interest inventories) are individuals more likely to cheat? Why?

   How might violating assumptions about psychological testing impact decisions that are made based on test results?

3. **Find an example of cheating on a high-stakes test (which is a test that is used to make important decisions) in the news and then answer the questions below.**

   What cheating occurred, who was the cheater, and what might the possible motives have been behind the cheating?

   How could cheating have been avoided or caught earlier?

# Exercise 1.4: Can You Classify Psychological Tests?

**OBJECTIVE**

Be able to classify and describe different types of psychological tests.

**BACKGROUND**

There are some common ways that professionals refer to psychological tests. Sometimes professionals will refer to a test as a maximal performance test, a behavior observation test, or a self-report test. They might also refer to the same test as a standardized or nonstandardized test, objective or projective. In addition, they might refer to the same test based on what the test measures. For example, when speaking about the SAT, a professional might explain that the test is an objective, standardized test of maximal performance designed to predict academic success in college. To help you describe different psychological tests, in Exercise 1.4, you will identify and classify five of the tests included in Appendix A of your textbook.

**YOUR TASK**

1. **From the Test Spotlights in Appendix A of your textbook, select five different psychological tests of interest to you.** Document the name of the tests in the table below.

2. **Classify each test.** Review each test spotlight and conduct additional research if necessary. Then, for each test, indicate how you would classify the test by placing an "x" in the appropriate box. To refresh your memory of how tests can be similar and different, review the "Test Classification Methods" section of Chapter 1.

|   |   | Example | Test 1 | Test 2 | Test 3 | Test 4 | Test 5 |
|---|---|---------|--------|--------|--------|--------|--------|
|   |   | The SAT |        |        |        |        |        |
| 1 | **Maximal Performance** (Test takers perform a well-defined task, and success is measured by answering questions correctly.) | x |  |  |  |  |  |
|   | **Behavior Observation** (Test takers are observed by others; often the test taker is not aware that he or she is being observed.) |  |  |  |  |  |  |
|   | **Self-Report** (Test takers describe their feelings, beliefs, opinions, or mental states.) |  |  |  |  |  |  |

*(Continued)*

(Continued)

|   |   | Example<br>The SAT | Test 1 | Test 2 | Test 3 | Test 4 | Test 5 |
|---|---|---|---|---|---|---|---|
| 2 | **Standardized**<br>(There are specific directions for scoring; scores are interpreted by comparing with a standardization sample.) | x |  |  |  |  |  |
|   | **Nonstandardized**<br>(Scores are not interpreted using standardization samples.) |  |  |  |  |  |  |
| 3 | **Objective**<br>(There are predetermined correct answers, requiring little subjective judgment of the person scoring the test.) | x |  |  |  |  |  |
|   | **Projective**<br>(Test takers respond to unstructured or ambiguous stimuli such as images or incomplete sentences.) |  |  |  |  |  |  |

## Exercise 1.5: Where Can I Locate Online Information About Psychological Tests?

**OBJECTIVE**

Locate online resources to obtain information about psychological tests.

**BACKGROUND**

Individuals in educational, clinical/counseling, and organizational settings use psychological tests for many reasons. Finding the most appropriate one for a specific purpose is not always easy. To choose an appropriate test for a particular circumstance, we must know the types of tests that are available and their merits and limitations. Numerous resources are available for finding information about psychological tests. While some of these resources contain information about tests that are available commercially through test publishers, others have been designed and used by researchers and are not available commercially but are available through the other resources identified in Chapter 1. To increase your understanding on how to locate resources, in Exercise 1.4, you will explore various online resources described in the textbook for researching and locating psychological tests.

**YOUR TASK**

1. **Identify a psychological construct that has personal meaning to you** (e.g., intelligence, aggression, anxiety, addiction). For example, perhaps as a child you were in a gifted program due to your above-average *intelligence*. Or, perhaps a friend of yours or a family member has been struggling with *aggression, anxiety,* or *addiction*.

2. **Search available online resources to find as many tests as you can that measure your chosen construct**.
   - Conduct a search of a minimum of four different online resources to find *commercially available tests* designed to measure the construct you identified.
   - Conduct a comprehensive search of a minimum of two different online resources to find *unpublished tests* designed to measure the construct you identified.
   - See the "Locating Information About Tests" section in Chapter 1 for examples of the numerous resources available to you.

3. **Document your findings in the table on the following page.**

   For your identified construct, list the tests you identified. For each test, identify the resource you found the test in, whether the test is commercially available or unpublished, the purpose of the test (what it is designed to measure and/or predict), and type of information contained in the resource where you gathered information about the test.

**Psychological Construct:** _____

| Name of Test | Resource | Commercially Available or Unpublished? | Purpose of the Test | Type of Information Available About the Test |
|---|---|---|---|---|
| Children's Personality Questionnaire **(EXAMPLE)** | Buros Test Reviews Online | Commercially available | This test measures personality traits to predict and evaluate the course of personal, social, and academic development. | Author, purpose, publication date, acronym, publisher, publisher address, publisher URL, where to find a test review, and price. |
| 1. | | | | |
| 2. | | | | |
| 3. | | | | |
| 4. | | | | |
| 5. | | | | |
| 6. | | | | |
| 7. | | | | |
| 8. | | | | |
| 9. | | | | |
| 10. | | | | |

4. **Reflect on and document your answers to the questions below.**

   How were the resources you searched to find information about available tests similar and different?

   Which resource(s) did you find most valuable, and why?

   Why might these resources be valuable to a professional in an educational, clinical/counseling, and/or organizational setting?

## Exercise 1.6: Reflect on Your Learning

**OBJECTIVE**

Describe key takeaways and confusing concepts from Chapter 1.

**BACKGROUND**

In Chapter 1 of the textbook, you were introduced to psychological testing. You read about what a psychological test is and learned a little history of psychological testing. You were introduced to the three defining characteristics of psychological tests, the assumptions we must make when using tests, and the different ways we classify tests. You were also introduced to four concepts that students often confuse: psychological assessment, psychological tests, psychological measurement, and surveys. Last, you learned about a variety of resources that are available for locating information about commercially available and unpublished psychological tests. For Exercise 1.6, you will reflect on your learning from Chapter 1 of the textbook and identify key takeaways from the chapter.

**YOUR TASK**

1. **Identify your "Aha!" moments from Chapter 1.**
    - Identify 3 to 4 new insights or realizations you had after reading Chapter 1, referred to as "Aha!" moments.
    - Consider things that made you look at a concept, your life, or an issue in a completely different way than you had in the past.
    - Document your insights and realizations below, providing details of your learning.

2. **Identify some muddy moment discussion questions.**
    - Identify 2 to 3 concepts that are still "muddy" for you from the chapter.
    - Consider concepts you still don't understand, concepts you need clarified, and/or questions you want to ask.
    - Develop 1 to 3 questions to initiate a discussion in class to further your understanding of the concepts and get your questions answered.

| | |
|---|---|
| **Insights and Realizations** | 1. _____ <br> 2. _____ <br> 3. _____ <br> 4. _____ |
| **Muddy Moments Discussion Questions** | 1. _____ <br> 2. _____ <br> 3. _____ |

# Chapter-Level Projects

## Project 1

**BACKGROUND**

Imagine a large financial institution called to ask if they could hire you to identify psychological tests to integrate into their management development program. The purpose of the organization's 12-month management development program is to ensure nominated employees receive necessary leadership training. Individuals who are interested in pursuing senior leader positions within the organization acquire the leadership knowledge and skills necessary to contribute effectively toward the growth and success of the organization. Once a month, individuals in the management development program participate in a half a day instructor-led, face-to-face course. Participants also complete online learning courses each month. The knowledge and skills taught vary from month to month. While the management development program focuses on developing critical knowledge and leadership skills, there are no existing tests built into the program to measure whether participants are indeed learning the knowledge and skills needed to be successful in a leadership position. Before agreeing to help the financial institution, you need to have some questions answered. You've scheduled a 30-minute online meeting with the organization to obtain answers to your questions.

**YOUR TASK**

1. **Identify the questions you need answered.** Based on the information presented in Chapter 1, identify what questions you might need answers to in order to identify psychological tests the organization could incorporate into their management development program.

2. **Create a well-thought-out visual learning aid.** Create a professional-looking visual learning aid to share your questions with the organization during your online meeting. Include in the visual why answers to your questions are important for ensuring the right tests are identified.

## Project 2

**BACKGROUND**

Pretend that you are a manager for an automotive manufacturing company. You were first hired 10 years ago to work on the line, were cross-trained in multiple departments, and now you are the manager. However, recently you have noticed that many of your new line employees don't appear to have the knowledge needed to effectively perform their job. Knowing that Human Resources recently started using a new knowledge test as part of the selection process for line employees, you decide to ask Human Resources to share with you any information available on what knowledge the test is measuring. Upon reviewing the information Human Resources provided to you, you find that some of the knowledge the test is measuring is no longer required to effectively run the automotive manufacturing system, and running the system is the primary job of the line staff. It now makes sense to you why recently hired line staff don't appear to have the knowledge needed to effectively perform their job. You talk to your supervisor about the situation and your concerns about the continued use of the test, who suggests that you should share what you learned, your concerns, and your recommendations at the next managers meeting.

**YOUR TASK**

1. **Based on the scenario above, create a deliverable.** Create a detailed deliverable (something that you can deliver or provide for a person or group, such as a document or plan that displays the product/process) that captures your learning, concerns, and recommendations to share with others at the next managers meeting. Your deliverable can be a PowerPoint presentation, a Prezi, or other platform as directed by your instructor.

2. **At a minimum, include the following information in your deliverable**:
   - The issues you are experiencing with your new line employees.
   - What you learned by reviewing the information Human Resources shared with you.
   - Why you are concerned about continued use of the test.
   - Your recommendations for moving forward to ensure new line employees have the knowledge needed to effectively perform their job.

3. **Integrate learnings from Chapter 1 when creating your deliverable.** When expressing your concern and sharing your recommendation, refer to concepts in Chapter 1 to support your concerns and recommendations.

# Project 3

**BACKGROUND**

Imagine you were in graduate school serving as the teaching assistant for a psychology instructor. Because some of the students in the course are struggling with the concepts in Chapter 1, the instructor has asked you to spend 1 hour with these students to help increase their understanding of the Chapter 1 material. In addition to meeting with the students, the instructor requested that you create a visual learning aid you can use not only as an instructional tool when meeting with the students, but that students can take with them and use as a study tool for future exams.

**YOUR TASK**

1. **Search the Internet to learn more about visual learning aids.** Conduct a search of the Internet to learn more about the value of visual learning aids and the different types of learning aids. When searching, consider using key terms such as *visual learning aids, graphic organizer, concept maps, cognitive organizer, concept diagrams,* and *story maps.*

2. **Create a visual learning aid of Chapter 1 material.** Review the learning objectives at the beginning of Chapter 1. Create a well-thought-out visual learning aid to enhance student understanding of the important concepts associated with each learning objective. Your visual learning aid should be professional-looking and include visual symbols and words to express Chapter 1 concepts, as well as the connections between them. Creativity is encouraged.

## Practice Questions

### Multiple Choice

1. What do all psychological tests require an individual to do?
   a. Answer questions
   b. Fill out a form
   c. Perform a behavior
   d. Sign a consent form

2. Who published the first test of intelligence in 1905?
   a. Lewis Binet
   b. Alfred Simon
   c. Robert Woodworth
   d. Alfred Binet

3. Who published the Stanford–Binet?
   a. Henry Murray
   b. Robert Woodworth
   c. Lewis Terman
   d. Alfred Binet

4. What test did Robert Woodworth develop during WW I to help the U.S. military detect soldiers unable to handle combat stress?
   a. Thematic Apperception Test
   b. Stanford–Binet
   c. Personal Data Sheet
   d. Rorschach inkblot test

5. What was the first widely used personality inventory?
   a. MMPI
   b. Woodworth Psychoneurotic Inventory
   c. Rorschach Inkblot Test
   d. Thematic Apperception Test

6. A test requiring individuals to demonstrate their driving ability is best classified as what type of test?
   a. Test of maximal performance
   b. Self-report test
   c. Behavior observation test
   d. Projective test

7. A test requiring individuals to respond to test questions about their feelings and beliefs can best be described as what type of test?
   a. Test of maximal performance
   b. Self-report test
   c. Behavior observation test
   d. Projective test

8. Which one of the following types of tests does not have answers that can be scored as correct or incorrect?
   a. Objective test
   b. Projective test
   c. Standardized test
   d. Self-report test

9. What type of test is administered to a large group of individuals who are similar to the group for whom the test has been designed?
   a. Nonstandardized test
   b. Standardized test
   c. Projective test
   d. Subjective test

10. What type of test would a classroom teacher most likely administer?
    a. Achievement test
    b. Aptitude test
    c. Intelligence test
    d. Interest inventory

11. If Jose took a test to identify his potential for learning or his ability to perform in an area in which he had not been specifically trained, what type of test would he be taking?
    a. Achievement test
    b. Intelligence test
    c. Aptitude test
    d. Vocational test

12. Joe took three tests. One required him to respond to true/false questions, one to multiple-choice questions, and one to rating scales. What type of tests did Joe take?

    a. Projective tests

    b. Nonstandardized tests

    c. Subjective tests

    d. Objective tests

13. What type of test would a career development counselor most likely administer?

    a. Achievement test

    b. Aptitude test

    c. Intelligence test

    d. Interest inventory

14. If you wanted to locate a professional test review for a published test, which one of the following would be the best source?

    a. Tests in Print

    b. Tests in Microfiche

    c. Mental Measurements Yearbook

    d. Measures for Psychological Assessment

## Short Answer

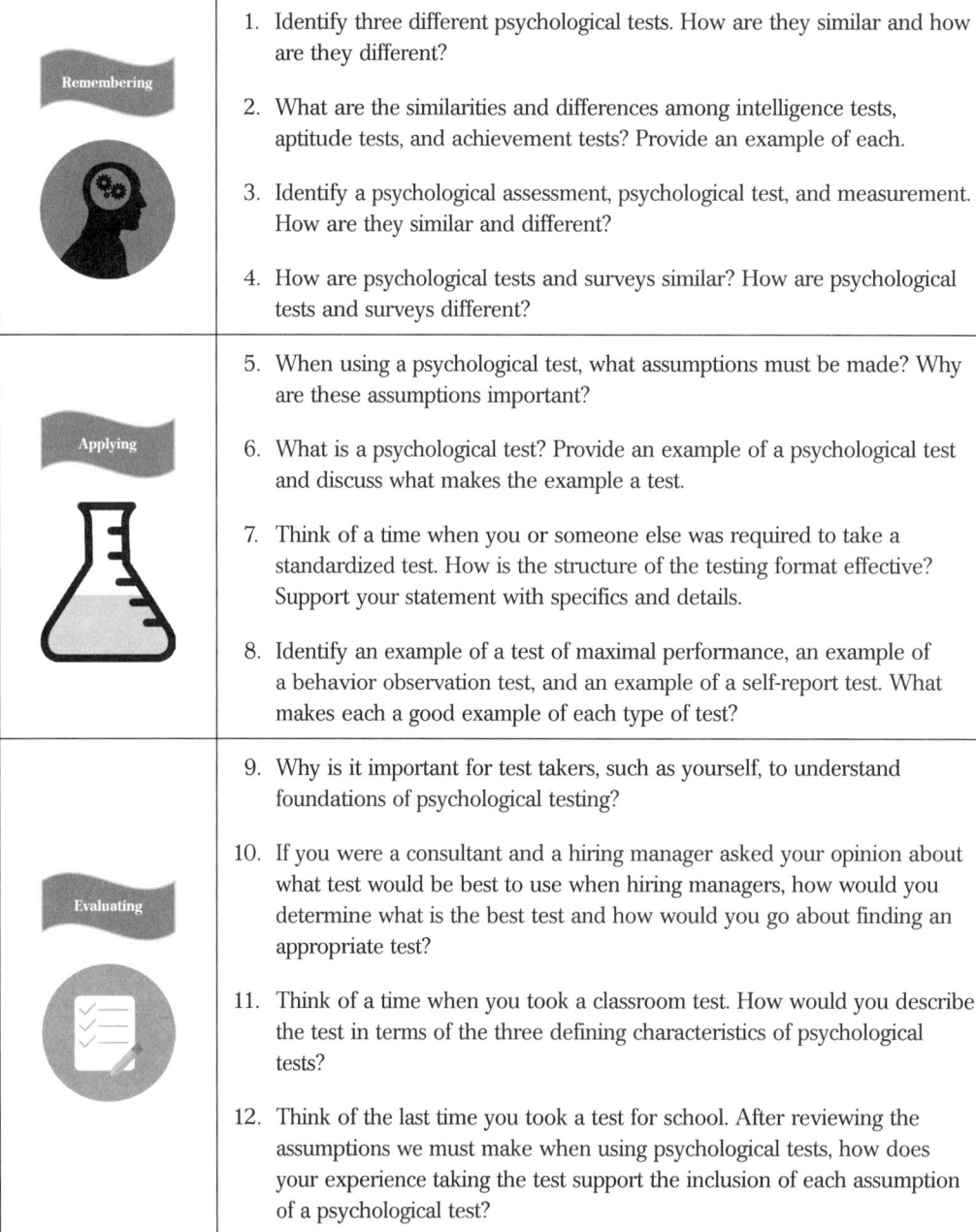

**Remembering**

1. Identify three different psychological tests. How are they similar and how are they different?

2. What are the similarities and differences among intelligence tests, aptitude tests, and achievement tests? Provide an example of each.

3. Identify a psychological assessment, psychological test, and measurement. How are they similar and different?

4. How are psychological tests and surveys similar? How are psychological tests and surveys different?

**Applying**

5. When using a psychological test, what assumptions must be made? Why are these assumptions important?

6. What is a psychological test? Provide an example of a psychological test and discuss what makes the example a test.

7. Think of a time when you or someone else was required to take a standardized test. How is the structure of the testing format effective? Support your statement with specifics and details.

8. Identify an example of a test of maximal performance, an example of a behavior observation test, and an example of a self-report test. What makes each a good example of each type of test?

**Evaluating**

9. Why is it important for test takers, such as yourself, to understand foundations of psychological testing?

10. If you were a consultant and a hiring manager asked your opinion about what test would be best to use when hiring managers, how would you determine what is the best test and how would you go about finding an appropriate test?

11. Think of a time when you took a classroom test. How would you describe the test in terms of the three defining characteristics of psychological tests?

12. Think of the last time you took a test for school. After reviewing the assumptions we must make when using psychological tests, how does your experience taking the test support the inclusion of each assumption of a psychological test?

Chapter 1 ■ What Are Psychological Tests?    21

## Multiple-Choice and Short-Answer Practice Question Answer Key

### Multiple Choice

| Question | Answer | Textbook Page | Explanation |
|---|---|---|---|
| 1. | c | 7 | All psychological tests require a person to perform a behavior. Furthermore, a behavior is an observable and measurable action. Some examples of common behaviors associated with testing include solving a math problem or answering an interview question such as, "How would you deal with a difficult customer?" In fact, reading and then circling the best answer option for the question, "What do all psychological tests require that you do?" is an observable and measureable action. |
| 2. | d | 13 | Alfred Binet published the first intelligence test in 1905 in France. However, he did have a coauthor: Theodore Simon. The test was based on Binet's work with his own children and French school children, and Parisian school officials used the test to identify kids who could not perform well in school. |
| 3. | c | 13 | American psychologist Lewis Terman adapted Binet's original intelligence test in 1916 and published it under the name Stanford–Binet Intelligence Scales. Today it is still one of the most used intelligence tests. |
| 4. | c | 14 | Woodworth developed the Personal Data Sheet during World War I, wanting to identify individuals who might not be able to handle the stress of combat. The test originally consisted of 200 questions, which was reduced to 116 questions answered in a yes/no fashion. The test covered topics such as anxiety, depression, fears, impulse control, sleepwalking, nightmares, and memory problems. |
| 5. | b | 14 | Woodworth was not able to finish his Personal Data Sheet, and it was not used in World War I. However, after the war, he completed the Woodworth Psychoneurotic Inventory for use with civilians. The Woodworth Psychoneurotic Inventory was the first self-report test, becoming the first widely used personality inventory. |
| 6. | a | 20 | Tests of maximal performance require test takers to try their best. Many tests, however, fall into more than one category; therefore, the test could also be classified as a behavior observation test because the test taker's driving is observed. The textbook indicates that many times, for behavior observation tests, the test taker does not know he or she is being observed, which is different from a driving ability test. |

*(Continued)*

(Continued)

| Question | Answer | Textbook Page | Explanation |
|---|---|---|---|
| 7. | b | 21 | Tests made up of questions that ask the test taker about opinions, beliefs, feelings, and so on, are classified as self-report tests. Generally, for these tests, there are no right or wrong answers. An example of such a test is the Hogan Personality Inventory. |
| 8. | b | 22 | Projective tests are unstructured and require the test taker to respond to vague or ambiguous stimuli. There are no objectively correct or incorrect answers. This is different from the other answer options, which tend to be structured and as clear as possible. |
| 9. | b | 21 | Standardized tests are specifically designed to be given to a large group of people who share common characteristics. The goal is to establish a frame of reference for comparing and interpreting scores, and the results are group norms. The SAT is an example of a standardized test because it allows colleges to compare students' scores to one another. |
| 10. | a | 23 | Achievement tests are designed to measure a person's learning. As a result, these tests are often called knowledge tests and are most likely to be used in a classroom learning setting. In contrast, aptitude tests measure a person's ability to perform in new situations, intelligence tests measure a person's ability to cope with the environment, and interest inventories measure a person's likes and dislikes. |
| 11. | c | 23 | Aptitude tests assess a test taker's potential for learning or ability to perform in a new job or situation. Aptitude tests measure the product of cumulative life experiences—or what one has acquired over time. Thus, they help determine what "maximum" can be expected from a person. |
| 12. | d | 21 | Objective tests most often use three types of answering—yes/no, multiple choice, and rating scales. Objective tests are characterized by structure, clarity, and a correct answer. |
| 13. | d | 23 | Interest inventories are commonly used for career counseling and making career decisions. They are not used, however, to predict job success; rather, they are used to identify how well a person's characteristics match different careers or jobs. |
| 14. | c | 27 | While both Tests in Print and the Mental Measurements Yearbook are both very popular sources for test information, the Mental Measurements Yearbook tends to contain more information about a test (e.g., validity information, reliability information, test reviews, a list of references to pertinent literature). |

## Short Answer

| Question | Explanation |
|---|---|
| 1. | Although all psychological tests require a behavior to be performed to measure attributes, traits, or characteristics used to predict outcomes, there are many differences across tests. According to your textbook, these differences can be defined in terms of the behavior performed, the attribute measured, the content, the administration and format, the scoring and interpretation, and the psychometric quality. The Stanford–Binet Intelligence Scales, the Wechsler Adult Intelligence Scale, and the Rorschach inkblot test are three commonly used psychological tests. The Stanford–Binet and the Wechsler intelligence scales are very similar in all of the areas stated above. However, they are substantially different from the Rorschach. The Rorschach requires test takers to project themselves into the test and interpret content, whereas intelligence scales require individuals to identify correct answers. Thus, the content, administration, and interpretation are all vastly different. In addition, intelligence scales tend to have excellent psychometric qualities, while the Rorschach has much lower quality psychometric qualities. |
| 2. | To laypersons, intelligence, achievement, and aptitude tests often get confused because of their similarities. All three can be used to predict similar outcomes, such as success in an education program or job performance. However, there are differences. An achievement test measures learned skill or knowledge in a specific area. This is different from aptitude and intelligence tests, which measure a person's ability. Aptitude tests specifically measure a person's ability to learn or perform in a new situation, and intelligence tests measure a more general ability to cope with one's environment. |
| 3. | Psychological assessments, tests, and measurements have similarities, as they are all commonly used to collect information and make decisions about individuals. However, there are important differences. A psychological assessment is a much broader concept than a test. Psychological assessment involves collecting and assembling information to make a decision. Some of that information may involve test results, but things such as personal histories can also be included. In addition, assessment generally includes some subjective components. In contrast, measurement refers to processes and rules used to assign numbers. Thus, while most psychological tests involve measurement, not all psychological tests meet the definition of measurement. |
| 4. | Psychological tests and surveys are both used to collect information. However, there are two important distinctions. First, tests focus on individual outcomes, while surveys focus on group outcomes. For example, an organization may give a test to employees to decide whom they want to promote. That same organization may also administer a survey to employees to determine if they are happy with the promotion process as a group. Also, test results are usually reported as a single score, but survey results are often reported at the individual-item level. |
| 5. | There are many assumptions that are made when using psychological tests. A test user must assume that<br><br>• the tests measure what they claim to measure,<br>• the behavior and scores will remain stable over time,<br>• test takers understand and interpret items similarly,<br>• test takers will (and can) accurately report about themselves, |

*(Continued)*

(Continued)

| Question | Explanation |
|---|---|
| | - test takers will honestly report their thoughts and feelings, and<br>- the test score represents the test takers' true score plus some random error.<br><br>These assumptions are important because they affect our confidence in the meaning and interpretation of the scores and relate to their usefulness. There are many actions that test administrators and test users can take to increase our confidence that each of the assumptions is true. |
| 6. | Perhaps the best way to define a test is to describe the two features common to all psychological tests. First, they all require a person to perform some observable and measurable action (i.e., behavior). Second, the behavior is used to indicate a personal attribute, trait, or characteristic, or to predict an outcome. For example, a multiple-choice job knowledge test requires the test taker to read and respond to test questions (behavior). The responses are used to indicate a person's level of knowledge. |
| 7. | One example could be when my child took the High School Exit Exam, and it's a standardized test because everyone in high school must take and pass the test so they can graduate from high school. Students can begin to take the test at the end of their sophomore year and every year after if they do not pass it the first time. Students' scores have a norm specific to the state we live in but not to the nation and is beneficial to all students. Our child's scores are compared to other students' who live in the same state and who are subjected to the same school standards. |
| 8. | Student answers will vary, but the answer should have included three different psychological tests and a description of what makes each a good example of the type of test. For a test of maximal performance, the test must require test takers to perform a particular well-defined task. For a behavior observation test, the test taker would need to be observed. For a self-report test, the test must require test takers to report or describe their feelings, beliefs, opinions, or mental states. |
| 9. | It is important to understand the foundations of psychological testing because testing is widely used in modern society. For example, test results are used to diagnose and treat disorders, to determine who to hire for a job, and to determine whom to admit to college. In each case, test scores are used to make decisions that have significant life impact. As a test taker, it is helpful to understand the foundations of psychological testing so that you can better understand if the tests you are taking are well-designed tests and if the resulting test scores are being properly interpreted and used. As a test user, it is important to ensure that you use tests appropriately, leading to the best possible decisions. |
| 10. | Student answers will vary, but the answer should include a discussion about how there is no one best test, but rather an appropriate test cannot be determined until the consultant knows what psychological construct needs to be measured. To determine what psychological construct needs to be measured, the consultant would need to understand what it takes to be successful as a manager. A good answer might also have included the importance of finding a test that meets the three defining characteristics of a good test (they representatively sample behaviors, behavior samples are obtained under standardized conditions, there are rules for scoring). To find an appropriate test, the students should have included discussion of leveraging some of the commonly used resources discussed in the "Locating Information About Tests" section of Chapter 1. |

| Question | Explanation |
|---|---|
| 11. | Student answers will vary, but the answer should have included a description of the test in terms of the three defining characteristics of psychological tests: (a) All good tests representatively sample the behaviors thought to measure an attribute or thought to predict an outcome, (b) all good tests include behavior samples that are obtained under standardized conditions, and (c) all good tests have rules for scoring. |
| 12. | Student answers will vary, but the answer should have included an evaluation of the student's experience taking the test referencing whether each of the 6 assumptions listed in the chapter was satisfied or violated. For instance, a student may describe a time when he or she took a final examination. Referencing the Assumption 1 (psychological tests measure what they purport to measure or predict what they are intended to predict), students could claim that while the instructor indicated the test would measure student knowledge of the American Civil War, most of the questions on the test appeared to be related to World War I. The student could then have concluded the test did measure what it purported to measure, violating Assumption 1. |

# 2 Why Is Psychological Testing Important?

## Overview

In Chapter 2 of the textbook, you were introduced to the importance of psychological testing. Hopefully, after reading the chapter, you have a clearer understanding of the types of decisions made using psychological test results, which professionals use psychological tests, for what reasons, and some of the controversies associated with psychological testing. While Chapter 2 of the textbook included foundational information about the importance of psychological testing, Chapter 2 of the workbook provides you with the opportunity to demonstrate your understanding of material presented in the textbook and apply your learning by completing some practical and critical-thinking exercises linked to specific learning objectives. Chapter 2 of the workbook also allows you to complete chapter-level projects to demonstrate your understanding of multiple topics within the chapter. Chapter 2 of the workbook ends with some multiple-choice and short-answer questions you can use to self-assess your understanding of the material.

# Practical and Critical-Thinking Exercises

## Purpose

This section contains five exercises you can complete to demonstrate your understanding and apply your learning (Exercises 2.1–2.5) and one exercise you can complete to reflect on your learning (Exercise 2.6). The exercises, linked to learning objectives, are displayed below.

**Exercise 2.1**
Can You Classify the Decision Being Made?
- **Learning Objective:** Classify decisions as individual or institutional decisions and absolute or comparative.

**Exercise 2.2**
What Types of Individual and Institutional Decisions Might Be Made?
- **Learning Objective:** Identify the types of decisions that might be made for a single psychological test.

**Exercise 2.3**
Who Uses Psychological Tests, and Why?
- **Learning Objective:** Identify who uses test scores and the types of decisions they make based on test scores.

**Exercise 2.4**
Why Are Integrity Tests Controversial?
- **Learning Objective:** Explain the pros and cons of integrity tests.

**Exercise 2.5**
What Is the Controversy Over Use of the General Aptitude Test Battery?
- **Learning Objective:** Identify the controversy over use of the General Aptitude Test Battery and suitable alternatives.

**Exercise 2.6**
Reflect on Your Understanding.
- **Learning Objective:** Describe key takeaways and confusing concepts from Chapter 2.

## Exercise 2.1: Can You Classify the Decision Being Made?

**OBJECTIVE**

Classify decisions as individual or institutional decisions and absolute or comparative.

**BACKGROUND**

If you recall from Chapter 2, psychological tests are important because individuals and institutions make different types of decisions based on test scores. When institutions use test scores to make decisions, they make them using a comparative or absolute method. To help you distinguish between the different types of decisions, in Exercise 2.1, you will review a few testing scenarios and then classify the decisions described in each scenario as *individual* or *institutional*, and if an institutional decision, as *comparative* or *absolute*.

**YOUR TASK**

1. **Review the testing scenarios below.** Carefully review each testing scenario, paying particular attention to who is using the test score to make a decision, and how the decision, if an institutional decision, is being made.

    **Scenario 1**: As required by the two medical schools she is applying to, Jane submits her Medical College Admission Test scores as part of the application process. Both medical schools admit 100 students a year, in a top-down fashion, using only scores from the Medical College Admission Test.

    **Scenario 2**: After completing the mandatory educational requirements, which include taking a test, a radiologist is granted certification because her test score met the minimum required to earn the certification.

    **Scenario 3**: A law school evaluates a student's score on the Law School Admissions Test to determine if the student achieved the minimum score required by the school for admittance.

    **Scenario 4**: John is uncertain what type of career he should pursue, so he takes the Strong Interest Inventory to learn about his interests/work preferences and identify jobs he might be most compatible with.

    **Scenario 5**: A public safety organization requires job applicants to take a job knowledge test. The 30 highest scoring individuals then partake in a personal interview. Scores on the test and interview are combined, and the 10 highest scoring individuals are offered a job.

    **Scenario 6**: A mental health professional administers a test to a client and, based on the client's test score, determines if the individual meets the diagnostic criteria for a disorder.

    **Scenario 7**: A government organization decides that it will offer jobs to the top 25% highest scoring applicants on an entrance exam.

2. **Classify the decisions.** For each scenario, first identify if the decision being made is an individual or institutional decision. Then, if an institutional decision, determine if the decision is being made using an absolute or comparative method. Document your responses in the chart below.

|  | Type of Decision | |
| --- | --- | --- |
| **Testing Scenario** | **Individual or Institutional Decision?** | **Absolute or Comparative Decision?** |
| Scenario 1 | | |
| Scenario 2 | | |
| Scenario 3 | | |
| Scenario 4 | | |
| Scenario 5 | | |
| Scenario 6 | | |
| Scenario 7 | | |

3. **Answer the question below.**

   Why is it important to understand the different types of decisions that could be made based on psychological tests?

## Exercise 2.2: What Types of Individual and Institutional Decisions Might Be Made?

**OBJECTIVE**

Identify the types of decisions that might be made for a single psychological test.

**BACKGROUND**

Both individuals and institutions use the results of psychological tests to make important decisions. If a test taker uses his or her test score to make decisions about himself or herself, these are referred to as individual decisions. However, if another entity (typically representing an educational, clinical/counseling, or organization setting) uses a test score to make a decision about the test taker, these are referred to as institutional decisions. To help you distinguish between the different individual and institutional decisions that might be made using test scores, in Exercise 2.2, you will conduct research on one measurement instrument and then answer some questions.

**YOUR TASK**

1. **Read the following.**

    In organizational settings, many human resource professionals and industrial-organizational psychologists use assessments and tests as leadership development tools to help employees understand their leadership strengths and development needs. The Leadership Practices Inventory (LPI) is one such assessment.

2. **Research the LPI.** Review the general information about the LPI found in On the Web Box 2.1 in Chapter 2 of the textbook. Thoroughly explore the content found within the LPI website (URL provided in the textbook). Read the general information about the LPI, examine the sample reports, read the customer stories, and watch the provided videos.

3. **Answer the questions below.**

    How would you describe the LPI to another person? For example, what is the purpose of the LPI, and what does the LPI measure?

    _____
    _____
    _____
    _____
    _____

    Why can we consider the LPI an assessment? (Be specific)

    _____
    _____
    _____
    _____
    _____

If you participated in the LPI, how might you use the results? What type of decisions might you make based on the results?

_____

_____

_____

_____

_____

If you participated in the LPI, how might an organization use your results? What type of decisions might an organization make based on the results?

_____

_____

_____

_____

_____

# Exercise 2.3: Who Uses Psychological Tests, and Why?

**OBJECTIVE**

Identify who uses test scores and the types of decisions they make based on test scores.

**BACKGROUND**

A variety of professionals use psychological tests for many different purposes in three different settings: educational, clinical, and organizational. For example, in educational settings, administrators, teachers, school psychologists, and career counselors use test scores to place students in programs and measure student learning. In clinical settings, counseling and clinical psychologists use test scores to diagnose disorders and plan treatment programs. In organizational settings, human resource professionals use test scores to make hiring decisions and determine training needs. To increase your understanding of who uses psychological tests and why, for Exercise 2.3, you will conduct research on six psychological tests, documenting what each test measures/predicts, which professionals use each test, and the types of decisions users make based on the test scores. You will then answer some questions.

**YOUR TASK**

1. **Complete the table below.** Review Table 2.1 in your textbook to refresh your memory about who uses psychological tests and for what purposes. Then, identify six specific tests (two used in each setting) by either thinking about the psychological tests you, or someone you know, have previously taken, or by conducting an Internet search to find different psychological tests. Conduct research on each test to better understand what the test is designed to measure or predict, which professionals use the test, and what types of decisions users make based on the test scores. Document your answers in the table below.

| Test | What does the test measure/predict? | Which professionals use the test? | What types of decisions do users make based on the test scores? |
|---|---|---|---|
| 1. | | | |
| 2. | | | |
| 3. | | | |
| 4. | | | |
| 5. | | | |
| 6. | | | |

2. **Answer the questions below.**

   Why is it important to understand who uses psychological test scores?

   _____

   _____

   _____

   _____

   _____

   Why is it important to understand the different settings in which professionals use psychological test scores?

   _____

   _____

   _____

   _____

   _____

   Why is it important to understand how professionals use test scores?

   _____

   _____

   _____

   _____

   _____

## Exercise 2.4: Why Are Integrity Tests Controversial?

**OBJECTIVE**

Explain the pros and cons of using integrity tests.

**BACKGROUND**

Integrity tests measure a person's honesty, trustworthiness, and dependability. For many years, organizations have used integrity tests as pre-screening and selection tools because a lack of integrity is associated with counterproductive workplace behaviors. Such counterproductive behaviors include absenteeism, discipline problems, theft, and sabotage. However, use of integrity tests is controversial. To increase your understanding of the pros and cons of integrity tests, in Exercise 2.4, you will conduct research to learn more about the use of integrity tests in organizational settings and then answer some questions.

**YOUR TASK**

1. **Enhance your understanding of the controversies surrounding integrity test use.** Review "The Controversy Over Aptitude and Integrity Tests" section in Chapter 2 and the "Integrity Testing" section in Chapter 14 of the textbook. Conduct additional research on the Internet or through your university library to learn more about the controversies surrounding the use of integrity tests in organizational settings. During your research, find four credible sources where the author discusses the pros and/or cons of integrity testing. For each source, after documenting the author(s) and title of the source, write a summary of the key points in the table below.

| Authors and Title | Summary |
|---|---|
|  |  |
|  |  |
|  |  |
|  |  |

2. **Answer the questions below.**

   What are three benefits organizations might realize by using integrity tests?

   _____
   _____
   _____
   _____
   _____
   _____

   What are three reasons organizations might choose not to use integrity tests?

   _____
   _____
   _____
   _____
   _____
   _____

   Would you use integrity tests as a pre-screening or selection tool? Why or why not?

   _____
   _____
   _____
   _____
   _____
   _____

# Exercise 2.5: What Is the Controversy Over Use of the General Aptitude Test Battery?

**OBJECTIVE**

Identify the controversy over use of the General Aptitude Test Battery and suitable alternatives.

**BACKGROUND**

The General Aptitude Test Battery (GATB) is a work-related aptitude test that measures aptitudes that can be used to help assess the likelihood that an individual will be successful in specific careers or training programs. Developed in the 1940s by the U.S. Employment Service, the GATB was used extensively by state and federal agencies to assess those seeking jobs. While the GATB use in the United States has declined considerably, Canadians continue to use the GATB as a pre-employment test and for vocational counseling and rehabilitation. To increase your understanding of the controversies surrounding use of the GATB for pre-employment screening, in Exercise 2.5, you will conduct research to not only explore historical and current controversies associated with the GATB use, but also to find alternatives to the GATB.

**YOUR TASK**

1. **Enhance your understanding of the controversies surrounding the GATB.** Review "The Controversy Over Aptitude and Integrity Tests" section in Chapter 2 of the textbook. Conduct an Internet search to learn more about current controversies regarding use of the GATB.

2. **Explain why organizations may not want to use the GATB.** Imagine you are working at a local job placement organization when you are introduced to a new employee, Rita, from Canada who has had prior experience in job placement companies. During her orientation and training, she is shocked to learn that the GATB is not used in the United States as a standard test for both pre-employment screening and job placement services. What would be your explanation to Rita for why your organization does not use the GATB for employment screening and job placement services?

_____

_____

_____

_____

_____

_____

_____

_____

_____

3. **Find more suitable tests to assist with job placement.** Conduct an Internet search to find the National Center for O*NET Development's resource center website. Explore O*Net's products page to find two to three other tests that would be suitable to assist in job placement, exploring careers, and making career decisions. In the table below, document the tests you found, provide a brief description of each, and state how each is more suitable to assist in job placement than the GATB.

| Name of Test | Description | What Makes the Test More Suitable? |
|---|---|---|
|  |  |  |
|  |  |  |
|  |  |  |

4. **Locate and take two Armed Service Vocational Aptitude Battery (ASVAB) practice tests.** Conduct an Internet search for free ASVAB practice tests. Take 2 of the practice tests you find.

5. **Answer the following questions based on your ASVAB results.**

   Why might the ASVAB be a better aptitude test than the GATB?

   What did you learn by reviewing your ASVAB test results?

   How would you feel about employers using your ASVAB results to make job placement decisions? Why would you feel this way?

# Exercise 2.6: Reflect on Your Understanding

**OBJECTIVE**

Describe key takeaways and confusing concepts from Chapter 2.

**BACKGROUND**

In Chapter 2 of the textbook, you were introduced to the importance of psychological testing. You read about the types of decisions made using psychological test results, which professionals use psychological tests and for what reasons, and some controversies associated with psychological testing. For Exercise 2.6, you will reflect on your learning from Chapter 2 of the textbook and identify key takeaways from the chapter.

**YOUR TASK**

1. **Identify your "Aha!" moments from Chapter 2.**
   - Identify 3 to 4 new insights or realizations you had after reading Chapter 2, referred to as "Aha!" moments.
   - Consider things that made you look at a concept, your life, or an issue in a completely different way than you had in the past.
   - Document your insights and realizations below, providing details of your learning.

2. **Identify some muddy moment discussion questions.**
   - Identify 2 to 3 concepts that are still "muddy" for you from the chapter.
   - Consider concepts you still don't understand, concepts you need clarified, and/or questions you want to ask.
   - Develop 1 to 3 questions to initiate a discussion in class to further your understanding of the concepts and get your questions answered.

| | |
|---|---|
| **Insights and Realizations** | 1. _____ <br> 2. _____ <br> 3. _____ <br> 4. _____ |
| **Muddy Moments Discussion Questions** | 1. _____ <br> 2. _____ <br> 3. _____ |

# Chapter-Level Projects

## Project 1

**BACKGROUND**

Imagine you are preparing to deliver a presentation at a national conference. The topic of your presentation is the widespread use of psychological tests. As part of your presentation, you will prepare an informational handout to demonstrate how psychological tests are used in different settings to make important decisions.

**YOUR TASK**

1. **Identify six psychological tests.** Review the "Who Uses Psychological Tests and For What Reasons" section of Chapter 2 in your textbook. Conduct an Internet search and locate 6 psychological tests, two used in each of the following settings: educational, clinical/counseling, and organizational. Identify tests not discussed in Chapter 2 of your textbook.

2. **Evaluate your six identified psychological tests.** Conduct additional research on each test to gather the information below:
   - The purpose of the test (i.e., what is the test designed to measure or predict)
   - The setting(s) the test is used in. Remember, a specific test may be used in more than one setting.
   - The specific professionals who use the test in the identified setting(s)
   - The types of decisions made using the test results
   - Whether the decisions are individual or institutional; if institutional, whether decisions are made using an absolute or comparative method.

3. **Prepare an informational handout.** Design an informational handout to display findings from your research. Include research you feel is most relevant to know considering your audience. Ensure the handout is easy to read and professional-looking.

# Project 2

**BACKGROUND**

You've likely taken a number of psychological tests in the past. And chances are good that you've likely made some important decisions based on the test results. Others have also probably made important decisions about you based on your test results. For example, you may have decided which colleges/universities to apply to based on your SAT or ACT results, or what major to pursue based on the results of an aptitude test or interest inventory. Likewise, college/university admission professionals may have decided whether or not to offer you admission or award you a scholarship based on your test results.

**YOUR TASK**

1. **Make a list of the psychological tests you have taken.**
   - What was the test designed to measure or predict?
   - What decisions did you or others make based on your test results?
   - If others made decisions about you, did they use a comparative or absolute method?

2. **Interview three professionals to learn about the tests they use.** Identify and schedule time to talk with three professionals who regularly use test results to make decisions. Each professional should come from a different setting: educational, clinical/counseling, or organizational/business. Interview each professional to gather the following information:
   - What tests do they administer most frequently?
   - For each test, what are they measuring or trying to predict?
   - How do they use the results of each test?
   - What type of decisions are made using psychological test results?
   - Who uses tests results and for what settings?
   - What concerns are there for the use of psychological tests?

3. **Write a newspaper article.** Reflect on your learnings from the two activities above. Write a newspaper article about why psychological testing is important. In your article, capture not only your learnings from the two activities, but the major concepts presented in Chapter 2 of your textbook.

# Project 3

**BACKGROUND**

Imagine you were in graduate school serving as the teaching assistant for a psychology instructor. Because some of the students in the course are struggling with the concepts in Chapter 2, the instructor has asked you to spend 1 hour with these students to help increase their understanding of the Chapter 2 material. In addition to meeting with the students, the instructor requested that you create a visual learning aid you can use not only as an instructional tool when meeting with the students, but that students can take with them and use as a study tool for future exams.

**YOUR TASK**

1. **Search the Internet to learn more about visual learning aids.** Conduct a search of the Internet to learn more about the value of visual learning aids and the different types of learning aids. When searching, consider using key terms such as *visual learning aids, graphic organizer, concept maps, cognitive organizer, concept diagrams,* and *story maps.*

2. **Create a visual learning aid of Chapter 2 material.** Review the learning objectives at the beginning of Chapter 2. Create a well-thought-out visual learning aid to enhance student understanding of the important concepts associated with each learning objective. Your visual learning aid should be professional-looking and include visual symbols and words to express Chapter 2 concepts, as well as the connections between them. Creativity is encouraged.

## Practice Questions

### Multiple Choice

1. What type of decision is made when a high school administrator uses your test score to determine if you should be in a gifted program?
   a. Absolute
   b. Comparative
   c. Individual
   d. Institutional

2. Hector completed several interest inventories at the career center at his college. He used the results to decide on a college major. What kind of decision did Hector make?
   a. Institutional
   b. Individual
   c. Comparative
   d. Absolute

3. What method is an organizational leader using to make a decision when the leader continues to consider your job application because your score was one of the highest on a pre-employment test?
   a. Absolute
   b. Comparative
   c. Individual
   d. Institutional

4. A manager at XYZ Corporation administers an employment test to help determine which job candidates will be offered a job. The manager first decides what minimum score she will accept and then offers jobs to individuals who scored equal to or more than the minimum score. The manager used the test to make what kind of decision?
   a. Individual
   b. Absolute
   c. Comparative
   d. Normative

5. In educational settings, teachers, administrators, school psychologists, and career counselors use psychological tests for all of the following purposes EXCEPT
   a. measuring student learning.
   b. awarding scholarships.
   c. identifying career interests.
   d. planning treatment programs.

6. In organizational settings, human resources professionals and industrial-organizational psychology practitioners use psychological tests for all of the following purposes EXCEPT
   a. making hiring decisions.
   b. diagnosing disorders.
   c. determining training needs.
   d. evaluating employee performance.

7. Which one of the following beliefs has been a major concern of the general public regarding the use of psychological tests?
   a. Test publishing companies make too much money selling psychological tests.
   b. Psychological tests unfairly discriminate against certain racial groups.
   c. Psychological tests have no evidence of reliability/precision or validity for intended use.
   d. Local and federal government regulation of psychological testing is too prevalent.

8. What debate centers on whether people are born with their intelligence or acquire their intelligence during their lives?
   a. Innate versus learned
   b. Mature versus learned
   c. Innate versus nurture
   d. Nature versus nurture

9. What test is used to determine whether individuals qualify for specific jobs in military branches?
   a. Rorschach Inkblot Test
   b. General Aptitude Test Battery (GATB)
   c. Armed Service Vocational Aptitude Battery (ASVAB)
   d. Leadership Practices Inventory (LPI)

10. What process was introduced because an examination of GATB scores showed that more Whites were being referred for jobs than African Americans and Hispanics?
    a. Ethnic norming
    b. Situational norming
    c. Within-group norming
    d. Between-group norming

11. What is the term used to describe when test takers' raw scores are compared with those of their own racial or ethnic group?
    a. Ethnic norming
    b. Situational norming
    c. Race norming
    d. Between-group norming

12. What do integrity tests claim to measure?
    a. Ability to perform a job
    b. Personality
    c. Individuals' ethics
    d. Honesty

## Short Answer

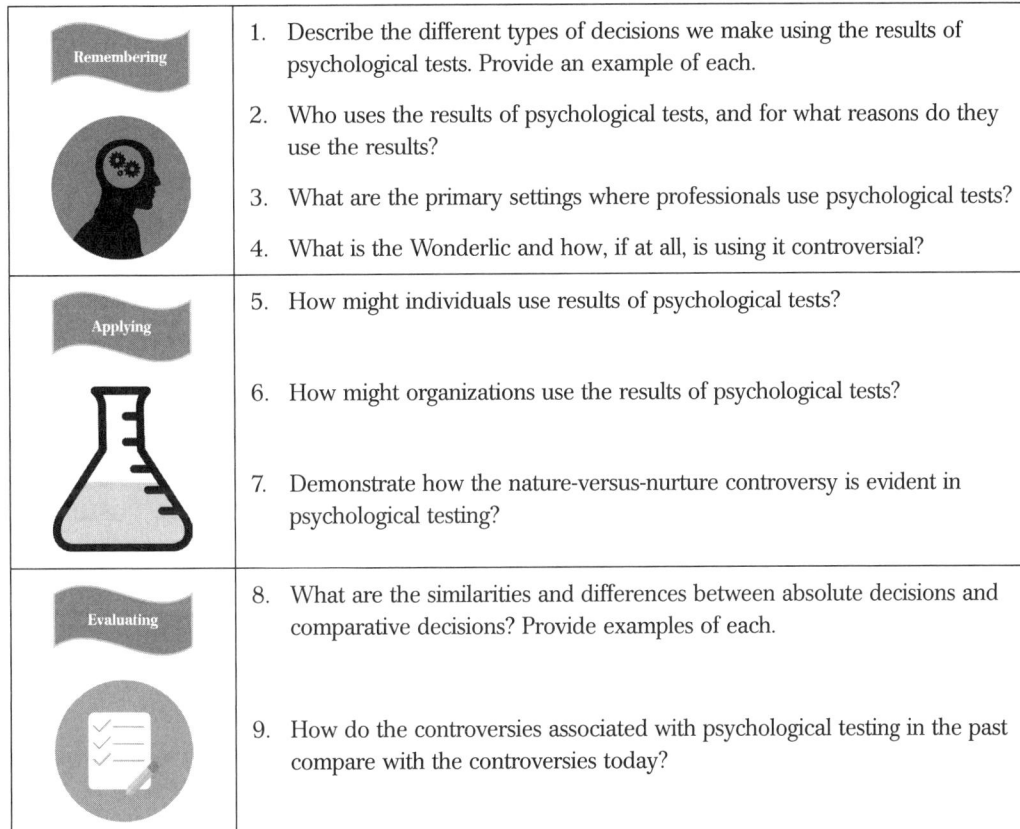

**Remembering**
1. Describe the different types of decisions we make using the results of psychological tests. Provide an example of each.
2. Who uses the results of psychological tests, and for what reasons do they use the results?
3. What are the primary settings where professionals use psychological tests?
4. What is the Wonderlic and how, if at all, is using it controversial?

**Applying**

5. How might individuals use results of psychological tests?

6. How might organizations use the results of psychological tests?

7. Demonstrate how the nature-versus-nurture controversy is evident in psychological testing?

**Evaluating**

8. What are the similarities and differences between absolute decisions and comparative decisions? Provide examples of each.

9. How do the controversies associated with psychological testing in the past compare with the controversies today?

# Multiple-Choice and Short-Answer Practice Question Answer Key

## Multiple Choice

| Question | Answer | Textbook Page | Explanation |
|---|---|---|---|
| 1. | d | 37 | Institutional decisions are those made based on a test score by someone other than the test taker. For example, a company may decide to hire an individual based on an interview, or a college may decide to admit an applicant based on his or her SAT score. |
| 2. | b | 36 | Based on a test score, a person may make decisions that directly concern himself or herself. These decisions are called individual decisions because they are made by the individual who took the test. Consider a person who takes the Graduate Record Examination—a test many graduate programs use as a part of the admission process. If the individual performs well on the test, he or she may choose to apply to schools that are more selective. However, if he or she does not perform well on the test, a less selective school may be the person's choice. |
| 3. | b | 37 | The leader is making a comparative decision because the leader is comparing your score to others who have taken the test. With this type of decision, test takers are generally rank ordered based on their test score. Decisions are often made in order, so if the company needed to hire five employees, and the top five performed well, all five might be offered a job. If a person turned the job down, then the sixth person on the list might be offered the job, and so on. Alfred Binet published the first intelligence test in 1905 in France. However, he did have a coauthor: Theodore Simon. The test was based on Binet's work with his own children and French school children, and Parisian school officials used the test to identify kids who could not perform well in school. |
| 4. | b | 37 | The manager made an absolute decision. These types of decisions are based on the test taker's score in relation to some defined standard and do not consider the scores of other test takers when decisions are made. For example, the Praxis test is a test that measures teacher candidates' knowledge and skills. States set a minimum score that the candidate must achieve to become licensed in that state. |

| Question | Answer | Textbook Page | Explanation |
|---|---|---|---|
| 5. | d | 38 | Planning treatment programs is outside the area of expertise of these individuals, and therefore they should not be using tests for this purpose. The only individuals who should be planning treatment programs are individuals specifically trained in this area—such as clinical psychologists, psychiatrists, social workers, and other health care workers. |
| 6. | b | 38 | Diagnosing disorders is outside the area of expertise of human resource professionals and industrial-organizational psychologists. While industrial-organizational psychologists have "psychologist" in their title, they do not have training in such areas, are not licensed health care providers, and should not provide such services. |
| 7. | b | 41–42 | While some individuals may have some of the concerns listed in the answer options, a deeply rooted issue is concern over discrimination in psychological testing. In the United States, concerns about discrimination and cultural bias date back to one of the first large-scale testing efforts, the Army Alpha and Beta tests. Such concerns continue today, as evidenced by laws such as the Civil Rights Act and court cases affecting the nature and practices of psychological testing. |
| 8. | d | 43 | The nature-versus-nurture debate centers the relative importance of genetically inherited factors (nature) versus environmental or learned factors (nurture) and their importance in determining a person's intelligence. What makes this debate important is that certain racial and ethnic groups tend to score lower than other racial and ethnic groups, and explanations as to why this occurs often incorporate and emphasize one side of the nature-versus-nurture debate. However, there is widespread scientific agreement that both nature and nurture play an important role in the determination of intelligence, but the relative significance of each factor is still an open question. |
| 9. | c | 46–47 | The military uses the ASVAB to predict personal future academic and occupational success in the military. The ASVAB is administered at over 14,000 locations and to over 1 million people a year. |

*(Continued)*

(Continued)

| Question | Answer | Textbook Page | Explanation |
|---|---|---|---|
| 10. | c | 46 | Within-group norming is a score adjustment procedure that used to be recommended to deal with group differences between minority and majority groups when making hiring decisions. While the practice was endorsed by a National Research Council study, the practice was controversial and was outlawed by the 1991 Civil Rights Act. |
| 11. | c | 46 | Race norming is also known as within-group norming. In this practice, raw scores within a racial group are compared and ranked based on their relative standing within the group. The relative ranking for each group is combined into a single overall ranking of candidates. Under this practice, the highest scoring individual in each group would be treated the same regardless of their raw scores. Race norming was a controversial practice and was outlawed by the 1991 Civil Rights Act. |
| 12. | d | 49 | Integrity tests measure a person's attitudes and experiences toward honesty. They also touch on characteristics such as dependability, trustworthiness, reliability, and prosocial behavior. One type of integrity test requires that test takers answer questions about their experiences, based on the notion that past behavior predicts future behavior. A second type requires test takers to share preferences and is similar to a personality measure. There is controversy surrounding the use of integrity tests, but employers regularly use them because of large monetary losses related to counter-productive work behaviors. |

## Short Answer

| Question | Explanation |
|---|---|
| 1. | Decisions based on psychological tests can be classified along two dimensions. The first dimension is individual-versus-institutional decisions. An example of an individual decision is a test taker's decision to apply or not apply to a specific school based on his or her test results. In contrast, an institutional decision involves another entity making a decision concerning the test taker. For example, based on test results, a school may decide to accept or not accept a test taker.<br><br>The second dimension is comparative-versus-absolute decisions. A comparative decision involves comparing a test taker's score to other people who have taken the test. For example, an employer may offer jobs to the top five scoring individuals with the understanding that they are the best applicants for the job. On the other hand, an absolute decision involves only looking at an individual's specific score and its relation to some set standard. For example, if a test taker achieves a certain score, he or she may become certified in an area of professional practice. This indicates the test taker has a level of knowledge at or above what has been identified as the minimum required amount for the profession. |
| 2. | The textbook includes discussion of test uses in three different settings: educational, clinical, and organizational. In educational settings, test users can be administrators, teachers, school psychologists, and career counselors. They use test results for a variety of reasons, including to award scholarships, measure learning, identify problems, and identify career interests. In clinical settings, test users can be clinical psychologists, psychiatrists, social workers, and counselors. They use test results to diagnose disorders, plan treatment, assess treatment, and counsel others. In organizational settings, test users can be human resource professionals and industrial-organizational psychologists. They use test results to make hiring decisions, determine training needs, and evaluate performance. |
| 3. | There are three primary settings where professionals use psychological tests: educational, clinical, and organizational settings. Some examples of educational settings are primary schools, secondary schools, and colleges. Clinical settings may include private practices, surgical centers, public health clinics, or residential programs. Organizational settings may include organizations, consulting practices, and consulting companies. |
| 4. | The Wonderlic Personnel Test is a highly regarded psychological test that is commonly administered in the NFL. It includes 50 questions and takes about 10 min to complete. The purpose is for football executives to measure potential NFL players' cognitive intelligence. Scores have historically varied widely with the average score being around 20; however, officials consider scores below 10–12 to be a "serious red flag" for the potential NFL player. There is controversy around the use of the Wonderlic due to bias against players who scored exceptionally well on the Wonderlic. The theory is that the higher the score, the greater the IQ and the less likely the individual would be aggressive enough on the field. However, no empirical evidence has shown a correlation. |
| 5. | There are many ways that both individuals and organizations might use test results. For example, a high school student may take a vocational assessment helping him or her decide on career options. Organizations may also give the same vocational assessment when deciding on what type of job to put an employee into. |

*(Continued)*

(Continued)

| Question | Explanation |
|---|---|
| 6. | There are many ways that both individuals and organizations might use test results. For example, a high school student may take a vocational assessment helping him or her decide on career options. Organizations may also give the same vocational assessment when deciding on what type of job to put an employee into. |
| 7. | The nature (heredity or innate) component refers to natural intellectual abilities, whereas nurture (learned experiences) refers to what an individual learns through cultural and environmental influence. The nature-versus-nurture controversy applies to psychological testing in that the test questions need to be developed without cultural or group biases. A good example provided in the textbook is that of the Army Alpha and Beta tests. They were found to be biased against African American men and foreign-born recruits. |
| 8. | Comparative and absolute decisions are methods institutions commonly use to make decisions using test scores. Comparative decisions involve comparing a person's performance relative to others who have taken the test, while absolute decisions involve comparing a person's performance in relation to some set standard. Although they are different decision-making methods, they can sometimes be used together. For example, an employer may decide to set a minimum test score to establish basic proficiency. Any applicant who scored higher would be considered employable. This is an absolute decision. Then a comparative decision might be made, and jobs offered to the two highest scores (above the minimum cut score). If no one scores above the cut score, then the job is offered to no one. |
| 9. | Many of the past controversies over testing are quite similar to current controversies and involve bias and discrimination. For example, the first large-scale testing effort during WWI, the Army Alpha test, had language and cultural issues. As a result, a second test, the Army Beta test, was developed, and this kicked off a nature-versus-nurture debate concerning intelligence. This debate has continued with Arthur Jensen's 1969 article, where Jensen stated that 80% of group differences in intelligence are a result of genetic factors. And the concern continued into the 1990s with the publication of the Bell curve where the authors stated that intelligence is between 40% and 80% heritable. An American Psychological Association task force publication, *Intelligence: Knowns and Unknowns*, did not necessarily disagree with the Bell curve, but stated that there is no support to conclude that the difference is due to genetics. |

# 3 What Are the Ethical Responsibilities of Test Publishers, Test Users, and Test Takers?

## Overview

In Chapter 3 of the textbook, you were introduced to the ethical use of psychological tests. After reading the chapter, you should have a clearer understanding of what we mean by ethics; the professional practice standards relevant to the field of psychological testing; where to locate ethical standards and guidelines; the general responsibilities of test publishers, test users, and test takers; and some of the issues related to testing special populations. Chapter 3 of the workbook provides you with the opportunity to demonstrate your understanding of material presented in the textbook and apply your learnings by completing some practical and critical-thinking exercises linked to specific learning objectives. Chapter 3 of the workbook will also allow you to complete chapter-level projects to demonstrate your understanding of multiple topics within the chapter. Chapter 3 of the workbook ends with some multiple-choice and short-answer questions you can use to self-assess your understanding of the material.

# Practical and Critical-Thinking Exercises

## Purpose

This section contains five exercises you can complete to demonstrate your understanding and apply your learning (Exercises 3.1–3.5) and one exercise you can complete to reflect on your learning (Exercise 3.6). The exercises, linked to learning objectives, are displayed below.

**Exercise 3.1**
**What Are Potential Consequences of Not Demonstrating General Responsibilities When Using Tests?**
- **Learning Objective:** Identify general responsibilities and potential consequences when using a test for selection.

**Exercise 3.2**
**What Are Some Standards, Guidelines, and Principles for Maintaining Ethical Testing Practices?**
- **Learning Objective:** Distinguish between four common publications developed to help test users achieve and maintain ethical testing practices.

**Exercise 3.3**
**Are All Test User Qualifications the Same?**
- **Learning Objective:** Compare and contrast the test user qualifications of different publishers and psychological tests.

**Exercise 3.4**
**Were My Test Taker Rights Violated?**
- **Learning Objective:** Apply understanding of test taker rights and responsibilities to personal testing experiences.

**Exercise 3.5**
**What Accommodations Are Appropriate for Persons With Disabilities?**
- **Learning Objective:** Describe potential testing modifications and predict consequences for not accommodating persons with disabilities.

**Exercise 3.6**
**Reflect on Your Learning.**
- **Learning Objective:** Describe key takeaways and confusing concepts from Chapter 3.

# Exercise 3.1: What Are Potential Consequences of Not Demonstrating General Responsibilities When Using Tests?

**OBJECTIVE**

Identify general responsibilities and potential consequences when using a test for selection.

**BACKGROUND**

How a test is used is just as important as choosing an appropriate test. Remember, various types of professionals use tests to make important decisions in educational, clinical, and organizational settings, so proper use of a test is critical. Unfortunately, misuse by those administering and taking tests, as well as those scoring and interpreting test results, can harm individuals and society. For individuals, test misuse may result in inappropriate decisions and improper diagnoses. Test misuse reflects poorly on professional organizations and properly trained test users. To increase your understanding of the consequences of improper test use, for Exercise 3.1, you will imagine you are involved in a testing situation and, after identifying some relevant test user and/or test taker responsibilities, determine the potential consequences of not abiding by the identified responsibilities.

**YOUR TASK**

1. **Read the information below.**

    Assume you are the Director of Training and Development for a home loan servicing bank. After earning a master's degree in psychology about 15 years ago, you spent 2 years as a loan officer at the bank. You then took a training position within the Human Resources (HR) Department, where you were quickly promoted into positions of increasing responsibility. Last year, you were promoted into the Director role.

    Recently, the bank's Board of Directors voted and agreed that the bank needs to reorganize departments and combine units with similar job functions into one department. Per the Board, current supervisors will remain in their position, but individual units will move to a different department that share similar functions to form three new departments. Given the new departments, the Board has directed HR to hire three new supervisors.

    The Board would like to fill the three supervisory roles with internal candidates to reduce the need to train outside employees, to maintain some consistency during the reorganization process, and to promote opportunities for growth for current employees. The Board asked you to design a test that will be used as part of the selection process to measure the supervisory skills of applicants for the supervisory roles. You've never designed a test before but did as the Board directed.

    Your son-in-law, who also works for the bank, expressed interest in applying for one of the jobs. Your son-in-law and daughter are expecting their first child, and you know this promotion would greatly help them. Your son-in-law has worked for the company for a year and wants to advance within the company. However, given your knowledge of what the test measures, you are not confident he will be able to pass the test.

2. **Document your findings in the table on the following page.** Complete the table below to summarize potential ethical issues given the information above. Access three of the Professional Practice Standards relevant to psychological testing found in On the Web Box 3.1. From each of the three standards selected, identify one general responsibility of a test user or test taker and the potential ethical issue(s) that might result from not abiding by

the responsibility. Describe each responsibility and the potential ethical issue(s) in the following chart, using the example as a guide.

| Professional Practice Standard | General Responsibility | Potential Ethical Issue and Consequence |
|---|---|---|
| (*Example*) American Psychological Association's Ethical Principles of Psychologists and Code of Conduct | According to ethical standard 3.06 (Conflict of Interest), as a psychologist, I should not take on a professional role when personal, scientific, professional, legal, financial, or other interests or relationships could reasonably be expected to (1) impair my objectivity, competence, or effectiveness in performing my function or (2) expose me or the bank to harm or exploitation. | Given my role in the organization and what I've been asked to do, my objectivity may be compromised. In my current position, my knowledge of the test content and my close personal relationship with a candidate may result in a potential conflict. If I provide my son-in-law with information regarding the test, I would be . . . |
| 1. | | |
| 2. | | |
| 3. | | |

# Exercise 3.2: What Are Some Standards, Guidelines, and Principles for Maintaining Ethical Testing Practices?

### OBJECTIVE

Distinguish between four common publications developed to help test users achieve and maintain ethical testing practices.

### BACKGROUND

Many professionals use psychological tests in a variety of settings, including educational, clinical, and organizational settings, to make important decisions. Unfortunately, misuse by those administering and taking tests, as well as those scoring and interpreting test results, is a chronic and disturbing problem that can harm individuals and society. For individuals, test misuse may result in inappropriate decisions and improper diagnoses. Test misuse also reflects poorly on professional organizations and properly trained test users, resulting in poor decisions that can harm individuals and the public. Often those who administer tests do not misuse tests intentionally; rather, they do so because of inadequate technical knowledge and misinformation about proper testing procedures. To prevent test misuse, psychologists and others have developed technical and professional standards, guidelines, and principles for constructing, evaluating, administrating, scoring, and interpreting psychological tests. For Exercise 3.2, you will explore some of the standards, guidelines, and principles developed to help test users achieve and maintain ethical testing practices.

### YOUR TASK

1. **Review four publications on achieving and maintaining ethical testing practices**. Access the American Psychological Association (APA) Science Directorate's Testing and Assessment website using the link in On the Web Box 3.2. After accessing the FAQ: Finding Information About Psychological Tests link, click on the link titled Additional Information on the Proper Use of Tests. Review each of the four publications to learn more about the standards, guidelines, and principles developed to help test users achieve and maintain ethical testing practices.

2. **Document your findings in the chart on the following page.** For each publication, identify who should abide by the guidelines in the publication and why (e.g., a member of a specific association, an educator designing a districtwide assessment), what valuable information is contained within the publication, and one or two unique elements found in each publication.

| Publication Name | Who should abide by the guidelines, and why? | What valuable information is contained within the publication? | What makes the publication unique from the others? |
|---|---|---|---|
| 1. | | | |
| 2. | | | |
| 3. | | | |
| 4. | | | |

Chapter 3 ■ What Are the Ethical Responsibilities of Test Publishers, Test Users, and Test Takers?

# Exercise 3.3: Are All Test User Qualifications the Same?

**OBJECTIVE**

Compare and contrast the test user qualifications of different publishers and psychological tests.

**BACKGROUND**

Test publishers have thousands of psychological tests and assessment tools commercially available for purchase. Test publishers market their tests in test catalogues and on their websites. Ethically, test publishers should sell psychological tests only to individuals who are appropriately trained to administer, score, and interpret them. Therefore, to purchase any one psychological test or assessment, test publishers require that individuals meet specific qualifications. Many test publishers classify each test they market with a user qualification code (for example, Level A, Level B, Level C). To help you recognize the similarities and differences in test user qualifications across publishers and tests, for Exercise 3.3, you will identify six psychological tests, document information about each test, and then answer some short-answer questions.

**YOUR TASK**

1. **Identify six psychological tests.** Search test publisher websites, or Appendix A of your textbook, to identify six psychological tests of interest to you (two Level A from different publishers, two Level B from different publishers, and two Level C from different publishers).

2. **Determine the construct measured by each test.** Read information provided on the test publisher's website to determine what each of the six tests is designed to measure.

3. **Determine the test user qualifications for each test.** Search the test publisher website for each test to determine what qualifications a person must have to purchase each test.

4. **Document your findings in the table below.** For each test, document the name of the test, the construct the test measures, the test publisher, and the user qualifications in the table below.

| Test Name | Test Publisher | Construct Measured | User Qualifications |
|---|---|---|---|
| Wechsler Intelligence Scale for Children—Fourth Edition (WISC-IV) (EXAMPLE) | Pearson | Measures children's intellectual ability | • This test has a Qualification Level C.<br>• To purchase this test, a person must have significant expertise interpreting tests. To purchase the test, a person must meet one of three criteria: (a) have a doctorate degree in psychology, education, or a closely related field with formal training in the ethical administration, scoring, and |

*(Continued)*

(Continued)

| Test Name | Test Publisher | Construct Measured | User Qualifications |
|---|---|---|---|
| Wechsler adult intelligence scale (4th edition) | Pearsons assessment | intellectual ability of adults | interpretation of clinical assessments related to the intended use of the assessment; (b) be licensed or have certified practice in his or her state in a field related to the purchase; or (c) be an active member of or have a certification from a professional organization that requires training and experience in the relevant area of assessment. level C |
| Stanford-Binet intelligence scale | PRO-ED | assess intelligence and cognitive abilities of children + adults ages 2-89 | level C qualifications doctorate in psych or related field. licensed or certified to practice in your state. |
| Myers Briggs type indicator | CPP | personality test. helps individuals understand personality preferences | level B qualifications either, masters in psych (related field) certified or active member of group, degree or license, or formal mental health / edu training |
| NEO personality inventory-3 | PAR | assess normal personality in children + adults ages 12+ | level B ↓ |
| Graduate record examination | educational testing service | gauge undergrad achievement in 8 fields of study | Level A no qualifications are required |
| SAT | educational testing service | college entrance exam | Level A no qualifications are required |

5. **Answer the questions below**. Review what you learned about each test and write one paragraph (three to five sentences) to answer each question below.

   How are publisher descriptions of user qualifications within qualification levels (e.g., for Level A) similar and/or different?

   _____

   _____

   _____

   _____

   _____

   _____

   _____

   _____

   How are different publisher descriptions of user qualification levels (Level A, B, C) similar and/or different?

   _____

   _____

   _____

   _____

   _____

   _____

   _____

   _____

   Why do you think there are different qualification levels for the tests you selected?

   _____

   _____

   _____

   _____

   _____

   _____

   _____

   _____

## Exercise 3.4: Were My Test Taker Rights Violated?

**OBJECTIVE**

Apply understanding of test taker rights and responsibilities to personal testing experiences.

**BACKGROUND**

Professionals in educational, clinical, and organizational settings use results from psychological tests to make important decisions about people. For example, college admission staff may have used your SAT or ACT score when making a decision about whether to admit you. Likewise, individuals like you who take psychological tests use the results to learn about themselves and make personal decisions. For example, you may have considered your performance on the SAT or ACT when deciding which colleges and universities you would apply to. Or, when reading a magazine, you may have taken a brief test to find your perfect skin routine or determine what your college major should be. To help you recognize the similarities and differences in test user qualifications across publishers and tests, for Exercise 3.4, you will identify six psychological tests, document information about each test, and then answer some short-answer questions.

**YOUR TASK**

1. **Think about your experience with psychological testing.** Identify two experiences taking a psychological test. Have one experience be when a professional used your test score to make a decision about you, and one experience be when you took a test and used the results to learn or make a personal decision about yourself. Describe each experience in one of the tables below (e.g., Experience 1: An HR professional administered a personality test to me when I applied for a sales manager job at a local retail store).

2. **Identify the test taker rights afforded and violated.** Review the "Test Taker Rights" section of Chapter 3. For each testing experience you identified, find up to three test taker rights that you were afforded (actively observed) and three test taker rights that you feel were violated or that could have been violated. Document each test taker right in the table provided and include a description of the situation where the right was afforded or violated. For each actively observed right, document the impact affording you that right had on you. For each right violated or that could have been violated, document the potential or realized negative consequences. Document your findings in Chart 1.

3. **Identify the test taker responsibilities fulfilled and not fulfilled.** Review the "Test Taker Responsibilities" section of Chapter 3. After reflecting on each experience, identify up to three test taker responsibilities that you fulfilled and three test taker responsibilities that you did not fulfill or may not have fulfilled. Document each responsibility in the table below, including a description of the situation where you did or did not fulfill your responsibility. For each fulfilled responsibility, document the positive implication(s). For each responsibility not fulfilled, document the potential or realized negative consequences. Document your findings in Chart 2.

| CHART 1 | | | |
|---|---|---|---|
| **Experience 1** | **Test Taker Right** | **Situation** | **Implication/ Consequence** |
| **Rights Afforded** | 1. | | |
| | 2. | | |
| | 3. | | |
| **Rights Violated** | 1. | | |
| | 2. | | |
| | 3. | | |
| **Experience 2** | **Test Taker Right** | **Situation** | **Implication/ Consequence** |
| **Rights Afforded** | 1. | | |
| | 2. | | |
| | 3. | | |
| **Rights Violated** | 1. | | |
| | 2. | | |
| | 3. | | |

| CHART 2 | | | |
|---|---|---|---|
| **Experience 1** | **Test Taker Responsibility** | **Situation** | **Implication/ Consequence** |
| **Responsibilities Fulfilled** | 1. | | |
| | 2. | | |
| | 3. | | |
| **Responsibilities Not Fulfilled** | 1. | | |
| | 2. | | |
| | 3. | | |
| **Experience 2** | **Test Taker Responsibility** | **Situation** | **Implication/ Consequence** |
| **Responsibilities Fulfilled** | 1. | | |
| | 2. | | |
| | 3. | | |
| **Responsibilities Not Fulfilled** | 1. | | |
| | 2. | | |
| | 3. | | |

4. **Prepare a short argument about the importance of ensuring test takers receive all deserved rights.** Reflect on your two test-taking experiences and the rights you were afforded and the rights that were violated. Write a one-paragraph argument about why it's important for professionals to ensure test takers receive all deserved rights.

5. **Prepare a short argument about the importance of test takers fulfilling their responsibilities.** Reflect on your two test-taking experiences and the responsibilities you did and did not fulfill. Write a one-paragraph argument about why it's important for test takers to fulfill their responsibilities when taking tests.

## Exercise 3.5: What Accommodations Are Appropriate for Persons With Disabilities?

**OBJECTIVE**

Describe potential testing modifications and predict consequences for not accommodating persons with disabilities.

**BACKGROUND**

According to the *Standards for Educational and Psychological Testing*, test scores should accurately reflect the construct that is being measured by a test. When individuals with disabilities take a test, their test scores may not accurately reflect that construct due to the disability. For instance, a test taker may not be able to complete a test because of the way in which it was delivered (e.g., delivering a paper and pencil test to someone who has a motor skill deficiency, which makes it difficult for them to write quickly enough). As you learned prior, we often use psychological test scores to make important decisions. If an individual, due to a disability, is unable to complete a test or achieves a score that does not accurately measure the construct that the test is designed to measure, decisions made based on the interpretation of those test scores may not be valid. As a result, individuals with disabilities might need special accommodations during testing to ensure that their test scores properly represent their capability on the construct that the test is designed to measure. The accommodations depend on the specific disability. To increase your understanding of administration and interpretation accommodations when testing individuals with disabilities, in Exercise 3.5, you will explore some of the administration and interpretation modifications test developers or users might make for individuals with visual, hearing, motor, and cognitive impairments; identify the potential consequences of not making modifications; and explore tests developed specifically for persons with physical or mental challenges.

**YOUR TASK**

1. **Identify administration and interpretation modifications.** Review the *Guidelines for Accommodating Test Takers with Disabilities* found in For Your Information Box 3.2. Select one modification from each of the four categories of impairments (visual, hearing, motor, and cognitive). Identify one modification from each category and document the modification in the chart below. Reflect on possible ramifications (consequences) for a test developer or a user not making the modifications.

   | Visual Impairment | Modification: |
   |---|---|
   | • Ramification: | |

   | Hearing Impairment | Modification: |
   |---|---|
   | • Ramification: | |

   | Motor Impairment | Modification: |
   |---|---|
   | • Ramification: | |

   | Cognitive Impairment | Modification: |
   |---|---|
   | • Ramification: | |

2. **Identify tests developed specifically for persons with disabilities**. Review the Tests Developed Specifically for Persons With Physical or Mental Challenges found in Table 3.1. Select one test from each category. Document the selected tests in the appropriate place below. Conduct research to learn as much as you can about each identified test. For each test, write one paragraph answering the following questions:
   - What does the test measure?
   - How is the test modified for the specific impairment?
   - What comparable test could be used for individuals without the disability?

**Visual Impairment Test:** _____

_____
_____
_____
_____
_____
_____

**Hearing Impairment Test:** _____

_____
_____
_____
_____
_____
_____

**Motor Impairment Test:** _____

_____
_____
_____
_____
_____
_____

**Cognitive Impairment Test:** _____

_____
_____
_____
_____
_____
_____

# Exercise 3.6: Reflect on Your Learning

**OBJECTIVE**

Describe key takeaways and confusing concepts from Chapter 3.

**BACKGROUND**

In Chapter 3 of the textbook, you read about the ethical use of psychological tests. You learned what we mean by ethics. You also learned about some of the professional practice standards most relevant to the field of psychological testing, as well as the general responsibilities of test publishers, test users, and test takers. Finally, you were also introduced to some of the issues related to testing special populations. For Exercise 3.6, you will reflect on your learning from Chapter 3 of the textbook and identify key takeaways from the chapter.

**YOUR TASK**

1. **Identify your "Aha!" moments from Chapter 3**.
   - Identify 3 to 4 new insights or realizations you had after reading Chapter 3, referred to as "Aha!" moments.
   - Consider things that made you look at a concept, your life, or an issue in a completely different way than you had in the past.
   - Document your insights and realizations below, providing details of your learning.

2. **Identify some muddy moment discussion questions.**
   - Identify 2 to 3 concepts that are still "muddy" for you from the chapter.
   - Consider concepts you still don't understand, concepts you need clarified, and/or questions you want to ask.
   - Develop 1 to 3 questions to initiate a discussion in class to further your understanding of the concepts and get your questions answered.

| **Insights and Realizations** | 1. _____ <br> 2. _____ <br> 3. _____ <br> 4. _____ |
|---|---|
| **Muddy Moments Discussion Questions** | 1. _____ <br> 2. _____ <br> 3. _____ |

# Chapter-Level Projects

## Project 1

**BACKGROUND**

Imagine you've been working at a distribution center for 15 years, and currently you're a senior team lead and trainer. The distribution center stores and distributes products to online e-retailers and e-commerce businesses. In the last 5 years, the distribution center has incorporated new technology, based on technological advances, to improve the automation processes for moving products in, around, and out of the facility. These changes have significantly affected the knowledge, skills, and abilities distribution center employees need to effectively perform their jobs. This change in required knowledge, skills, and abilities of distribution center employees has significant implications for the tests the distribution center currently uses as part of the process for selecting distribution center employees and for evaluating staff learning during the new hire training program. New tests will need to be identified or created to be integrated into the selection and new hire training program.

Because of a prior lawsuit a former employee brought against the distribution center as a result of improper test use, your manager is very concerned that professional practice guidelines are followed when selecting, administering, and using the results of tests when selecting employees and training employees. Because you have the most experience as the team lead, and due to the trust the HR Director has in you, she has requested that you work closely with her to ensure the steps taken to select or develop the tests, implement the tests, and use the test scores to follow ethical guidelines and professional practice standards.

**YOUR TASK**

1. **Review Chapter 3**. Thoroughly review the content in the following three sections of Chapter 3:
   - Professional Practice Standards
   - General Responsibilities of Test Publishers, Test Users, and Test Takers
   - Testing Special Populations

2. **Prepare a recommendation report**. Write a 2- to 3-page recommendation report that comprehensively and clearly documents the steps you believe need to be taken to ensure all professional practice guidelines are followed when selecting, administering, and using the results of the tests to be used as part of the selection process and training program.

# Project 2

**BACKGROUND**

Imagine that you are an undergraduate student pursuing a degree in psychology. During your final year of college, you experienced the three situations below in different classes:

**Situation 1**: On the first day of class, your professor informed the entire class that each student would be required to either participate in a research study she was conducting on personality *or* write a 10-page paper at the end of class. She explained that participation in the study would take approximately 60 minutes and would involve taking several cognitive ability tests. The professor also explained that she definitely preferred that students participate in her study, rather than writing the paper.

**Situation 2:** When discussing the concept of personality disorders in an abnormal psychology course, your professor (who is a clinical psychologist and has his own clinical psychology practice) brought to class his materials for the Rorschach Inkblot test. He showed you each of the test's 10 inkblots, which were printed on cards. He also explained that the Rorschach Inkblot test is the primary test he uses in his practice.

**Situation 3:** One of the required activities at the end of your Psychology of Leadership course was to participate in a multi-rater (or 360-degree) feedback process. The purpose of the feedback process was for you to obtain feedback from individuals you worked closely with throughout the semester on the extent to which you demonstrated key leadership behaviors you learned about during the semester. The entire process was implemented online, requiring that you, your instructor, and each of your classmates complete a survey rating the extent to which you demonstrated each of 25 leadership behaviors throughout the course. Upon completing the process, your instructor sent you an individualized report with detailed results, including your leadership strengths and opportunities for improvement. Your instructor asked that you bring your report to class, and after breaking into smaller groups, exchange, review, and discuss one another's results.

**YOUR TASK**

1. **Review Chapter 3**. Thoroughly review the content in the following two sections of Chapter 3:
   - Professional Practice Standards
   - General Responsibilities of Test Publishers, Test Users, and Test Takers

2. **Prepare a PowerPoint or Prezi presentation**. Prepare a 9-slide PowerPoint or Prezi presentation. Prepare three slides for each situation listed above and describe, in detail, the following:
   - The situation
   - The potential ethical issues you identified based on your review of professional practice standards *and* the general responsibilities of test publishers, test users, and test takers
   - How the ethical issue(s) could have been avoided

# Project 3

**BACKGROUND**

Imagine you were in graduate school serving as the teaching assistant for a psychology instructor. Because some of the students in the course are struggling with the concepts in Chapter 3, the instructor has asked you to spend 1 hour with these students to help increase their understanding of the Chapter 3 material. In addition to meeting with the students, the instructor requested that you create a visual learning aid you can use not only as an instructional tool when meeting with the students, but that students can take with them and use as a study tool for future exams.

**YOUR TASK**

1. **Search the Internet to learn more about visual learning aids.** Conduct a search of the Internet to learn more about the value of visual learning aids and the different types of learning aids. When searching, consider using key terms such as *visual learning aids, graphic organizer, concept maps, cognitive organizer, concept diagrams,* and *story maps.*

2. **Create a visual learning aid of Chapter 3 material**. Review the learning objectives at the beginning of Chapter 3. Create a well-thought-out visual learning aid to enhance student understanding of the important concepts associated with each learning objective. Your visual learning aid should be professional-looking and include visual symbols and words to express Chapter 3 concepts, as well as the connections between them. Creativity is encouraged.

## Practice Questions

### Multiple Choice

1. Which one of the following statements about ethical standards is FALSE?
   a. Members of professional organizations can be expelled for violating ethical standards.
   b. Ethical standards are laws federal or local government agencies pass.
   c. Ethical standards are statements by professionals regarding appropriate behavior.
   d. No one can be tried or sued in a court of law for violating an ethical standard.

2. Which one of the following statements about misuse of psychological tests is TRUE?
   a. Misuse is not a problem in today's society.
   b. Misuse is sometimes a problem, but rarely with serious consequences.
   c. Misuse is a chronic and disturbing problem that can result in serious harm.
   d. Misuse is only a concern to researchers who are likely to be most affected.

3. Which one of the following is a right of test takers?
   a. Keep a copy of any test they take
   b. Receive a copy of the test manual
   c. Review the test before administration
   d. Have their test score kept private

4. A group of teachers at Alfred E. Newman High School decided that it would be helpful to administer intelligence tests to first-year students to be used for placing students in appropriate classes. They also decided that it would be best not to tell the students what they were being tested for and not to tell them their scores on the intelligence tests. When teachers discussed their plan with the school psychologist, he strongly opposed it because he said it violated students' right to
   a. assemble.
   b. withdraw.
   c. know their IQ.
   d. informed consent.

5. Belinda conducted a research project in which she interviewed workers about their work standards and integrity on the job. She assured her study participants that all personal information they disclosed would be kept private and would not be disclosed without their permission. Which one of the following did she guarantee her participants?
   a. Anonymity
   b. Reliability
   c. Confidentiality
   d. Obscurity

6. Phillip is a supervisor at the LMNOP Corporation. He is very concerned about helping his workers and meeting their needs. Therefore, he sent a request to the HR Department asking for the scores on pre-employment tests that his workers had taken. The HR Department replied they could not give him the scores because the test takers had been assured of what?
   a. Their right to informed consent
   b. Their right to confidentiality
   c. Protection from invasion of privacy
   d. Protection from stigma

7. Coding test materials in such a way that test takers can be identified without their knowledge or consent would be a violation of test users' promise of what?

   a. Anonymity
   b. Protection from invasion of privacy
   c. Protection from stigma
   d. Confidentiality

8. For whom are ethical standards written?

   a. Test publishers and test users
   b. Members of a professional organization
   c. Test takers with disabilities
   d. Everyone involved in the testing process

9. Test publishers ensure every psychological test has

   a. adequate marketing.
   b. an unlimited number of test users.
   c. a complete test manual.
   d. a record of satisfied test users.

10. When test questions are published or given to persons other than test takers, there may be a problem with

    a. test scoring.
    b. test security.
    c. evidence of validity.
    d. evidence of reliability.

11. Which one of the following is listed in your textbook as a responsibility of the test publisher?

    a. Ensuring that only qualified persons purchase its psychological tests
    b. Marketing the psychological tests it publishes
    c. Giving a copy of the test to each potential purchaser
    d. Giving a copy of the test manual to each potential purchaser

12. Intellectual disabilities, learning disabilities, and traumatic brain injuries are examples of what type of impairment?

    a. Cognitive
    b. Motor
    c. Sensory
    d. Personality

13. What do testing guidelines that protect people with physical and mental challenges require?

    a. Modifying the testing process to prevent impairments from affecting test outcomes
    b. Giving all tests individually (instead of in groups) and orally (instead of in written form)
    c. Relieving the challenged test taker from the ethical standard of informed consent
    d. Not administering tests to people with challenges in a specific way

14. A structured interview might need to be substituted for paper-and-pencil tests for individuals with what type of impairment?

    a. Visual
    b. Motor
    c. Hearing
    d. Cognitive

15. Which one of the following is TRUE about learning disabilities?

    a. They are much like physical and mental disabilities.
    b. They do not have visible signs.
    c. They do not require special testing administration.
    d. They do not affect test scores.

16. What is one of the best ways instructors can help students with learning disabilities?

    a. Tape-record their lectures
    b. Encourage learning-disabled students to self-disclose

c. Request reasonable accommodations for the student
   d. Determine how each student learns best

17. Which one of the following is TRUE?
   a. Most psychological tests are appropriate for test takers from various cultures and backgrounds.
   b. The Rorschach inkblot test is appropriate for Blacks and Hispanics as well as Whites.
   c. Tests appropriate for people with learning disabilities are also appropriate for normal Blacks and Hispanics.
   d. The MMPI provides a model for revising older tests that were not developed with minorities in mind.

18. Which one of the following organizations published the fourth edition of the Principles for the Validation and Use of Personnel Selection Procedures in 2003 to reflect the current research on selecting, developing, and using testing instruments to make employment-related decisions?
   a. American Psychological Association
   b. Association for Psychological Science
   c. Society for Human Resource Management
   d. Society for Industrial-Organizational Psychology

19. Who has the responsibility to request a test accommodation for a physical condition, illness, or language issue that may interfere with test performance?
   a. Test developer
   b. Test administrator
   c. Test user
   d. Test taker

## Short Answer

**Remembering**

1. Discuss three ethical issues of concern to testing professionals and consumers.
2. What documents about ethics are published by the APA? Why is it important for test users to be familiar with these documents? What would be the consequence of test users not being familiar with these documents?
3. Describe how organizations can and cannot enforce compliance with their ethical standards.
4. What rights do test takers have regarding privacy, anonymity, and informed consent?

**Applying**

5. What actions or activities would you see a test publisher performing if the publisher were fulfilling its ethical responsibilities?
6. Think of a time when you either witnessed or heard about the unethical use of a psychologist test. Based on information from the textbook, describe what made the situation unethical, supporting your answer with details.
7. Explain what the *Standards* (AERA, APA, & NCME, 2014) say about testing special populations.
8. Determine any issues associated with test takers from multicultural backgrounds.

**Evaluating**

9. Compare and contrast ethical standards and ethical guidelines.
10. What recommendations would you make to modify an assessment, whether for visual, hearing, motor, or cognitive impairments?
11. Defend the importance of the minimum qualifications Pearson, one test publishing company, deems essential to purchase and use specific psychological tests.
12. Formulate an argument supporting the right of a college student not to share test results with her parents as a 17-year-old dependent. Include ethical considerations in your argument.

## Multiple-Choice and Short-Answer Practice Question Answer Key

### Multiple Choice

| Question | Answer | Textbook Page | Explanation |
|---|---|---|---|
| 1. | b | 56 | Ethical standards are established by professional organizations stating what they believe to be acceptable and unacceptable professional behavior. Because they are not established by governmental agencies, no one can be tried or sued in a court of law for violating an ethical standard. However, the professional organization can take action such as expulsion from the organization. |
| 2. | c | 55 | Unfortunately, test misuse is a continuing and chronic problem. Most times, misuse is unintentional and a result of poor technical knowledge. However, this does not lessen the serious consequences of misuse. For example, incorrect decisions can prevent an individual from being hired into a job or result in an individual receiving unneeded treatment. These poor decisions based on misuse of testing information can have emotional and financial impact harming both the individual and society. |
| 3. | d | 74 | The right to privacy and confidentiality is a core standard of the *APA Ethical Principles and Code of Conduct*. The standard assures test takers that all personal information they disclose will not be divulged without their explicit permission, except as mandated by law. However, a court order can overrule this principle. |
| 4. | d | 75 | All test takers have a right to determine their involvement. This is called informed consent. In addition, they are entitled to an explanation of why they are being tested, how the test data will be used, and what their test scores mean. Because this scenario involves high school students (minors), informed consent from both the parent and the student should have been obtained. |
| 5. | c | 74 | In this case, the researcher assured the participant confidentiality. Anonymity, a closely related concept, is achieved when personal identifying information is not collected and therefore the responses of any individual cannot be known. In this scenario, that is not the case because she interviewed the workers and collected personal information. |

| Question | Answer | Textbook Page | Explanation |
|---|---|---|---|
| 6. | c | 74 | Although the manager has good intentions, test takers have a right to privacy. This means the HR Department acted in accordance with the APA ethical principles by safeguarding the private information that the employees had disclosed. HR could release the information if the employees approved it, but they would need to ensure that the employees were doing so without any undue pressure or fear of reprisals from the manager. |
| 7. | a | 74 | Anonymity means that no data are collected that can tie an individual to his or her test results. Thus, if the test user promises anonymity, but collects and codes data in ways that allow results to be tied to a specific individual, then this has violated the person's promised anonymity. |
| 8. | b | 58 | Ethical standards are specifically written for the members of a professional organization. However, these same organizations can state what they believe the rights of test takers are, but rights are not ethical standards that the test takers need to live up to. In addition, test organizations are not required by law to follow the ethical standards, but they do voluntarily attempt to be consistent with them, such as ensuring user qualifications. |
| 9. | c | 69 | Test publishers should ensure that all tests have a comprehensive test manual that includes information about the psychometrics of the test, detailed administration information, proper use of the test, and norms. The textbook does discuss test marketing, but it does so in terms of ensuring that the publisher truthfully markets the test, not with extent of marketing. |
| 10. | b | 70 | Test security concerns the safe keeping of test information ensuring the fair and equitable opportunity for all who take the test. If information is released giving access to some test takers but not others, then the test security has been compromised, and some individuals may have an unfair advantage. |
| 11. | a | 69 | Test publishers voluntarily follow testing ethical standards, which state that they should only sell tests to qualified users. The publishers often create guidelines and standards stating the minimum training, education, and experience a user must have to purchase and administer a test. |

*(Continued)*

(Continued)

| Question | Answer | Textbook Page | Explanation |
|---|---|---|---|
| 12. | a | 76 | *Cognitive impairments* is a broad term used to describe deficiencies or characteristics that affect intellectual performance. The textbook lists intellectual disabilities, learning disabilities, and traumatic brain injuries as examples of cognitive impairments. By contrast, motor impairments include paralysis and missing limbs, and sensory impairments include deafness and blindness. |
| 13. | a | 76 | According to professional testing standards, test results and outcomes should indicate the intended skills or attributes accurately and not be affected by a disability. In other words, an unrelated disability should not affect the outcome of a test. As a result, test users often alter testing procedures and score interpretation to accurately reflect the skills or attributes being measured. |
| 14. | a | 77 | Depending on the extent of the visual impairment, these individuals will most likely be unable to read the paper-and-pencil test. Therefore, a structured interview, which is conducted orally, is a reasonable accommodation. Other accommodations might include large print and braille test materials. |
| 15. | b | 76–77 | Learning disabilities, like physical and mental disabilities, may require special testing accommodations. Unlike other disabilities, however, they do not have visible signs. A learning disability is a disability that affects any aspect of learning. This can include language abilities, mathematical abilities, and focus and attention. Some examples include dyslexia, dyscalculia, and dysgraphia. |
| 16. | b | 80 | Instructors can indeed make adjustments that allow the students to learn in the manner appropriate for their disability and test more effectively. However, before instructors can do this, the student must self-declare to school administrators who will ensure that the diagnosis was made by an appropriately qualified professional. |
| 17. | d | 81 | The MMPI was originally developed in the 1930s using a sample of White residents of Minnesota, which was mostly rural at the time. This sample with little diversity led psychologists to question if the test provided accurate information for individuals with a different background. As a result, the test was revised using a more diverse sample. |

| Question | Answer | Textbook Page | Explanation |
|---|---|---|---|
| 18. | d | 58 | In 2003, the Society for Industrial and Organizational Psychology (SIOP) published the fourth edition of the *Principles for the Validation and Use of Personnel Selection Procedures* to reflect current research and to be consistent with the *Standards for Educational and Psychological Testing*. The *Principles* reflect the official statement from SIOP regarding professionally accepted practices for selecting, developing, and using testing instruments to make employment-related decisions. The *Principles* include four main sections:<br><br>Overview of the Validation Process<br><br>Sources of Validity Evidence<br><br>Generalizing Validity Evidence<br><br>Operational Considerations in Personnel Selection |
| 19. | d | 73 | The 2014 *Standards* has an extensive discussion concerning the responsibilities of test takers. One of the explicitly stated responsibilities of test takers is to request an accommodation if he or she believes there is a physical condition, illness, or language issue that might affect his or her test performance. |

## Short Answer

| Question | Explanation |
|---|---|
| 1. | Ethical issues and concerns abound in testing, and they are practically limitless in number. For example, many scenarios could be conceived that relate to the four issues of primary concern: the right to privacy, the right to informed consent, the right to know and understand test results, and the right to protection from stigma. The right to privacy means that test information will not be released to others unless expressly authorized by the test taker. The right to informed consent means that individuals have the right of self-determination of participation (i.e., the right to freely choose whether to continue with testing). The right to know and understand the results means that test takers should be provided a nontechnical explanation of their scores. Finally, the right to protection from stigma means that they should not be labeled with derogatory terms. Instead, testing should facilitate growth and development. |
| 2. | The APA has published several documents concerning general ethics for psychologists and others specifically for testing. For example, the APA has published *Ethical Principles of Psychologists and Code of Conduct*, which includes five general principles, and specific ethical standards to guide psychologists. They have also published the *Standards for Educational and Psychological Testing* jointly with the American Educational Research Association (AERA) and National Council on Measurement in Education (NCME), *Test User Qualifications: A Data-Based Approach to Promoting Good Test Use*, and *Report of the Task Force on Test User Qualifications*. While these documents are not laws, it is important to be familiar with (and follow) them because the APA can sanction or expel member psychologists who do not adhere to the published standards and guidelines. |
| 3. | Ethics and law are different things. Law is created and enforced by governments to control or mediate the behavior of individuals, while ethical standards concern what people believe is right and wrong. The APA's ethical standards are what the professional organizational believes is the appropriate behavior of a psychologist. No one can be sued or tried in a court of law for violating the APA's ethical standards. However, the APA can sanction or even expel member psychologists who do not adhere to their ethical standards. |
| 4. | The APA's *Ethical Principles of Psychologists and Code of Conduct* addresses each of these issues. Test takers have privacy rights, meaning that their personal and test information will not be disclosed unless they expressly approve the disclosure (or as required by law). Taking steps to ensure anonymity can help to guarantee the test taker's right to privacy. To ensure anonymity, no information is collected that could be used to identify the test taker; therefore, he or she cannot be identified. Finally, informed consent means that test takers have the right to know why they are being tested, how the data are being used, and what their test scores mean. The information should be communicated in plain nontechnical language. Often, the test taker will provide written consent indicating that he or she has been informed about and understands the information shared. |

| Question | Explanation |
|---|---|
| 5. | Test publishers should follow the ethical guidelines. Test publishers should ensure they have defined minimum test user qualifications for each test they publish, stating the required training, education, and experience that a test user must have to purchase the test. Test publishers should also ensure that all of their marketing practices are accurate and truthful. They should ensure the security of the test. Finally, test publishers should also make available to test users a comprehensive test manual that includes the psychometric properties of the test, detailed administration instructions and scoring information, proper norms, and proper scoring interpretation practices. |
| 6. | Student answers will vary, but answers to the question should include a discussion of the unethical use witnessed or heard of, with reference to specific professional practice standard(s) violated. For instance, an answer could include a confidentiality violation if your test results were shared with one or more individuals without your explicit permission. For example, perhaps your test results were shared with your spouse or other family member). Or, perhaps you heard of an instance where a professional therapist shared a client's test results in a lobby full of other clients. |
| 7. | The *Standards* state that test users should make sure test outcomes accurately represent the intended skills or attributes. Those outcomes should not be inadvertently altered because of an individual's disability. Because of this standard, test users often use information in addition to test scores for diagnostic and intervention decisions. Test users may also modify a test's administration or score interpretation to ensure that the interpretation and use is accurate and consistent with the test's purpose. |
| 8. | As diversity of the United States has increased, so has attention to cultural issues and their effect on testing. One obvious concern is language, as different demographic groups have different levels of English proficiency. There has also been an increase in the numbers of individuals for whom English is their second language. Another important issue concerns the sample of people used to develop the test. For example, the Exner scoring system for the Rorschach inkblot test appears to be inappropriate for several groups because of large cultural differences within the norming group. The MMPI is another example. This test was developed using a rural White population. The test has been updated using a diverse sample more representative of the population of the United States. |
| 9. | Ethical standards and ethical guidelines both state expected appropriate behaviors and inappropriate behaviors. Where they differ is that standards developed by an organization such as the APA explicitly apply only to their members. As a result, these same organizations may publish broader reaching guidance or guidelines to others outside their membership to help shape and influence their behaviors. |
| 10. | Before you could be considered for a test modification, you would need to self-disclose to the appropriate individuals using official diagnosis information. Once a learning disability has been established and confirmed, there are many possible modifications, and their use depends on the specific diagnosis. Some common modifications include more testing time, allowing verbal rather than written responses, allowing breaks, and arranging for individual testing rooms with fewer distractions. |

*(Continued)*

(Continued)

| Question | Explanation |
|---|---|
| 11. | Student answers will vary, but the defense should include a well-substantiated discussion of why the minimum training, education, and experience in each of Pearson's three qualification levels (A, B, and C) is critical to proper test use. Test user qualifications are important because misuse of tests is a chronic and disturbing problem that harms individuals and society as a whole. Most test misuse is unintentional and results from a lack of knowledge. One way to combat the problem of test misuse is by ensuring test purchasers meet minimum test user qualifications. This helps to ensure that only knowledgeable individuals use the tests, decreasing the likelihood of misuse. |
| 12. | Student answers will vary, but the argument should include discussion of the college student's right to privacy even though she is a college student. A student may elect to give her parents access to college records, but the college must respect her rights. For instance, even though her parents have the right to access the student's records, any conversation that results from this access should also include the student, not just the parents. Another example is when a professor receives an email from a parent asking about the status of his or her child using the child's school email. |

# 4 How Do Test Users Interpret Test Scores?

## Overview

In Chapter 4 of the textbook, we introduced you to the procedures used to interpret test scores. Hopefully, after reading the chapter, you have a clearer understanding of the levels of measurement, the visual and statistical procedures we use for interpreting test scores, the purpose of standard scores and how we calculate them, and the role and use of norms when interpreting test scores. While Chapter 4 of the textbook included foundational information about the procedures used to interpret test scores, Chapter 4 of the workbook provides you with the opportunity to demonstrate your understanding of material presented in the textbook and apply your learning by completing some practical and critical thinking exercises linked to specific learning objectives. Chapter 4 of the workbook will also allow you to complete chapter-level projects to demonstrate your understanding of multiple topics within the chapter. Chapter 4 of the workbook ends with some multiple-choice and short-answer questions you can use to self-assess your understanding of the material.

# Practical and Critical-Thinking Exercises

## Purpose

This section contains five exercises you can complete to demonstrate your understanding and apply your learning (Exercises 4.1–4.5) and one exercise you can complete to reflect on your learning (Exercise 4.6). The exercises, linked to learning objectives, are displayed below.

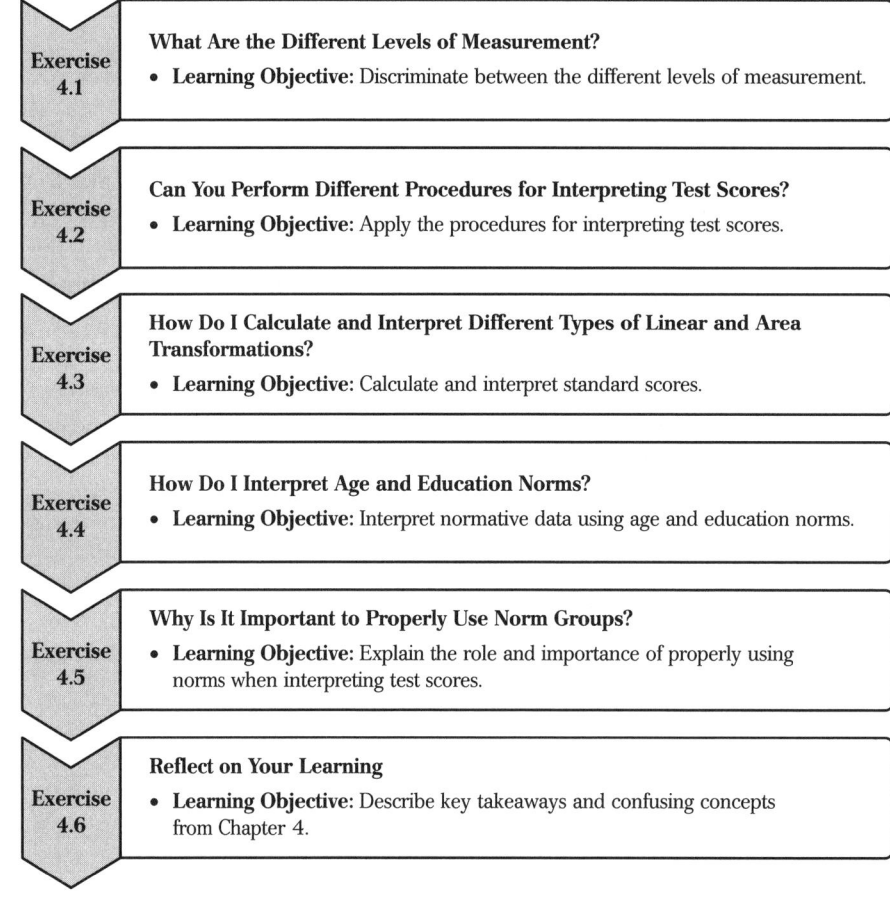

**Exercise 4.1** — **What Are the Different Levels of Measurement?**
- Learning Objective: Discriminate between the different levels of measurement.

**Exercise 4.2** — **Can You Perform Different Procedures for Interpreting Test Scores?**
- Learning Objective: Apply the procedures for interpreting test scores.

**Exercise 4.3** — **How Do I Calculate and Interpret Different Types of Linear and Area Transformations?**
- Learning Objective: Calculate and interpret standard scores.

**Exercise 4.4** — **How Do I Interpret Age and Education Norms?**
- Learning Objective: Interpret normative data using age and education norms.

**Exercise 4.5** — **Why Is It Important to Properly Use Norm Groups?**
- Learning Objective: Explain the role and importance of properly using norms when interpreting test scores.

**Exercise 4.6** — **Reflect on Your Learning**
- Learning Objective: Describe key takeaways and confusing concepts from Chapter 4.

# Exercise 4.1: What Are the Different Levels of Measurement?

**OBJECTIVE**

Discriminate between the different levels of measurement.

**BACKGROUND**

In Chapter 4, you learned that to accurately describe and interpret psychological test scores at the item level, scale level, and test result level, it's important to understand the four levels of measurement: nominal, ordinal, interval, and ratio. Each test item, scale, and overall test result has one of the four levels of measurement. We must understand the specific level of measurement as the level of measurement dictates the statistical calculations we can perform and the claims we can make based on results. To increase your understanding of the different levels of measurement, for Exercise 4.1, you will determine the level of measurement for various situations and then identify examples on your own.

**YOUR TASK**

1. **Determine the level of measurement**. Review the "Levels of Measurement" section in Chapter 4 of your textbook. Read each of the following situations. Then, determine whether the level of measurement in each situation is nominal, ordinal, interval, or ratio.

| Situation | Level of Measurement |
|---|---|
| A professor scores a multiple-choice test by counting the number of correct answers. | |
| You participate in an interview with a psychologist who asks you the following question:<br><br>How do you feel today?<br><br>A. Very unhappy<br>B. Unhappy<br>C. OK<br>D. Happy<br>E. Very happy | |
| As you are completing an employee engagement survey, you are asked to indicate to what degree the statement to the left or right best describes ***your current perception*** by selecting the appropriate number.<br><br>1 = Strong agreement with left statement<br>2 = Moderate agreement with left statement<br>3 = Neutral<br>4 = Moderate agreement with right statement<br>5 = Strong agreement with right statement | |

*(Continued)*

(Continued)

| Situation | | | | | | | Level of Measurement |
|---|---|---|---|---|---|---|---|
| | 1 | 2 | 3 | 4 | 5 | | |
| I am paid *fairly* compared to other employees. | | | | | | I am paid *unfairly* compared to other employees. | |
| I believe my pension plan *is reasonable*. | | | | | | I believe my pension plan *is unreasonable*. | |
| I believe the current sick time policy *is reasonable*. | | | | | | I believe the current sick time policy is *unreasonable*. | |
| As you are completing a quiz in your Tests and Measurements class, you come across this question: Most psychological tests produce which level of measurement? A. Nominal and ratio  B. Ordinal and ratio  C. Ordinal and interval  D. Nominal and ordinal | |
| You are completing a survey that includes the following question: How much money, on average, do you spend on groceries per week? A. $0–$50  B. $51–$75  C. $76–$100  D. $101 and above | |
| You are taking a personality test and are asked the following: How many times have you taken this personality test? _____ | |

2. **Identify examples of each level of measurement in everyday life**. Conduct an Internet search to find three real-life examples of each level of measurement. Try and find unique examples from everyday life, avoiding examples provided in the textbook or from the exercise above. If necessary, review the "Levels of Measurement" section in Chapter 4 of your textbook. Document your examples in the table on the following page, including an explanation of why your example qualifies at that level of measurement.

| Level of Measurement | Examples | Explain Why Your Example Qualifies as That Level of Measurement |
|---|---|---|
| Nominal | | |
| Ordinal | | |
| Interval | | |
| Ratio | | |

### Exercise 4.2: Can You Perform Different Procedures for Interpreting Test Scores?

**OBJECTIVE**

Apply the procedures for interpreting test scores.

**BACKGROUND**

As you learned in Chapter 4 of the textbook, the most basic score calculated from psychological tests is the *raw score*. When a group of people take a test, we often make sense of the raw test scores by creating frequency distributions and/or calculating descriptive statistics. A frequency distribution is an orderly arrangement of a group of numbers or test scores. Descriptive statistics help us describe or summarize a distribution of test scores using numbers. To increase your knowledge of the procedures we use to interpret test scores, for Exercise 4.2, you will create frequency distributions and calculate descriptive statistics using a provided dataset.

**YOUR TASK**

1. **Review the raw scores below**. Imagine that the following set of raw scores is from a group of 20 individuals who completed a test in their philosophy course at the local college.

| Student | Raw Score | Student | Raw Score | Student | Raw Score | Student | Raw Score |
|---|---|---|---|---|---|---|---|
| 1 | 26 | 6 | 21 | 11 | 20 | 16 | 27 |
| 2 | 26 | 7 | 24 | 12 | 22 | 17 | 23 |
| 3 | 22 | 8 | 26 | 13 | 25 | 18 | 24 |
| 4 | 19 | 9 | 29 | 14 | 18 | 19 | 26 |
| 5 | 28 | 10 | 30 | 15 | 25 | 20 | 22 |

2. **Create a frequency table.** Create a frequency table using the raw test scores above. Use Table 4.3 in Chapter 4 of your textbook as a guide.

| Score | Frequency | Percentage |
|---|---|---|
| | | |
| | | |
| | | |
| | | |
| | | |
| | | |
| | | |
| | | |
| | | |
| | | |

| Score | Frequency | Percentage |
|---|---|---|
|  |  |  |
|  |  |  |
|  |  |  |
|  |  |  |
|  |  |  |
|  |  |  |
|  |  |  |
|  |  |  |
|  |  |  |
|  |  |  |

3. **Draw a stem-and-leaf plot.** Using the information in your frequency table, draw a stem-and-leaf plot. See Figure 4.1 in the textbook for an example.

| Stem | Leaf |
|---|---|
|  |  |
|  |  |
|  |  |
|  |  |
|  |  |
|  |  |

4. **Calculate measures of central tendency.** Using the raw test scores, calculate the three measures of central tendency (mean, median, and mode). Document your answers in the table below.

| Mean | Median | Mode |
|---|---|---|
|  |  |  |

5. **Calculate measures of variability.** Using the raw test scores in Task 1, calculate the three measures of variability (range, variance, and standard deviation). Follow your instructor's directions on whether to perform these calculations by hand, by using Excel, or using another data analysis software. Document your answers in the table below.

| Range | Variance | Standard Deviation |
|---|---|---|
|  |  |  |

6. **Answer the question below**.

   Imagine you were the faculty member who administered the philosophy test to the 20 students, and another faculty member asked you how your class performed on the test. What would you say using information from the frequency table and stem-and-leaf plot you calculated, and the measures of central tendency and measures of variation you calculated?

## Exercise 4.3: How Do I Calculate and Interpret Different Types of Linear and Area Transformations?

**OBJECTIVE**

Calculate and interpret standard scores.

**BACKGROUND**

Raw test scores tell us very little. To understand distributions of test scores, we use raw test scores to create frequency distributions and to calculate measures of central tendency, measures of variability, and measures of relationship. However, we also make sense of raw test scores by converting (or transforming) them into more meaningful units we call standard scores, which are universally understood units in testing. To increase your understanding of how to calculate and interpret standard scores, in Exercise 4.3, you will perform linear and area transformations by transforming raw test scores into percentages, standard deviation units, $z$ scores, $T$ scores, and percentiles.

**YOUR TASK**

1. **Read the scenario below.**

    Imagine you designed a 30-item knowledge test to measure college students' knowledge of psychological testing. You administered your test to a representative group of college students who have taken a psychological testing course. You obtain the raw scores below.

2. **Convert raw scores to standard scores using linear and area transformations.** Using the formulas provided in Chapter 4 of your textbook, perform the calculations necessary to use linear transformations to transform each raw score into a percentage, standard deviation unit, $z$ score, and $T$ score, and use area transformations to convert each raw score into a percentile. When calculating the mean and standard deviation, round to the nearest tenth (one decimal place) prior to conducting your transformations. Document your answers in the table below.

| Student | Raw Score | Linear Transformations ||||  Area Transformation |
|---|---|---|---|---|---|---|
| | | Percentage | Standard Deviation Unit | $z$ Score | $T$ Score | Percentile |
| John | 21 | | | | | |
| Kim | 23 | | | | | |
| Jose | 22 | | | | | |
| Sammy | 19 | | | | | |
| Alex | 28 | | | | | |
| Racine | 20 | | | | | |
| Jax | 24 | | | | | |
| Josie | 26 | | | | | |
| Ryan | 28 | | | | | |
| Don | 25 | | | | | |

3. **Interpret the standard scores.** Carefully read each of the 10 statements below. Using what you learned about standard scores in Chapter 4 of the textbook and the linear and area transformations you calculated above, properly interpret standard scores by marking each of the statements as either "T" (for true) or "F" (for false). Document any comments or questions you have as you think about whether each statement is true or false.

| Item | Answer | | Statement | Comments/Questions |
|---|---|---|---|---|
| 1 | T | F | One college student scores a percentile of 80. This means that the student answered 80% of the items correctly. | |
| 2 | T | F | Ryan scored a $T$ score between 60 and 70. | |
| 3 | T | F | Josie scored between the mean and one standard deviation unit above the mean. | |
| 4 | T | F | Alex and Ryan had a raw score of 28. This means that both students had a percentile rank of 90. | |
| 5 | T | F | One college student scores a 70%. This means that the student scored equal to or better than 70% of others. | |
| 6 | T | F | Sammy scored between two and three standard deviation units below the mean. | |
| 7 | T | F | Jon scored below average, with a negative $z$ score. | |
| 8 | T | F | Both Jax and Josie scored between the mean and one standard deviation above the mean. | |
| 9 | T | F | Don scored equal to or better than 60% of the others. | |
| 10 | T | F | Jax scored 80%. This means that Jax had a percentile rank of 55. | |

# Exercise 4.4: How Do I Interpret Age and Education Norms?

**OBJECTIVE**

Interpret normative data using age and education norms.

**BACKGROUND**

To help interpret test scores from standardized tests, we will sometimes compare an individual's test score to norms, which are test scores achieved by some identified group of individuals. These norms provide us with a standard against which we can compare an individual's test score. Using norm-based interpretation, we can answer the question "Where does a test taker stand in comparison with a group that defines the standards?" We often report norms in charts or tables that describe the performance of a large group of individuals who were administered the test in the past (referred to as the norm group). When a person takes a test, we then compare his or her test score to the norm group to interpret his or her score. Comparing a person's score to the norm group allows us to determine the relative standing of the individual compared to those who have taken the test in the past. Two common types of norms are age norms and education norms. They allow us to determine at what age level or grade level, based on the person's test score, an individual is performing. We can determine whether an individual's test score is the same as, lower, or higher than the scores of others at the same age or education level. To increase your understanding of how to interpret age and education norms, for Exercise 4.4, you will use the Mini Mental State Exam (MMSE) normative data to interpret test takers' scores.

**YOUR TASK**

1. **Read the information below.**

   The MMSE is a commonly used test for assessing cognitive impairment. Typically completed in 5–10 minutes, the test consists of 11 items measuring five cognitive functions: orientation, registration, attention and calculation, recall, and language. A person's cognitive status is determined by comparing his or her raw score with the descriptive statistics of a norm group of test takers of similar ages and educational levels. The maximum score is 30, and a score of 23 or lower is indicative of cognitive impairment. As measured by the MMSE, cognitive performance varies by age and educational level. In general, cognitive performance tends to increase with education, yet decline with age. For example, the median score for 18- to 24-year-olds is 29, and the median score for those 80 or older is 25.

2. **Interpret the normative data.** Review the Normative Data for the MMSE found in On the Web Box 4.2 in your textbook. Imagine that you were a clinical psychologist and administered the MMSE to five individuals. The age, educational level, and raw score of each individual is listed below. Use the MMSE Normative Data to determine if each individual scored lower than, the same as, or higher than the norm group. To do this, compare each individual's raw score with the average score of individuals who are the same age and have similar educational levels. Document the implications of your findings in the table on the following page.

| Individual | Age | Education | MMSE Raw Score | Norm Group Comparison | | | Implications |
|---|---|---|---|---|---|---|---|
| | | | | Lower | Same | Higher | |
| 1 | 43 | High School | 24 | | | | |
| 2 | 81 | 8th grade | 27 | | | | |
| 3 | 27 | College | 29 | | | | |
| 4 | 69 | 4th grade | 22 | | | | |
| 5 | 39 | College | 28 | | | | |

# Exercise 4.5: Why Is It Important to Properly Use Norm Groups?

**OBJECTIVE**

Explain the role and importance of properly using norms when interpreting test scores.

**BACKGROUND**

Standardized tests often have norms groups. We use these norm groups to interpret a test taker's score by comparing the test taker's score to the scores of others in the norm group. While norms are very valuable for helping us interpret individual test scores, care must be taken to ensure the appropriate norm group is used to make the comparison. Using an inappropriate norm group can result in very important decisions being made based on poor interpretation of test data. To increase your understanding of the different types of norms available and the proper use of norms, in Exercise 4.5, you will write an article for a local newspaper about proper use of norm groups.

**YOUR TASK**

1. **Learn as much as you can about norm groups.** Learn as much as you can about norm groups by reviewing *The Role of Norms* section in Chapter 4 of your textbook and conducting an Internet and library search. At a minimum, gather the information needed to answer the questions in the table below. Before searching the Internet and the library, brainstorm some key search terms to ensure that you search for relevant information needed to thoroughly answer the questions below. For example, some of your key words might be

   - Norm-referenced tests
   - Norm-based or -referenced interpretation
   - Proper use of test norms
   - Interpreting psychological tests using norms

   Document your findings in the table below.

| Questions | Notes |
|---|---|
| What are norms? | |
| Why do we use norms? | |
| What are the different types of norms? | |

| Questions | Notes |
|---|---|
| What is the proper use of norms? | |
| What are the implications of inappropriately using norms? | |
| What are some examples of improperly used norms? | |
| Other important information about norms | |

2. **Write an article for a local newspaper.** Imagine you were a testing expert and were contacted by a local newspaper due to a recent event involving improper use of test norms in the local school system. The editor asked you to submit an article to educate the public on proper use of norms, asking that you address, at a minimum, the following:

- What norms are
- Why we use norms
- The different types of norms
- The proper use of norms
- The implications of inappropriately using norms
- Some examples of improperly used norms and the consequences

Using the answers to the questions in the first part of this exercise, write a 2- to 3-page article that you could submit to the editor.

## Exercise 4.6: Reflect on Your Learning

**OBJECTIVE:**

Describe key takeaways and confusing concepts from Chapter 4.

**BACKGROUND:**

In Chapter 4 of the textbook, you were introduced to the procedures used to interpret test scores. You read about the different levels of measurement and how we use frequency distributions, measures of central tendency, measures of variability, and measures of relationship to interpret test scores. You also learned about the purpose of standard scores, as well as how to calculate and interpret them. In addition, you learned about the role of norms when interpreting test scores, including the importance of using the correct norm groups. For Exercise 4.6, you will reflect on your learning from Chapter 4 of the textbook and identify key takeaways from the chapter.

**YOUR TASK**

1. **Identify your "Aha!" moments from Chapter 4**.
    - Identify 3 to 4 new insights or realizations you had after reading Chapter 4, referred to as "Aha!" moments,
    - Consider things that made you look at a concept, your life, or an issue in a completely different way than you had in the past.
    - Document your insights and realizations below, providing details of your learning.

2. **Identify some muddy moment discussion questions.**
    - Identify 2 to 3 concepts that are still "muddy" for you from the chapter.
    - Consider concepts you still don't understand, concepts you need clarified, and/or questions you want to ask.
    - Develop 1 to 3 questions to initiate a discussion in class to further your understanding of the concepts and get your questions answered.

| | |
|---|---|
| **Insights and Realizations** | 1. _____<br>2. _____<br>3. _____<br>4. _____ |
| **Muddy Moments Discussion Questions** | 1. _____<br>2. _____<br>3. _____ |

# Chapter-Level Projects

## Project 1

**BACKGROUND**

Imagine you are a professor at a local college who is well informed on techniques for interpreting test scores. The Dean of Academic Affairs has reached out to you and asked that you create material to share with faculty that may help them understand how to best interpret student test scores. You are excited about the opportunity to help your colleagues by showcasing your knowledge about test score interpretation and decide to design a reference guide.

**YOUR TASK**

1. **Reflect on what you have learned about test score interpretation.** Reflect on the information you learned in Chapter 4 of the textbook on the procedures we use for interpreting test scores. While you review Chapter 4, consider the different levels of measurement, frequency distributions, measures of central tendency, measures of variability, standard scores, and norms.

2. **Create a well-thought-out reference guide.** Create a well-thought-out and professional-looking reference guide with suggested best practices for interpreting test scores. *The reference guide should read like a quick reference sheet that highlights the different ways to interpret test scores.* Integrate in your reference guide a minimum of 5–10 concepts and tips discussed in Chapter 4, including, but not limited to frequency distributions, measure of central tendency, measures of variability, standard scores, and norms. Include what the best practice is, when it would be appropriate to use, and how the best practice will help faculty interpret test scores.

# Project 2

**BACKGROUND**

Imagine you designed a 50-item test to measure your classmates' knowledge of how to properly interpret test scores. You administered the test at the beginning of the semester (the pretest) to measure the class's initial knowledge, and then again at the end of the semester (the posttest) to measure the class's knowledge after the 16-week course. Imagine you obtained the scores below:

| Student | Pretest Scores | Posttest Scores |
|---|---|---|
| 1 | 8 | 25 |
| 2 | 32 | 46 |
| 3 | 31 | 44 |
| 4 | 20 | 38 |
| 5 | 10 | 39 |
| 6 | 33 | 40 |
| 7 | 29 | 48 |
| 8 | 15 | 40 |
| 9 | 27 | 49 |
| 10 | 31 | 39 |

**YOUR TASK**

1. **Calculate measures of central tendency, measures of variation, and measures of relationship.** For both distributions of test scores, calculate the measures of central tendency and measures of variation. Calculate a measure of relationship between the pre- and posttest scores.

2. **Transform the raw test scores to more meaningful units of measurement.** Perform the calculations necessary to use linear transformations to transform each raw score into a percentage, standard deviation unit, $z$ score and $T$ score, and use area transformations to convert each raw score into a percentile.

3. **Create a presentation.** Create a PowerPoint or Prezi presentation to clearly display the results of your calculations. Also use speaker notes that will include a well-written and comprehensive discussion of the results, demonstrating your understanding of how to use the calculations to interpret the results.

# Project 3

**BACKGROUND**

Imagine you were in graduate school serving as the teaching assistant for a psychology instructor. Because some of the students in the course are struggling with the concepts described in Chapter 4, the instructor has asked you to spend 1 hour with these students to help increase their understanding of the Chapter 4 material. In addition to meeting with the students, the instructor requested that you create a visual learning aid you can use not only as an instructional tool when meeting with the students, but that students can also take with them and use as a study tool for future exams.

**YOUR TASK**

1. **Search the Internet to learn more about visual learning aids.** Conduct a search of the Internet to learn more about the value of visual learning aids and the different types of learning aids. When searching, consider using key terms such as *visual learning aids, graphic organizer, concept maps, cognitive organizer, concept diagrams,* and *story maps*.

2. **Create a visual learning aid of Chapter 4 material**. Review the learning objectives at the beginning of Chapter 4. Create a well-thought-out visual learning aid to enhance student understanding of the important concepts associated with each learning objective. Your visual learning aid should be professional-looking and include visual symbols and words to express Chapter 4 concepts, as well as the connections between them. Creativity is encouraged.

## Practice Questions

### Multiple Choice

1. If 10 students arrange themselves from shortest to tallest, and we assign the shortest a score of 1 and the tallest a score of 10, what level of measurement would we be using?
   a. Interval scale
   b. Nominal scale
   c. Ordinal scale
   d. Ratio scale

2. Most psychological tests produce which level of measurement?
   a. Nominal and ratio
   b. Ordinal and ratio
   c. Ordinal and interval
   d. Nominal and ordinal

3. Which one of the following provides us with a visual representation of distribution scores?
   a. Measures of variation
   b. Measures of central tendency
   c. Descriptive statistics
   d. Frequency distributions

4. What would you calculate to find out more about the middle of a distribution of scores?
   a. Levels of measurement
   b. Frequency of distributions
   c. Measures of variability
   d. Measures of central tendency

5. What would you calculate if you wanted to find out whether individuals who took a test performed similarly to or differently from one another?
   a. Measures of variation
   b. Measures of central tendency
   c. Descriptive statistics
   d. Frequency distributions

6. What would be the most accurate index or indices when a distribution of scores has outliers?
   a. Mode and median
   b. Mean and mode
   c. Mean and median
   d. Mean only

7. The correlation between two distributions of scores can range from
   a. −10.0 to +10.0
   b. −1.0 to +1.0
   c. 0 to +1.0
   d. −0.5 to +0.5

8. Which one of the following correlation coefficients would you most likely see if students' performance on a midterm exam was inversely related to their performance on a final exam?
   a. −10.0
   b. −0.6
   c. +0.2
   d. +6.0

9. What type of distribution is skewed to the left, has one high point, and has many high scores?
   a. Negatively skewed distribution
   b. Positively skewed distribution
   c. Evenly distributed distribution
   d. Peaked distribution

10. In a normal distribution, approximately what percentage of test scores will fall between 2 and 3 standard deviations above the mean?
    a. 68%
    b. 34.1%
    c. 13.6%
    d. 2.1%

11. In a normal distribution, approximately what percentage of test scores will fall between one standard deviation below the mean and one standard deviation above the mean?

    a. 95%

    b. 68%

    c. 34.1%

    d. 13.6%

12. Which one of the following standard scores always has a mean of 50 and a standard deviation of 10?

    a. *T* scores

    b. *z* scores

    c. Percentiles

    d. Standard deviation units

13. If your score on a test is calculated to be equivalent to a percentile rank of 80, which one of the following is TRUE?

    a. You scored better than 79% of the norm group.

    b. You scored equal to or better than 80% of the norm group.

    c. You scored equal to or less than 80% of the norm group.

    d. 80% of the norm group scored higher than you.

14. If the mean of a distribution of test scores is 70, and the standard deviation is 5, what would John's *z* score be if he scored an 80?

    a. 0

    b. 1

    c. 2

    d. 3

15. Which one of the following is FALSE about the use of norms?

    a. There is one right population that is regarded as the normative group.

    b. Test publishers often develop and publish the results of various norm groups.

    c. Test users should always be careful to use up-to-date norms.

    d. The smaller the norm group, the more likely the norm group is not representative.

## Short Answer

| | |
|---|---|
| **Remembering** | 1. What are the potential consequences of not understanding the level of measurement of data?<br><br>2. Describe the characteristics of the normal probability distribution.<br><br>3. What procedures are used to interpret test scores?<br><br>4. What is the purpose of transforming raw scores into standard scores? |
| **Applying** | 5. Show how normal probability distribution help us understand a distribution of test scores.<br><br>6. Illustrate how to make the calculations for three commonly used standard scores.<br><br>7. Demonstrate how outliers can affect the distribution of scores and measures of central tendency. |
| **Evaluating** | 8. Compare and contrast the different levels of measurement. Provide examples of each.<br><br>9. Defend the value of calculating measures of central tendency. Give examples.<br><br>10. Summarize how norms help us understand test scores.<br><br>11. Relate how norms may be used incorrectly when interpreting test scores. Describe the potential consequences. |

# Multiple-Choice and Short-Answer Practice Question Answer Key

## Multiple Choice

| Question | Answer | Textbook Page | Explanation |
|---|---|---|---|
| 1. | c | 92 | Ordinal scales are rank orderings. This type of scale indicates an individual's or object's value based on its relationship to others in the group. The rank only has meaning in relationship to the group being compared. For example, if you were one of the tallest in the group, it would matter greatly if the group was composed of third graders or professional basketball players. In addition, the magnitude of difference between individuals is not known. Continuing with a height example, if you were the second tallest, you could be 1 inch shorter or 2 feet shorter, and it does not matter because it is your position in the rank that has meaning. |
| 2. | c | 92–94 | Very few psychological tests have a true zero point indicating a complete absence of an attribute. For example, a person cannot have a complete absence of a personality. In addition, nominal scales group individuals into categories. While this is sometimes used in psychological testing, ordinal and interval scales are most characteristic of psychological tests. |
| 3. | d | 96 | A frequency distribution is a visual summary of scores. It is often presented in a table or a histogram. The data are summarized showing the count of occurrences at a specific value or range of values. |
| 4. | d | 101 | Measures of central tendency are descriptive statistics we use to describe the central, middle, or most characteristic score in a distribution. There are three commonly used measures of central tendency: mean, median, and mode. Each has its use, so there is not one best measure of central tendency; instead selection and use depend on the situation and the test user's needs. |
| 5. | a | 105 | Variability refers to the spread of scores in a distribution, and therefore measures of variation can be used to determine if test scores are close together or far apart. There are three commonly used measures of variation: range, variance, and standard deviation. Each has their strengths and weaknesses, but the most commonly used measure is the standard deviation. |
| 6. | a | 104 | In a skewed distribution or a distribution with outliers, the mean is more affected than the mode or median. This is because the mean gets "pulled" toward the extreme values. In contrast, the mode and median are much less affected and as a result can be considered better descriptions at the center of the distribution. |

*(Continued)*

(Continued)

| Question | Answer | Textbook Page | Explanation |
|---|---|---|---|
| 7. | b | 113 | The correlation coefficient is a measure describing the relationship between two variables. The correlation can range from −1.00 to +1.00. A correlation of −1.00 indicates a perfect negative correlation, showing that as one variable increases, there is an exact matching decrease in the other variable. A correlation of +1.00 indicates a perfect positive correlation showing that as one variable increases, the other variable increases an equal amount. Perfect correlations rarely, if ever, occur. |
| 8. | b | 113 | A correlation coefficient can range from −1.00 to +1.00. Therefore, the correct answer cannot be −10.0 or +6.0. A positive correlation indicates that as one variable increases, the other also increases. A negative correlation indicates that as one variable increases, the other variable decreases, which is another way of describing an inverse relationship. Thus, the correct answer is −0.6. |
| 9. | a | 102 | A negatively skewed distribution is the one that has a single high point to the right and a long tail to the left. One way to remember the difference between positive and negative skew is that a negatively skewed distribution has a long tail in the negative direction, and a positively skewed distribution has a long tail in the positive direction. |
| 10. | d | 101 | A normal distribution is a theoretical distribution that is useful for interpreting test scores. Figure 4.3 in your textbook shows the percentage of scores falling between various standard deviations. Approximately 34.1% of the scores will fall between the mean and one standard deviation above the mean. Approximately 13.6% of the scores will fall between one standard deviation and two standard deviations above the mean. Finally, about 2.1% of the scores will fall between two and three standard deviations above the mean. Because the normal distribution is symmetric, these percentages hold for standard deviations below the mean as well. These percentages are very important in testing and statistics in general, and it is worthwhile to memorize these percentages. |
| 11. | b | 101 | This question can easily be answered by referring to Figure 4.3 in your textbook, which shows the normal probability distribution. Looking at the figure, we can see that approximately 34.1% of the scores will fall between the mean and one standard deviation above the mean. Because we know that the normal distribution is symmetrical, we then also know that approximately 34.1% of the scores will fall between the mean and one standard deviation below the mean. Thus, adding these values together, approximately 68% of the scores will fall between one standard deviation below the mean and one standard deviation above the mean. |

| Question | Answer | Textbook Page | Explanation |
|---|---|---|---|
| 12. | a | 116 | Raw scores are often difficult to interpret. Therefore, they are often transformed into a different score allowing for easier interpretation and comparison with other test scores. The *T* score is a common linear transformation based on the standard deviation. The *T* score has a mean of 50 and standard deviation of 10. |
| 13. | b | 116 | A percentile is a common area score transformation. A score's percentile indicates the percentage of scores that fall at or below that score. Thus, if the percentile is 80, then 80% of the scores were at or below the score. Put another away, the score is equal to or better than 80% of the scores. |
| 14. | c | 116 | A *z* score is a linear transformation that converts the raw score into standard deviation units. Using the *z* score formula, we subtract the mean from the obtained score and then divide by the standard deviation. Thus, $z = (80 - 70)/5 = 2$. |
| 15. | a | 124 | Because psychological tests produce scores that are at the ordinal or interval levels of measurement, scores generally only have meaning in relation to other scores. Norms provide us with the ability to compare scores and are used as the comparison group. There is *not* one norm group. Instead, the norm group should be selected based on the individual(s) to whom the test is to be administered. For example, we would not use norms based on third graders if we are testing college students. |

## Short Answer

| Question | Explanation |
|---|---|
| 1. | Because psychological tests produce scores that are at the ordinal or interval levels of measurement, scores generally only have meaning in relation to other scores. Norms provide us with the ability to compare scores and are used as the comparison group. There is *not* one norm group. Instead, the norm group should be selected based on the individual(s) to whom the test is to be administered. For example, we would not use norms based on third graders if we are testing college students. |
| 2. | Most heights would be in the middle, and numbers would gradually taper off symmetrically as we move away from the center peak. We would find that approximately 34.1% of the individuals would fall between the mean and one standard deviation, approximately 13.6% would fall between one standard deviation and two standard deviations away from the mean, and approximately 2.1% would fall between two and three standard deviations from the mean. These characteristics have important statistical implications. |
| 3. | Descriptive statistics, such as central tendency and variability, describe test scores, allowing us to understand key features of the distribution and interpret test scores. |
| 4. | Raw scores are transformed into standard scores to aid in the interpretation of test results and scores. With a transformed score, it is often easier to compare individual scores on the same test or similar tests. |
| 5. | The normal distribution is important because many human traits conform to this theoretical distribution. For example, if we created a graph showing heights of adults from the general population, the graph would look like a normal distribution. |
| 6. | Three common transformations are percentages, *z* scores, and percentiles. To calculate a percentage, divide the raw score by the total possible score. To calculate a *z* score, subtract the mean from the raw score, and then divide this amount by the standard deviation. Finally, to calculate the percentile rank, find the number of scores below the given score, add 0.5 for each score that is exactly the same as the given score, and then divide this total by the number of people who took the test. |
| 7. | Outliers can greatly influence the central tendency in skewed distributions. Outliers are extreme values in a distribution because outliers lie outside the overall pattern of a distribution, being significantly higher or lower than most other values. Outliers may lead to a more pronounced positive or negative skew and cause misleading results when calculating measures of central tendency. For example, if a distribution of test scores has one extremely low value, then the calculated mean is likely to be much lower than the median and mode. In this case, the mean would not be a good measure of central tendency, as it would not really reflect the average score in the distribution. |
| 8. | The levels of measurement can be thought of as a hierarchy, with each successive level possessing the characteristics of the lower levels plus additional characteristics. The nominal level is the lowest level on the hierarchy. This level of data is for classification into categories, and math operations are inappropriate. The next level is ordinal, which has the property of rank order. At this level, math operations, such as addition, subtraction, multiplication, and division, are inappropriate. However, you can determine rank ordering in terms of magnitude of the characteristic or attribute measured. Interval level is the next level of measurement. Interval level has all the characteristics of the lower levels, plus the intervals between numbers are equidistant. |

| Question | Explanation |
|---|---|
| 9. | Measures of relationship, such as the correlation, allow us to easily understand how two variables are associated or vary together. Examples of measures of central tendency include the mean, median, and mode. Examples of measures of variability include the range, variance, and standard deviation. Finally, an example of a measure of relationship is the correlation. |
| 10. | Norms help us understand test scores because they provide a comparison group. Very few psychological tests produce scores at the ratio level of measurement. Therefore, scores must be compared to understand what the scores mean. |
| 11. | Norms provide us with a relative measure to make interpretations of test scores. However, selection of an appropriate norm group is an important consideration. For example, if you are testing fifth graders on math concepts, you would want to use a norm based on the general population of fifth graders and not a norm based on third graders or high school students. |

# 5 What Is Test Reliability/Precision?

## Overview

In Chapter 5 of the textbook, we introduced you to the concept of reliability/precision. Hopefully, after reading the chapter, you have a clearer understanding of what we mean by reliability/precision and also have a good understanding of classical test theory, the three categories of reliability coefficients, and the methods we used to estimate them. You should also have an understanding of how to calculate reliability coefficients, the standard error of measurement, and confidence intervals. While Chapter 5 of the textbook included foundational information about the concept of reliability/precision, Chapter 5 of the workbook provides you with the opportunity to demonstrate your understanding of material presented in the textbook and apply your learning by completing some practical and critical-thinking exercises linked to specific learning objectives. Chapter 5 of the workbook will also allow you to complete chapter-level projects to demonstrate your understanding of multiple topics within the chapter. Chapter 5 of the workbook ends with some multiple-choice and short-answer questions you can use to self-assess your understanding of the material.

# Practical and Critical-Thinking Exercises

## Purpose

This section contains five exercises you can complete to demonstrate your understanding and apply your learning (Exercises 5.1–5.5) and one exercise you can complete to reflect on your learning (Exercise 5.6). The exercises, linked to learning objectives, are displayed below.

**Exercise 5.1**
**Do You Know How to Use the Test–Retest Method?**
- **Learning Objective:** Demonstrate your understanding of when the test–retest method is appropriate and your ability to calculate test–retest reliability and interpret the resulting reliability coefficient.

**Exercise 5.2**
**Do You Know How to Use the Internal Consistency Method?**
- **Learning Objective:** Demonstrate your understanding of when the internal consistency method is appropriate and your ability to calculate internal consistency and interpret the resulting reliability coefficient.

**Exercise 5.3**
**Can You Identify the Most Appropriate Methods for Estimating Reliability/Precision?**
- **Learning Objective:** Identify proper methods for estimating reliability/precision.

**Exercise 5.4**
**Can You Identify Examples of Random Error?**
- **Learning Objective:** Identify and assess examples of random error.

**Exercise 5.5**
**Can You Calculate and Interpret Confidence Intervals?**
- **Learning Objective:** Construct an argument on the reliability of a test that integrates confidence interval calculations.

**Exercise 5.6**
**Reflect on Your Understanding**
- **Learning Objective:** Describe key takeaways and confusing concepts from Chapter 5.

## Exercise 5.1: Do You Know How to Use the Test–Retest Method?

**OBJECTIVE**

Demonstrate your understanding of when the test–retest method is appropriate and your ability to calculate test–retest reliability and interpret the resulting reliability coefficient.

**BACKGROUND**

As described in Chapter 5, the most important attribute of a test is its reliability/precision. A reliable test is one we can trust to measure each person in approximately the same way every time it is used. A psychological test without evidence of reliability/precision is not valuable because it may produce inconsistent results every time it is used. One common method we use to estimate the reliability/precision of a test is the test–retest method. To increase your understanding of when the test–retest method is appropriate and how to estimate reliability using the test–retest method, for Exercise 5.1, you will answer some questions about the test–retest method of gathering evidence of reliability/precision and how to calculate test–retest reliability. You will also calculate and interpret test–retest reliability, calculate the standard error of measurement, and construct a 95% confidence interval.

**YOUR TASK**

1. **Read the information below.**

    Imagine you work as the Director of Recruiting and Selection in the Human Resources (HR) Department of an organization, and being trustworthy (dependable, honest, and responsible) is critical to the success of individuals for many of the positions within your organization. Therefore, you decide to look for a psychological test that you might integrate into the selection process that measures trustworthiness. After conducting research on available tests, you identify a test of trustworthiness. While the test publisher of the instrument claims the test is reliable, you can find little research to confirm there is indeed evidence of reliability/precision. Before deciding whether to integrate the test into your selection process, you decide to gather your own evidence of test–retest reliability.

2. **Answer the questions below.**

    What assumption(s) would you need to make if you were going to gather proof the test of trustworthiness had evidence of reliability/precision using the test–retest method? For what types of tests might the test–retest method of estimating reliability not be appropriate?

    _____

    _____

    _____

    _____

What steps would you take (including the setting and time) to gather evidence of test–retest reliability?

Who would you include in your test–retest study, and why?

How would you know if the test was reliable? What would you look for?

If your test–retest results indicated the test was not reliable, why might this be? What could you do to increase the test's reliability?

3. **Calculate the test–retest reliability and standard error of measurement.** Imagine your test–retest reliability study yielded the data below. Using the process suggested by your instructor (e.g., by hand, using Excel or another electronic spreadsheet program or software), calculate the test–retest reliability and standard error of measurement. Construct a 95% confidence interval around the score of Test Taker 1 and Test Taker 2 on the first administration. Document your answers below.

| Test Taker | First Administration Score | Second Administration Score |
|---|---|---|
| 1 | 75 | 82 |
| 2 | 69 | 75 |
| 3 | 45 | 45 |
| 4 | 59 | 60 |
| 5 | 77 | 78 |
| 6 | 60 | 80 |
| 7 | 50 | 70 |
| 8 | 55 | 60 |
| 9 | 78 | 80 |
| 10 | 78 | 76 |

A. Test–retest reliability coefficient: _____

B. Standard error of measurement: _____

C. 95% confidence interval of Test Taker 1 on First Administration: _____

D. 95% confidence interval of Test Taker 2 on First Administration: _____

4. **Interpret your results.** Given the results above, answer the following questions:

Do the test scores from the test–retest reliability study provide sufficient evidence of reliability/precision for the test of trustworthiness? Would you use the test in your selection process based on these results? Why, or why not?

_____
_____
_____
_____
_____

Given your calculated confidence intervals, would it be accurate to say that Test Taker 1 is definitely scored higher in trustworthiness than Test Taker 2? Why, or why not?

_____
_____
_____
_____
_____

# Exercise 5.2: Do You Know How to Use the Internal Consistency Method?

## OBJECTIVE

Demonstrate your understanding of when the internal consistency method is appropriate and your ability to calculate internal consistency and interpret the resulting reliability coefficient.

## BACKGROUND

As described in Chapter 5, we can't always use the test–retest method for gathering evidence of reliability and validity. Instead, sometimes we use the internal consistency method. To increase your understanding of when the internal consistency method is appropriate and how to estimate reliability using the internal consistency method, for Exercise 5.2, you will answer some questions about internal consistency reliability, including how to calculate it, and then calculate, as well as interpret, an internal consistency reliability coefficient.

## YOUR TASK

1. **Read the information below.**

    Imagine you work as the HR director at a large dental practice and the office manager is concerned that patients with high treatment anxiety require more time than patients who are not anxious. The office manager believes that having patients complete a dental anxiety assessment prior to their first appointment would be valuable so that additional time with the dentist can be scheduled, if needed. The office manager has found a 20-item dental anxiety assessment and would like to immediately begin using the assessment. However, you can find little research to confirm the assessment has evidence of reliability/precision. Before using the assessment with patients, you decide to gather your own evidence of reliability/precision.

2. **Answer the questions below.**

    What assumption(s) would you need to make if you were going to gather evidence of reliability/precision for the dental anxiety assessment using the internal consistency method? For what types of tests might the internal consistency method of estimating reliability not be appropriate?

    _____
    _____
    _____
    _____
    _____

What steps would you take (including the setting and time) to gather evidence of internal consistency reliability?

Who would you include in your internal consistency study, and why?

How would you know if the test was reliable? What would you look for?

If your internal consistency results indicated the test was not reliable, why might this be? What could you do to increase the test's reliability?

3. **Calculate the internal consistency reliability.** Imagine your internal consistency reliability study of the dental anxiety assessment (using the split-half approach) yielded the data below. Using the process suggested by your instructor (e.g., by hand, using Excel, or another electronic spreadsheet program or software), calculate the internal consistency reliability.

| Test Taker | Scores (Number Correct) | |
| --- | --- | --- |
| | First Half of Test | Second Half of Test |
| Sandy | 6 | 3 |
| Michael | 5 | 4 |
| Joe | 8 | 6 |
| Sara | 4 | 7 |
| Aimee | 5 | 8 |
| Leslie | 5 | 7 |
| Bob | 9 | 10 |
| Rick | 3 | 3 |

4. **Correct the obtained split half reliability using Spearman Brown.** Using the formula in For Your Information Box 5.1 of your textbook, correct your obtained split half reliability using Spearman Brown. Document your reliability coefficients in the space below.

   A. What is the internal consistency reliability coefficient? _____

   B. What is the reliability coefficient for the test when corrected using the Spearman-Brown formula? _____

   C. Is there enough evidence of internal consistency reliability for you to use the dental anxiety assessment in the dental practice? Why or why not?

   _____
   _____
   _____
   _____

# Exercise 5.3: Can You Identify the Most Appropriate Methods for Estimating Reliability/Precision?

**OBJECTIVE**

Identify proper methods for estimating reliability/precision.

**BACKGROUND**

There are various methods we can use to estimate the reliability/precision of a psychological test. We can estimate reliability using the test–retest method, the alternate-forms method, and/or the internal-consistency method. We can also estimate scorer reliability. There is not just one correct way to estimate reliability/precision. Depending on the test, we might use one or more methods to gather as much evidence of reliability/precision as possible. To increase your understanding of the proper use of each method, in Exercise 5.3, you will review four testing scenarios and select the most appropriate method(s) for estimating reliability/precision.

**YOUR TASK**

1. **Read each of the scenarios below.**

    A. An instructor has designed a comprehensive math exam for students entering community college. The exam contains multiple-choice questions that measure a student's ability to read formulas, carry out math calculations, and solve word problems. Because students may score higher on the second administration purely because they have taken the test one time already, when gathering evidence of reliability/precision, the instructor can give the exam only once. However, the instructor needs to know how reliable the test scores are.

    B. An HR professional wants to assess employee attitudes about quality of work life. She wants to be sure that her self-designed instrument is reliable. Her instrument contains 20 statements that employees will rate from 1 to 5. The HR professional has designed the instrument to be homogeneous.

    C. An Industrial and Organizational (I–O) psychology practitioner designed two parallel promotion tests for firefighters. Both tests required two fire chiefs to observe firefighters completing job-related activities (e.g., use and maintenance of safety equipment). Each firefighter was required to take two parallel tests rated by the same fire chiefs.

    D. A test developer is constructing a measure of critical thinking. The instrument consists of a number of anagrams and riddles—problems for which answers are not readily apparent until solved. The test score depends on the percentage of questions the test taker solved correctly.

2. **Select the most appropriate method(s) for estimating reliability/precision.** For each scenario, identify one or more possible methods you could use to estimate reliability/precision. Explain why you chose each method, including any assumptions you made when selecting the method. Document your findings in the chart on the following page.

| Scenario | Possible Method(s) for Estimating Reliability/Precision | Why Each Method Was Chosen and Assumptions Made |
|---|---|---|
| **A** | 1. | |
| | 2. | |
| | 3. | |
| | 4. | |
| **B** | 1. | |
| | 2. | |
| | 3. | |
| | 4. | |
| **C** | 1. | |
| | 2. | |
| | 3. | |
| | 4. | |
| **D** | 1. | |
| | 2. | |
| | 3. | |
| | 4. | |

## Exercise 5.4: Can You Identify Examples of Random Error?

**OBJECTIVE**

Identify and assess examples of random error.

**BACKGROUND**

Psychological tests are not 100% accurate, and all contain some error. Measuring psychological constructs is not as exact as measuring things such as height and weight. As described by classical test theory, the score we receive on a test reflects our true score plus some error. For example, if we earned an 80% on a classroom test of our knowledge of psychological testing concepts, this 80% would not be a 100% accurate representation of what we really know; rather on any given day, we may have scored a little lower or higher score due to error. One type of error is random error. To increase your understanding of potential sources of random error, in Exercise 5.4, you'll reflect on your experience taking one or more tests to obtain your driver's license and identify potential sources of random error.

**YOUR TASK**

1. **Read the information below.**

    If you have a driver's license, you probably recall taking one or more tests. For example, you may have taken a road test, a written test, and a vision test. The road test likely assessed your driving skills requiring that you ride with a Department of Motor Vehicles representative, perform basic maneuvers (e.g., a 3-point turn, stopping quickly) on a back lot, and/or demonstrate your safe-driving behaviors (e.g., staying in the proper lane, passing, obeying traffic signals) by driving on a road. The written test may have required that you answer multiple-choice questions to assess your knowledge of driving laws. For the vision test, you may have had your visual acuity tested using a machine or a wall chart. In each case, the score you received was likely not 100% accurate; rather, your score reflected your true score plus some random error.

2. **Identify potential *random* error.** Identify five examples of random error that might affect scores on tests taken to obtain a driver's license. When working on this exercise, think about when you (or people you know) were first obtaining a driver's license. Reflect about each test and then identify and describe how random error may influence reliability/precision.

| Type of Test | Identify an Example of Random Error | Describe Random Error as It Applies to Your Example |
|---|---|---|
| Road Test (EXAMPLE) | When performing a 3-point turn, there is a loud noise in the adjacent parking lot that distracts the driver. | The loud noise may have distracted the driver, taking the driver's full attention away from performing the 3-point turn, resulting in mistakes being made, lowering the driver's road test score. |

*(Continued)*

(Continued)

| Type of Test | Identify an Example of Random Error | Describe Random Error as It Applies to Your Example |
|---|---|---|
| Road Test | | |
| Written Test | | |
| Vision Test | | |

3. **Evaluate the effects of random error on the driver's license tests.** After completing the chart above, what can you determine about random error? Develop three statements that reflect your learning about random error based on this exercise.

   a. _____
   _____
   _____
   _____
   _____
   _____

   b. _____
   _____
   _____
   _____
   _____
   _____

   c. _____
   _____
   _____
   _____
   _____
   _____

# Exercise 5.5: Can You Calculate and Interpret Confidence Intervals?

## OBJECTIVE

Construct an argument on the reliability of a test that integrates confidence interval calculations.

## BACKGROUND

As described in Chapter 5, a test taker's observed score may differ (sometimes significantly) from his or her true score. Confidence intervals help us make informed decisions when interpreting observed scores, as they help us understand the range in which a test taker's true score is likely to fall. Constructing a confidence interval requires two simple calculations. First, we calculate the standard measurement error (SEM) for the psychological test. Once we know the SEM, we can compute a confidence interval for a particular observed score. To increase your understanding of confidence intervals, for Exercise 5.5, you'll consider a hypothetical situation involving two managers being considered for a promotion, construct confidence intervals around each manager's observed test score, and then create an argument for which manager you would promote.

## YOUR TASK

1. **Read the information below.**

   Imagine that leaders at your organization administer an emotional intelligence test to all individuals applying for manager-level positions. The test is administered only to those individuals who perform well on a structured interview. Currently, the organization has one manager position open, and two internal candidates who performed well on the structured interview took the test: Erin and Chris. Erin scored 80, and Chris scored 85. The organization would like to hire the individual who scored the highest, which appears to be Chris. However, the organization realizes that due to measurement error, on any given day, both Erin and Chris' observed scores may have been different.

2. **Construct a 95% confidence interval for Erin and Chris' observed test score.** To determine the range of scores we can feel confident that Erin and Chris' true scores would fall within, construct a 95% confidence interval for both test taker's scores. First, using the formula in For Your Information Box 5.4, calculate the SEM for the test. Then, construct a confidence interval around each person's score to provide a better estimate of the range in which each test taker's true score is likely to fall.

   Assume the following calculated reliability and standard deviation for the emotional intelligence test:

   - Reliability coefficient of the EI test $(r_{xx})$ = .90
   - Standard deviation $(\sigma)$ = 12.75

Document your answers in the table below.

| Test Taker | Observed Score | 95% Confidence Interval |
|---|---|---|
| Erin | 80 | |
| Carol | 85 | |

3. **Prepare an argument.** Demonstrate your understanding of confidence intervals and the confidence intervals you calculated above by preparing an argument about who the organization should hire.

## Exercise 5.6: Reflect on Your Understanding

**OBJECTIVE**

Describe key takeaways and confusing concepts from Chapter 5.

**BACKGROUND**

In Chapter 5 of the textbook, you were introduced to the concept of reliability/precision. You read about what we mean by reliability/precision and were introduced to classical test theory, the three categories of reliability coefficients, and the methods we used to estimate them. You were also introduced to how to calculate reliability coefficients and the standard error of measurement, and how to construct confidence intervals. Last, you learned about how to interpret test scores by evaluating SEM, confidence intervals, and reliability coefficients. For Exercise 5.6, you will reflect on your learning from Chapter 5 of the textbook and identify key takeaways from the chapter.

**YOUR TASK**

1. **Identify your "Aha!" moments from Chapter 5.**
   - Identify 3 to 4 new insights or realizations you had after reading Chapter 5, referred to as "Aha!" moments.
   - Consider things that made you look at a concept, your life, or an issue in a completely different way than you had in the past.
   - Document your insights and realizations below, providing details of your learning.

2. **Identify some muddy moment discussion questions.**
   - Identify 2 to 3 concepts that are still "muddy" for you from the chapter.
   - Consider concepts you still don't understand, concepts you need clarified, and/or questions you want to ask.
   - Develop 1 to 3 questions to initiate a discussion in class to further your understanding of the concepts and get your questions answered.

| Insights and Realizations | 1. _____ |
| --- | --- |
| | 2. _____ |
| | 3. _____ |
| | 4. _____ |
| Muddy Moments Discussion Questions | 1. _____ |
| | 2. _____ |
| | 3. _____ |

## Chapter-Level Projects

### Project 1

**BACKGROUND**

Imagine you work as the training and development specialist for a call center. Every quarter, a survey is randomly sent to the call center's customers to assess customer satisfaction and identify departmental training needs of customer service staff. While the analysis of the most recent quarter's responses revealed that customers rated customer service representatives as courteous and polite, over 90% of the customers reported customer service representatives were not able to answer their questions about products in a timely manner. After a review of the survey results, the HR director determined that while call center representatives were courteous and polite, more training needed to be done to ensure newly hired representatives had the product knowledge necessary to answer customer product questions in a timely manner.

**YOUR TASK**

1. **Read the information below.**

   Currently, newly hired customer service representatives participate in an onboarding process that includes 2 weeks of customer service training with daily quizzes of gained knowledge and skills, followed by 1 week of product training, again with daily quizzes. To better assess the product knowledge of customer service representatives, your boss recommends that the number of quizzes remains the same (15), but the number of questions on each test be reduced from 100 to 50 questions. By reducing the number of questions, trainers can cover more material without rushing through key information.

2. **Differentiate the various methods for measuring internal consistency.** Review the "Internal Consistency Method" section of Chapter 5 of your textbook to refresh your memory of the different methods for measuring the internal consistency of a test. Answer the following questions.

   If the number of questions on the quizzes was reduced, and new evidence of reliability/precision needed to be gathered, which method(s) for measuring internal consistency would be the most appropriate given the information above?

   _____
   _____
   _____
   _____
   _____

*(Continued)*

(Continued)

Which reliability coefficient would provide the best estimate of reliability?

_____

_____

_____

_____

_____

3. **Discuss the pros and cons of reducing the number of items on each quiz.** Review the "Factors That Affect Reliability" section of Chapter 5 of your textbook to refresh your memory of the factors that can increase or decrease the reliability of a test. Discuss the pros and cons of reducing the number of questions on each quiz, as suggested by the HR director.

_____

_____

_____

_____

4. **Prepare a recommendation report.** Reflect on the situation occurring at the call center, your learning from Chapter 5 of the textbook, and your answers above. What would you recommend to improve customer service representatives' ability to answer customer questions about products in a timely manner? Prepare a 1- to 2-page report providing the HR director with your recommendation for how best to address the situation occurring at the call center, ensuring that the reliability of the quizzes is not compromised. Include very specific recommendations, incorporating 5–10 concepts from Chapter 5 of your textbook to support your recommendation.

# Project 2

**BACKGROUND**

Imagine you are an industrial-organizational psychologist who specializes in test development. You recently received a phone call from a local grocery store manager who is in charge of opening a second location. The manager was hired because of her demonstrated skills managing employees and keeping training materials current. During the phone call, the manager shares that some of the grocery store's current training material will change because the new facility is equipped with state-of-the-art technology that is different than the original store, including store processes and layout. The manager also shares that she was just provided information on the new technology, processes, and layout. The store is scheduled to open in the next 4 months, and she needs to hire and train all new employees. You learn that the manager has already begun to update the training material, including the knowledge test that new hires take at the end of training to measure what they learned. The manager wants to make sure that the knowledge test measures the three areas covered in the training: new hires' knowledge of state-of-the-art technology, store processes, and layout. At the end of the phone call, the manager asked you to assist her with the testing component of the training process for the second location.

**YOUR TASK**

1. **Differentiate the different methods for assessing reliability/precision.** Review Chapter 5 of your textbook to refresh your memory of the different methods for estimating reliability/precision of a test. Given the information you have from the store manager, explain which method(s) you would use to estimate the reliability/precision of the revised test, and why.

   _____
   _____
   _____
   _____
   _____

2. **Identify the factors critical to test design.** Review Chapter 5 of your textbook to refresh your memory of important concepts related to estimating the reliability/precision of a test. Focus specifically on what factors, during the design of a test, affect the reliability/precision of a test. Document your insights below.

   _____
   _____
   _____
   _____
   _____

*(Continued)*

(Continued)

3. **Prepare a recommendation report for the store manager.** Reflect on the situation occurring at the call center, your learnings from Chapter 5 of the textbook, and your answers above. Prepare a 2- to 3-page report documenting the factors the store manager should take into account when designing the knowledge test and the process she should use to estimate the reliability/precision of the test. Support your recommendation by referring to 5–10 concepts from Chapter 5 of your textbook.

# Project 3

**BACKGROUND**

Imagine you were in graduate school serving as the teaching assistant for a psychology instructor. Because some of the students in the course are struggling with the concepts in Chapter 5, the instructor has asked you to spend 1 hour with these students to help increase their understanding of the Chapter 5 material. In addition to meeting with the students, the instructor requested that you create a visual learning aid you can use not only as an instructional tool when meeting with the students, but that students can take with them and use as a study tool for future exams.

**YOUR TASK**

1. **Search the Internet to learn more about visual learning aids.** Conduct a search of the Internet to learn more about the value of visual learning aids and the different types of learning aids. When searching, consider using key terms such as *visual learning aids, graphic organizer, concept maps, cognitive organizer, concept diagrams,* and *story maps.*

2. **Create a visual learning aid of Chapter 5 material.** Review the learning objectives at the beginning of Chapter 5. Create a well-thought-out visual learning aid to enhance student understanding of the important concepts associated with each learning objective. Your visual learning aid should be professional-looking and include visual symbols and words to express Chapter 5 concepts, as well as the connections between them. Creativity is encouraged.

## Practice Questions

### Multiple Choice

1. When we talk about how each inch on a yardstick is the same length, we are talking about the yardstick's
   a. reliability/precision.
   b. internal consistency.
   c. order effects.
   d. score reliability.

2. Which one of the following methods do we use to examine the performance of a test over time and provide an estimate of a test's stability?
   a. Test–retest reliability
   b. Split-half reliability
   c. Score reliability
   d. Alternative forms reliability

3. Marsha, a student teacher, wanted to check the reliability of a math test that she developed for her fourth graders. She gave the test to students on Monday morning and then again on Tuesday morning. On the first administration of her test, there was a wide variety of scores, but on the second administration, nearly all of the children made A's on the test. Marsha wondered, "Why did all the students make A's on Tuesday, but not on Monday?" Which one of the following would most likely account for this outcome?
   a. Order effects
   b. Practice effects
   c. Measurement error
   d. Scorer error

4. Researchers administered the Personality Assessment Inventory (PAI) to two samples of individuals. First, they administered the PAI twice to 75 adults, with the second administration following the first by an average of 24 days. They also administered the PAI to 80 college students who took the test twice, with an interval of 28 days. In each case, the researchers were conducting studies to measure the PAI's
   a. internal consistency.
   b. score reliability.
   c. split-half reliability.
   d. test–retest reliability.

5. Jon developed a math test for fourth graders, but he was not able to administer the test twice. What method can Jon use to estimate the reliability/precision of the math test?
   a. Criterion related
   b. Construct
   c. Internal consistency
   d. Test–retest

6. When using the split-half method, an adjustment must be made to compensate for splitting the test into halves. Which one of the following would we use to make this adjustment?
   a. Coefficient alpha
   b. Pearson product–moment correlation
   c. Spearman–Brown formula
   d. Kuder–Richardson formula (KR-20)

7. Which one of the following is the appropriate method for estimating reliability for tests with homogeneous questions that have more than two possible responses?
   a. Coefficient alpha
   b. Pearson product–moment correlation
   c. Spearman–Brown formula
   d. KR-20

8. While _____ describes the degree to which questions on a test or subscale are interrelated, _____ refers to whether the questions measure the same trait or dimension.

    a. homogeneity; coefficient alpha
    b. coefficient alpha; homogeneity
    c. heterogeneity; coefficient alpha
    d. homogeneity; test–retest reliability

9. Researchers conducted two studies on the reliability of the Wisconsin Card Sorting Test (WCST) using adult psychiatric inpatients. In these studies, more than one person scored the WCST independently. What kind of reliability/precision were the researchers interested in establishing?

    a. Test–retest reliability
    b. Scorer reliability
    c. Split-half reliability
    d. Internal consistency

10. Katie and Kathy are roommates who share the same bathroom scale. Neither Katie nor Kathy is on a special diet to lose or gain weight. Each morning, they both weigh themselves. From day to day, it seems that each gains or loses 2 to 3 pounds. Some days Katie gains 3 pounds, and Kathy loses 2 pounds. Other days Katie loses 2 pounds and Kathy gains 3 pounds. Every day their weights are different from their weights the previous day, and they cannot distinguish a pattern. Katie and Kathy decide to start weighing themselves on a scale at the wellness center. To their surprise, they neither gain nor lose weight from time to time when using the scale at the wellness center. Which one of the following best explains this situation?

    a. Their home scale has systematic error, and the wellness center scale is more accurate.
    b. Their home scale has random error, and the wellness center scale is more accurate.
    c. The scale at the wellness center has systematic error, and their home scale is accurate.
    d. The scale at the wellness center has random error, and their home scale is accurate.

11. Which one of the following formulas do test developers who wish to increase the reliability of a test use to estimate how many homogeneous test questions should be added to a test to raise its reliability to the desired level?

    a. Coefficient alpha
    b. KR-20
    c. Spearman–Brown
    d. Pearson product–moment correlation

12. Which one of the following is important for both interpreting individual test scores and calculating confidence intervals?

    a. Standard error of measurement
    b. Pearson product–moment correlation
    c. Test Variance
    d. Spearman–Brown formula

13. When test reliability is high, the standard error of measurement is _____. As test reliability decreases, the standard error of measurement _____.

    a. high; decreases
    b. low; decreases
    c. high; increases
    d. low; increases

14. As a rule, adding more questions that measure the same trait or attribute can _____ a test's reliability.

    a. increase
    b. decrease
    c. overestimate
    d. underestimate

15. What makes generalizability theory different from classical test theory?
    a. Generalizability theory focuses on identifying systematic error.
    b. Generalizability theory focuses on identifying random error.
    c. Generalizability theory focuses on identifying systematic and random error.
    d. Generalizability theory focuses on identifying systematic and random true scores.

16. Which one of the following is associated with generalizability theory?
    a. Pearson product–moment correlation
    b. Interrater reliability
    c. Analysis of variance
    d. Cohen's kappa

17. Who is the most likely to apply generalizability theory?
    a. Test taker
    b. Test user
    c. Test administrator
    d. Test developer

18. _____ is a characteristic of the test itself; _____ depends on how the test is used.
    a. Reliability; validity
    b. Validity; reliability
    c. Face validity; content validity
    d. Content validity; face validity

## Short Answer

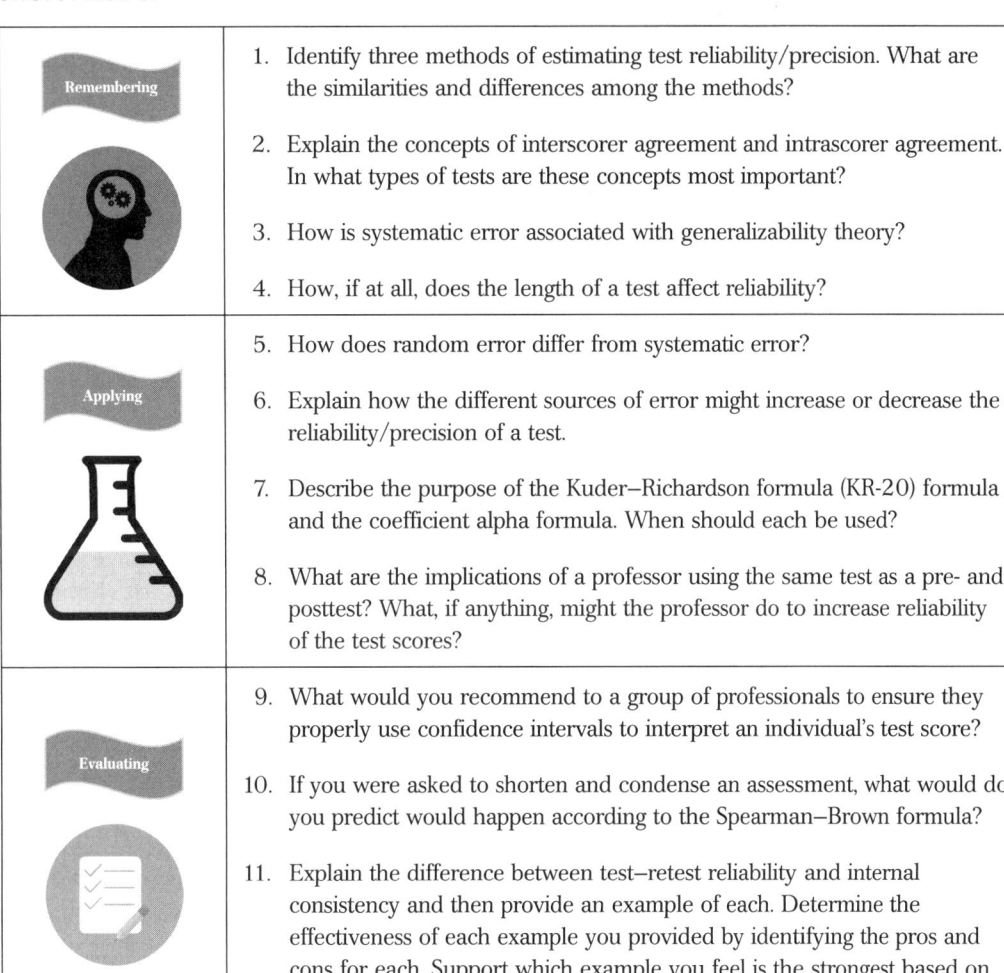

**Remembering**

1. Identify three methods of estimating test reliability/precision. What are the similarities and differences among the methods?

2. Explain the concepts of interscorer agreement and intrascorer agreement. In what types of tests are these concepts most important?

3. How is systematic error associated with generalizability theory?

4. How, if at all, does the length of a test affect reliability?

**Applying**

5. How does random error differ from systematic error?

6. Explain how the different sources of error might increase or decrease the reliability/precision of a test.

7. Describe the purpose of the Kuder–Richardson formula (KR-20) formula and the coefficient alpha formula. When should each be used?

8. What are the implications of a professor using the same test as a pre- and posttest? What, if anything, might the professor do to increase reliability of the test scores?

**Evaluating**

9. What would you recommend to a group of professionals to ensure they properly use confidence intervals to interpret an individual's test score?

10. If you were asked to shorten and condense an assessment, what would do you predict would happen according to the Spearman–Brown formula?

11. Explain the difference between test–retest reliability and internal consistency and then provide an example of each. Determine the effectiveness of each example you provided by identifying the pros and cons for each. Support which example you feel is the strongest based on your analysis as it applies only to the examples you provided.

# Multiple-Choice and Short-Answer Practice Question Answer Key

## Multiple Choice

| Question | Answer | Textbook Page | Explanation |
|---|---|---|---|
| 1. | b | 128 | In a measurement context, reliability refers to consistency, and internal consistency is a specific type of reliability. In this example, an inch is always a same length regardless if it is the first inch or the tenth inch on the yardstick. Thus, every inch is uniform in its measurement, and the yardstick is internally consistent. |
| 2. | a | 136 | Test–retest reliability requires that a test be given at two points in time. Then the scores from the first and second administration are compared using correlation. For a test to be reliable, the scores should be relatively stable over time; therefore, there should be a high correlation between the two sets of scores. |
| 3. | b | 137 | Practice effects are a common problem when using the test–retest method to establish reliability. Practice effects occur when test takers benefit from taking the test a second time. Because they are familiar with the test, test takers can answer the questions faster the second time and can potentially remember the questions and answers from the first administration. |
| 4. | d | 137 | When a test is administered to the same individuals more than once, the researchers are investigating test–retest reliability. Under this method, it is important to administer the test under similar conditions. In addition, the time spacing between administrations should be long enough to minimize the effect of remembering questions and answers, but not so long as to allow growth and learning. |
| 5. | c | 138 | Criterion-related and construct are types of validity evidence and therefore cannot be used to determine reliability. Because the test cannot be administered twice, Jon cannot use test–retest to establish the reliability of the test. Therefore, the answer must be internal consistency, which is a measure of reliability that helps us examine how related the items within the test are to each other. |
| 6. | c | 139 | There is a relationship between test length and reliability, such that the longer the test, the higher the reliability. This becomes an issue when using the split-half method because the test is divided into two halves, which results in a lower reliability estimate. To compensate for this, the Spearman–Brown formula is used to adjust the reliability coefficient to estimate what it would be for the full-length test. |

| Question | Answer | Textbook Page | Explanation |
|---|---|---|---|
| 7. | a | 139 | KR-20 and coefficient alpha are two methods for estimating the internal consistency of a test. However, the KR-20 can only be used when test items are scored in a dichotomous fashion such as right or wrong. In contrast, coefficient alpha can be used for scales as well as right or wrong questions. When coefficient alpha is used on dichotomous items, it will yield the same result as the KR-20. |
| 8. | b | 140 | Coefficient alpha is a specific method that measures the internal consistency of a test, which is just another way of saying that the items are interrelated. In contrast, homogeneity is a broader term that means all test items measure the same trait or attribute. Heterogeneity, on the other hand, means that the test items measure more than one trait or attribute. A test can have a high coefficient alpha and still be heterogeneous. |
| 9. | b | 142 | When multiple scorers or judges are required to score an exam, their scores or ratings will often differ. Scorer reliability assesses the amount of consistency or agreement among the scorers. When there are only two raters or judges, the correlation coefficient between the ratings can be used to assess scorer reliability. When there are more than two judges, the intraclass correlation coefficient, a special type of correlation, is the statistical procedure generally used to assess scorer reliability. |
| 10. | b | 132–133 | Random error is just that—random. Neither Katie nor Kathy can distinguish a pattern in the fluctuations of the weight when they use their scale at home. This suggests that there is random error in the measurement. In contrast to their home scale, the wellness center scale does not have these fluctuations and is consistent in its measurement, which would suggest (but not guarantee) a higher degree of accuracy. |
| 11. | c | 143 | The Spearman–Brown formula represents the relationship between the length of a test and the test's reliability/precision. The formula is often used to adjust the reliability estimate when using the split-half method. However, it can also be used to estimate what the reliability of a test would be if the test were made shorter or longer or to determine the number of items that need to be added to a test to obtain a specific level of reliability. |

*(Continued)*

(Continued)

| Question | Answer | Textbook Page | Explanation |
|---|---|---|---|
| 12. | a | 149–150 | The standard error of measurement is an index of the amount of inconsistency or error that can be expected in a single test score. It indicates how much an individual's test score is likely to deviate from his or her true score and as a result, it is used when constructing confidence intervals. |
| 13. | d | 152 | When a test's reliability/precision is high, an individual's observed test score will be a better estimate of his or her true score, so the standard error of measurement will be low. In contrast, as reliability/precision decreases, an individual's observed score is a poorer estimate of his or her true score, and therefore the standard error of measurement will be larger. |
| 14. | a | 153 | Adding more questions that measure the same construct will increase the reliability of a test. Conversely, as a general rule, if you removed items from a test, the reliability would most likely decrease. Reliability would most likely decrease because there is a positive relationship between the length of the test and the reliability of the test. |
| 15. | c | 155–156 | Classical test theory only identifies random error. However, generalizability theory allows the researcher not only to identify random error, but also to identify sources of systematic error. Using a statistical procedure called analysis of variance, or ANOVA for short, the researcher can examine factors such as the administration as a source of systematic error. |
| 16. | c | 156 | Analysis of variance or ANOVA is the statistical method that is used in generalizability theory. This procedure allows the researcher to identify different sources that may systematically be introducing error into the test scores. This is different from classical test theory that only looks at random error and does not include systematic error. |
| 17. | d | 156 | Test developers are the individuals who are responsible for establishing the reliability of a test and therefore are the ones who are most likely to use generalizability theory. |
| 18. | a | 134 | Reliability refers to the consistency of test results and concerns itself only with the test. Therefore, reliability of the test is a characteristic of the test. In contrast, validity is related to the inferences the test that is used makes based on test results. Therefore, it is concerned with how the test is used and not just with the characteristics of the test. |

## Short Answer

| Question | Explanation |
|---|---|
| 1. | There are three main methods used to estimate reliability: test–retest, internal consistency, and scorer reliability or agreement. While each method is similar because they all assess the consistency of scores, each method has a unique approach and provides different types of evidence. First, test–retest assesses the consistency of scores across one or more administrations of the test. The second type, internal consistency, assesses how the items within the test are consistent with each other. The third and final approach, scorer reliability, is used when there are multiple raters or judges who score the test. The scorer reliability approach examines how consistent raters or judges scored the test takers. If the raters or judges have scored each test taker more than once, the degree to which each rater is consistent in his or her ratings can also be evaluated. |
| 2. | Interscorer and intrascorer reliability are important for tests that require judges in the scoring process. Interscorer reliability is the amount of agreement across different judges. For example, a test may require that each essay answer be assessed by two independent graders. Interscorer reliability would look at the agreement between the graders. In contrast, intrascorer reliability is the amount of agreement or consistency within a single judge. For example, a single grader may score the same essay more than once to determine his or her consistency. |
| 3. | The ability to assess systematic error is a key feature of generalizability theory. Unlike classical test theory that focuses only on random error, generalizability theory allows the test developer or researcher to segment measurement error into many different facets. Thus, he or she can see how aspects of administration, scoring, or even the test taker can affect test scores. This allows us to estimate the degree to which the results of testing will generalize to other people, places, or times. |
| 4. | Adding more questions to a test typically increases the test's reliability. Including more questions provides more opportunity to observe the construct a test is designed to measure (e.g., a test taker's knowledge, skills, abilities, or traits), reduces the impact of random error, and increases the accuracy of measurement. |
| 5. | Random errors have meaning within classical measurement theory. According to classical measurement theory, a person's observed score is equal to his or her true score, plus random error. Random means that the measurement errors are unpredictable and cannot be attributed to any known cause. While random measurement error may cause individual measurements to be higher or lower than a person's true score, over repeated measurements, the errors will cancel out. On the other hand, systematic error affects tests scores in a consistent way and can be attributed to some cause. For example, practice effects will consistently increase scores on the second administration of a test. Unlike random error, systematic error will not cancel itself out. |
| 6. | The textbook describes six factors that can affect a test's reliability: test length, test homogeneity, test–retest interval, test administration, scoring, and cooperation of the test takers.<br><br>1. Test length—Generally, adding items that measure the same trait or attribute will increase the test's reliability.<br><br>2. Homogeneity—Generally, if items measuring the same attribute or trait are added, reliability will increase; however, if heterogeneous items are added, test reliability is more likely to decrease.<br><br>3. Test–retest interval—As a general rule, the longer the interval between administrations of a test, the lower the reliability coefficient will be. |

*(Continued)*

(Continued)

| Question | Explanation |
|---|---|
|  | 4. Test administration—Standardization and consistency between administrations is expected to increase reliability because extraneous factors will be limited or at least controlled.<br>5. Scoring—As a general rule, the more qualitative judgments that graders must make, the lower the reliability will be.<br>6. Cooperation of the test taker—Test takers who are not motivated to cooperate with the test instructions are likely to add additional measurement error to test scores and therefore likely to reduce test reliability. |
| 7. | The KR-20 is the Kuder–Richardson formula. This formula measures the internal consistency of a test, using items that are dichotomously scored as either right or wrong. This dichotomous nature of the formula distinguishes it from coefficient alpha, which can be used on items with multiple possible responses or levels. However, when coefficient alpha is used on dichotomous items, the results are the same as with the KR-20. |
| 8. | The professor should consider how practice effects may influence students' performance on the posttest. Students may perform better because they are familiar with the test questions and format, remember them while they attend class, and take notes specific to the test questions. Students may remember the content from the questions throughout the course, which could help them study for the final. However, not all the students will remember the questions on the test if the interval between test administration is long enough, which may reduce practice effects. Long intervals or a change on any other factor is preferred, and the use of an alternate form is the better choice. |
| 9. | Psychological tests and surveys are both used to collect information. However, there are two important distinctions. First, tests focus on individual outcomes, while surveys focus on group outcomes. For example, an organization may give a test to employees to decide whom they want to promote. That same organization may also administer a survey to employees to determine if they are happy with the promotion process as a group. Also, test results are usually reported as a single score, but survey results are often reported at the individual–item level. |
| 10. | The Spearman–Brown formula was independently developed by two different researchers: Charles Spearman and William Brown. The formula provides an estimate of a test's reliability if test items measuring the same trait or attribute are added or subtracted from a test. This is possible because there is a relationship between test length and reliability, with longer tests being more reliable. For example, a test developer may have a test with 100 questions but may wish to cut down on testing time and only use 80 questions. The Spearman–Brown formula would allow the researcher to estimate what the reliability of the shortened test will be. |
| 11. | Test–retest assesses reliability by comparing test scores from two different testing occasions. In contrast, internal consistency looks at the items within a single administration of a test to confirm that the items share something in common (measure the same construct). An example of internal consistency is coefficient alpha, which is an index of how related the individual test items are. Thus, internal consistency and test–retest are different in that the test–retest method uses the total test score on two different testing occasions to estimate the reliability of the test, while the internal consistency method uses the correlation of the individual items from a single testing session. One test–retest method is called parallel forms. Rather than giving the same test twice, two very similar tests are given on different occasions in an attempt to avoid practice effects. |

# 6 How Do We Gather Evidence of Validity Based on the Content of a Test?

## Overview

In Chapter 6 of the textbook, you were introduced to the concept of validity, in general, and on gathering evidence of validity based on test content, more specifically. Hopefully, after reading the chapter, you have a clearer understanding of what we mean by validity, the different sources of evidence of validity, and how we develop evidence of validity based on test content. While Chapter 6 of the textbook included information about evidence of validity based on test content, Chapter 6 of the workbook provides you with the opportunity to demonstrate your understanding of material presented in the textbook and apply your learning by completing some practical and critical-thinking exercises linked to specific learning objectives. Chapter 6 of the workbook will also allow you to complete chapter-level projects to demonstrate your understanding of multiple topics within the chapter. Chapter 6 of the workbook ends with some multiple-choice and short-answer questions you can use to self-assess your understanding of the material.

# Practical and Critical-Thinking Exercises

## Purpose

This section contains five exercises you can complete to demonstrate your understanding and apply your learning (Exercises 6.1–6.5) and one exercise you can complete to reflect on your learning (Exercise 6.6). The exercises, linked to learning objectives, are displayed below.

**Exercise 6.1**
**What Are the Methods for Establishing Evidence of Validity?**
- **Learning Objective:** Recognize the different sources of validity evidence.

**Exercise 6.2**
**How Can We Establish Evidence of Validity Based on Test Content During Test Development?**
- **Learning Objective:** Create test specification tables demonstrating evidence of validity based on test content.

**Exercise 6.3**
**How Can We Establish Evidence of Validity Based on Test Content After Test Development?**
- **Learning Objective:** Demonstrate your ability to calculate and interpret content validity ratios.

**Exercise 6.4**
**Exactly How Important Is Validity Based on Test Content?**
- **Learning Objective:** Determine the importance of and standards for establishing evidence of content validity.

**Exercise 6.5**
**Should Professionals Consider Face Validity When Evaluating a Test?**
- **Learning Objective:** Construct an argument on whether to consider face validity when developing a test.

**Exercise 6.6**
**Reflect on Your Learning**
- **Learning Objective:** Describe key takeaways and confusing concepts from Chapter 6.

## Exercise 6.1: What Are the Methods for Establishing Evidence of Validity?

**OBJECTIVE**

Recognize the different sources of validity evidence.

**BACKGROUND**

Whenever a test is used to make a decision, we need to ensure the interpretations or inferences we make from the test score are likely to be correct. For example, to be a commercial pilot, one must first obtain a commercial pilot's license. In addition to various other requirements, to obtain a pilot's license, individuals must successfully pass a Federal Aviation Administration (FAA) knowledge test and a practical (flight) test to demonstrate they have the knowledge and skills to successfully pilot a commercial airplane. How would you feel about getting on a commercial flight with a pilot who "passed" both tests, but the inferences drawn from the test (that the pilot had the required knowledge and skills) were not good ones? That is, the tests did not really measure what the FAA thought it measured. According to the Standards for Educational and Psychological Testing (AERA, APA, & NCME, 2014), there are five types of evidence we can gather to ensure the interpretations or inferences we make from test scores are likely to be correct: evidence based on (a) test content, (b) response processes, (c) internal structure, (d) relations with other variables, and (e) consequences of testing. To increase your understanding of the different methods for establishing evidence of validity, for Exercise 6.1, you will review hypothetical evidence of validity for a test and identify what source best describes each piece of evidence.

**YOUR TASK**

1. **Read the information below.**

    Imagine you work in the career services department of a local university. Your responsibility is to find appropriate work study jobs for students receiving work study funds as part of their financial aid package. The accounting faculty at the university regularly rely on work study students to help tutor students taking accounting courses. The faculty have indicated that to be a successful tutor, students must have adequate knowledge of accounting principles. You recommend that the university accounting faculty find an existing, commercially available test that measures accounting knowledge and that this test be administered to students interested in working as tutors in the accounting department.

    The accounting faculty get together and identify an accounting test. They provide you with the name of the test. However, before administering the test to students interested in being accounting tutors, you want to make sure that the test has evidence of validity for its intended use. You conduct some research to determine what evidence of validity exists.

2. **Identify existing sources of evidence.** Review the "Sources of Evidence of Validity" section in Chapter 6 of your textbook. Imagine you found five sources of evidence of validity during your research. These five sources are listed below. Read each source of evidence. Based on the 2014 Standards, document, in the chart on the following page, what source best describes each piece of evidence.

| Evidence | Type of Evidence |
|---|---|
| 1. After the test was administered, the test developer analyzed the responses and found that the test was equally difficult for minorities and non-minorities, and that all test items had the same psychometric characteristics for both groups. | |
| 2. After the test was administered and job offers were made, the test developer found that males and females had unequal passing rates, but jobs offered to each group were at the same rate. | |
| 3. The test developer identified the relative importance of accounting knowledge areas required by the job. Then she developed the test ensuring that all knowledge areas were covered and that the number of items in each area was based on its relative importance. | |
| 4. After the test was administered, the test developer interviewed test takers and determined that their answers were based on logical reasoning and retrieval of information from memory. Very little guessing was taking place. | |
| 5. The test developer administered the test to accountants who currently were employed at the organization and also collected performance data for these accountants. She found that accountants who had higher accounting knowledge test scores also had better performance. | |

3. **Answer the questions below.**

   If you were the accounting test developer, which method(s) would you use to gather evidence of validity for intended use? Why?

   _____

   _____

   _____

   What is the value of thinking about validity in terms of the various types of evidence compared to using the traditional terms *content, criterion related*, and *construct validity*?

   _____

   _____

   _____

   What might be the consequences of using an accounting test without evidence of validity for intended use?

   _____

   _____

   _____

Chapter 6 ■ How Do We Gather Evidence of Validity Based on the Content of a Test? 145

## Exercise 6.2: How Can We Establish Evidence of Validity Based on Test Content During Test Development?

**OBJECTIVE**

Create test specification tables demonstrating evidence of validity based on test content.

**BACKGROUND**

There are two methods we can use to obtain evidence of validity based on test content. The first method involves performing a series of systematic steps during the test development process. The result of this method provides the test developers and test users with confidence the questions on the test are representative of the construct being measured. For example, if designing a test to measure the construct of reliability and validity knowledge, the outcome would demonstrate the test includes test questions that are representative of what is important to know about both reliability and validity. For example, if your professor told you that the test you were taking was designed to measure your knowledge of reliability and validity, but only included a few questions on reliability, this test would not have evidence of validity based on test content. To increase your understanding of how to establish evidence of validity during the test development process, for Exercise 6.2, you will create two test specification tables to establish evidence of validity for intended use based on test content.

**YOUR TASK**

1. **Create a test specification table to assess student knowledge of the material presented in Chapter 6 of your textbook.** Imagine you were tasked with developing a test to measure student knowledge of material presented in Chapter 6 of your textbook. Review the "Demonstrating Evidence of Validity Based on Test Content During Test Development" section of Chapter 6 in your textbook. Using the example provided in For Your Information Box 6.1 and your word-processing software, create a test specification table you could use to guide development of the test and demonstrate evidence of validity. Assume the test you will be developing contains multiple-choice questions only.

   Include the following information in the test specification table:

   - Type of test
   - Item format
   - Test length
   - Testing universe
   - General content areas and subareas
   - Content area or subarea weight
   - Number of items per content and subarea

2. **Create a test specification table to assess student knowledge of a *construct of interest to you*.** Imagine you are asked to develop a 20-item multiple-choice knowledge test to measure student knowledge of a concrete attribute. Select a concrete attribute you might measure (e.g., how to read music, characteristics of different types of birds, how to bake a cake). Be creative and select something that you know well. Using the example provided in For Your Information Box 6.1 and your word-processing software, create a

test specification table you could use to guide development of the test and demonstrate evidence of validity.

Include the following information in the test specification table:

- Type of test
- Item format
- Test length
- Testing universe
- General content areas and subareas
- Content area or subarea weight
- Number of items per content and subarea

3. **Answer the following questions.**

When creating your test specification tables, what did you find easy? What did you find difficult?

_____
_____
_____
_____
_____

Why are test specifications critical to developing a content-valid test?

_____
_____
_____
_____
_____

What might be the consequences of not carefully developing test specifications?

_____
_____
_____
_____
_____

# Chapter 6 ■ How Do We Gather Evidence of Validity Based on the Content of a Test?

## Exercise 6.3: How Can We Establish Evidence of Validity Based on Test Content After Test Development?

**OBJECTIVE**

Demonstrate your ability to calculate and interpret content validity ratios.

**BACKGROUND**

There are two methods we can use to obtain evidence of validity based on test content. One method involves performing a series of systematic steps during the test development process, while the other involves assessing evidence of validity based on test content after a test has been developed. A popular method for assessing validity based on test content after developing a test involves having experts review and rate how essential test items are to the attribute, trait, or characteristic the items are measuring. For each item, Lawshe's (1975) content validity ratio is then calculated to identify the level of agreement across raters. For Exercise 6.3, you will calculate content validity ratios for a 10-item hypothetical test and then answer some questions regarding the results.

**YOUR TASK**

1. **Calculate the content validity ratios.** Review the "Demonstrating Evidence of Validity Based on Test Content After Test Development" section of Chapter 6 in your textbook. Then imagine, after developing a 10-item knowledge test to measure student knowledge of test validity, you asked five raters to rate the extent to which the knowledge in each question was *essential (E), useful but not essential (UNE)*, or *not essential* (NE) for demonstrating knowledge of test validity. Review the hypothetical content validation results in the table below. The checkmarks indicate the rating each rater provided for each of the 10 items. For example, Rater 1 evaluated Item 1 as *essential*. In the workspace provided below, calculate the content validity ratio (CVR) for each item. Refer to the "Demonstrating Evidence of Validity Based on Test Content After Test Development" section of Chapter 6 to locate the formula needed to calculate the CVR. Use a spare sheet of paper for your calculations and ensure your CVR values in the table below.

| Item | Rater 1 | | | Rater 2 | | | Rater 3 | | | Rater 4 | | | Rater 5 | | | CVR |
|---|---|---|---|---|---|---|---|---|---|---|---|---|---|---|---|---|
| | E | UNE | NE | E | UNE | NE | E | UNE | NE | E | UNE | NE | E | UNE | NE | |
| 1 | ✓ | | | ✓ | | | ✓ | | | ✓ | | | ✓ | | | |
| 2 | | ✓ | | ✓ | | | ✓ | | | | ✓ | | ✓ | | | |
| 3 | | | ✓ | ✓ | | | ✓ | | | | ✓ | | ✓ | | | |
| 4 | ✓ | | | ✓ | | | ✓ | | | ✓ | | | ✓ | | | |
| 5 | ✓ | | | ✓ | | | ✓ | | | ✓ | | | ✓ | | | |
| 6 | ✓ | | | ✓ | | | ✓ | | | ✓ | | | ✓ | | | |
| 7 | ✓ | | | ✓ | | | ✓ | | | ✓ | | | ✓ | | | |
| 8 | | ✓ | | | ✓ | | | ✓ | | | ✓ | | | ✓ | | |
| 9 | ✓ | | | ✓ | | | ✓ | | | ✓ | | | ✓ | | | |
| 10 | ✓ | | | ✓ | | | ✓ | | | ✓ | | | ✓ | | | |

2. **Interpret your results.** Given the results above, answer the following questions.

Which items are essential? What criteria did you use to determine which items are essential?

Does the test have evidence of validity based on test content? Why or why not?

What additional information should you consider while calculating the CVR?

## Exercise 6.4: Exactly How Important Is Validity Based on Test Content?

**OBJECTIVE**

Determine the importance of and standards for establishing evidence of content validity.

**BACKGROUND**

Organizations often administer pre-employment tests to job candidates during the hiring process to assess their capabilities and traits. In recent years, the use of pre-employment tests to screen and manage large applicant pools has increased in popularity. These pre-employment tests allow organizations to measure the extent to which job candidates have the knowledge, skills, abilities, and/or other characteristics needed to be successful in a given job. One way that we can gather evidence of validity of a pre-employment test is to look at its content. Demonstrating evidence of validity based on test content is critical to ensuring a test is job related, meaning the test measures knowledge, skills, abilities, and/or other characteristics that are directly related to job performance. A pre-employment test that effectively and comprehensively measures the knowledge, skills, abilities, and/or other characteristics necessary to perform a job successfully has evidence of validity based on test content, and therefore evidence of its job-relatedness. To increase your understanding of the importance of validity based on test content, for Exercise 6.4, you will locate and read the Uniform Guidelines on Employee Selection Procedures provided by the Equal Employment Opportunity Commission (EEOC), then answer questions about this type of evidence of validity.

**YOUR TASK**

1. **Read the EEOC's Uniform Guidelines on Employee Selection Procedures.** Search the Internet to find the EEOC's Uniform Guidelines on Employee Selection Procedures. Read through the Guidelines and find the information necessary to comprehensively answer the following questions.

   According to the EEOC's Uniform Guidelines on Employee Selection Procedures, must all pre-employment tests have established evidence of validity based on test content? Explain your response.

   _____
   _____
   _____
   _____
   _____
   _____
   _____

According to the EEOC's Uniform Guidelines on Employee Selection Procedures, what are the standards for demonstrating evidence of validity based on test content?

According to the EEOC's Uniform Guidelines on Employee Selection Procedures, when, if at all, is it acceptable to use a pre-employment test with evidence of adverse impact?

According to the EEOC's Uniform Guidelines on Employee Selection Procedures, when, if at all, is documentation of established evidence of validity required?

# Exercise 6.5: Should Professionals Consider Face Validity When Evaluating a Test?

**OBJECTIVE**

Construct an argument on whether to consider face validity when developing a test.

**BACKGROUND**

*Face validity* is a term used to describe how items appear to relate to the purpose of a test. For example, if an employment test contained questions such as "I have a soft heart," or "I sympathize with others' feelings," you might not see any connection between the questions and the job requirements. In this case, the test would lack face validity for you. While face validity is not a recognized method for demonstrating evidence of the validity of a test, a person's perception of the test items and what the test is supposed to measure or predict could influence how a person responds to the test questions. For example, he or she may not take the test seriously if the items appear to not match the intended purpose. To increase your understanding of face validity, for Exercise 6.5, you will discuss the importance of face validity and the reasons it is not used as a formal method for establishing evidence of validity.

**YOUR TASK**

1. **Develop a list to document the pros and cons for the argument on the use of face validity.** Review the section on face validity in Chapter 6 of your textbook, including the online face validity resources provided in On the Web Box 6.1. Using the material presented in the textbook and the arguments provided online, create a list of three pros and three cons of professionals, including an evaluation of a test based on face validity. Include in your list a reflection on whether you agree or disagree with the arguments presented on face validity and highlight the importance of each argument. Document your findings in the chart below.

|  | Source | Argument | Do you agree or disagree with the argument? |
|---|---|---|---|
|  | Provide the location of the source. | What is the argument provided? | Provide a reason you either agree or disagree with the argument. |
| **PROs** | | | |
| 1. | | | |
| 2. | | | |
| 3. | | | |
| **CONs** | | | |
| 1. | | | |
| 2. | | | |
| 3. | | | |

2. **Construct an argument on whether to consider face validity when developing a test.**
   Review your responses to Task 1. Construct a 1-paragraph argument on whether to consider face validity when developing a test.

# Exercise 6.6: Reflect on Your Learning

**OBJECTIVE**

Describe key takeaways and confusing concepts from Chapter 6.

**BACKGROUND**

In Chapter 6 of the textbook, you were introduced to what test validity is, the five sources of validity evidence described in the *Standards for Educational and Psychological Testing* (AERA, APA, & NCME, 2014), and the appropriate use of various validation strategies. You read about the methods used for demonstrating evidence of validity based on the content of a test both during the test development process and after the test development process. Last, you were introduced to the nature and importance of face validity, and why it does not provide evidence for interpreting test scores. For Exercise 6.6, you will reflect on your learning from Chapter 6 of the textbook and identify key takeaways from the chapter.

**YOUR TASK**

1. **Identify your "Aha!" moments from Chapter 6.**
   - Identify 3 to 4 new insights or realizations you had after reading Chapter 6, referred to as "Aha!" moments.
   - Consider things that made you look at a concept, your life, or an issue in a completely different way than you had in the past.
   - Document your insights and realizations below, providing details of your learning.

2. **Identify some muddy moment discussion questions.**
   - Identify 2 to 3 concepts that are still "muddy" for you from the chapter.
   - Consider concepts you still don't understand, concepts you need clarified, and/or questions you want to ask.
   - Develop 1 to 3 questions to initiate a discussion in class to further your understanding of the concepts and get your questions answered.

| | |
|---|---|
| **Insights and Realizations** | 1. _____<br>2. _____<br>3. _____<br>4. _____ |
| **Muddy Moments Discussion Questions** | 1. _____<br>2. _____<br>3. _____ |

## Chapter-Level Projects

### Project 1

**BACKGROUND**

As you learned in Chapter 6 of the textbook, the first three steps test developers often take to gather evidence of validity based on the content of a test are (a) define the testing universe, (b) develop the test specifications (similar to a blueprint), and (c) establish the test format. The fourth step is to write the test items. Writing good test items depends on having a clear understanding of the concrete or abstract construct the test will be measuring, having a well-defined and documented plan containing details about a test's content, and knowing what type of test and what types of items are necessary for measuring the construct.

**YOUR TASK**

1. **Read the following information.**

    O*NET Online is a comprehensive database of occupational information maintained by the U.S. Department of Labor/Employment and Training Administration. The database allows anyone with Internet access to explore and research different occupations. In addition to other information, for each occupation in the database, there is a description of sample job titles within the occupation, the tasks and work activities performed by individuals in the occupation, and the knowledge, skills, and abilities required to effectively perform the tasks.

2. **Identify an occupation of interest to you.** Access the O*NET Online database at www.onetonline.org. Conduct an occupation search to find the Summary Report for an occupation of interest to you. For example, if you were interested in the occupation of a computer hardware engineer, you would type "computer hardware engineer" in the occupation search field.

3. **Review the steps to complete during the process of test development.** Review the "Demonstrating Evidence of Validity Based on Test Content During Test Development" section of Chapter 6 in your textbook.

4. **Develop test specifications for two tests.** Imagine you were tasked with designing two tests a company could use as part of their selection process for computer hardware engineers. Create two different test specifications tables using the example provided in your textbook (see For Your Information Box 6.1) as a guide.

5. **Develop a presentation**. Develop a PPT or Prezi presentation capturing the following:
   - The name of your test and your two test specification tables
   - How you determined what content to include in each of your test specification tables
   - If you had to choose one of the test specifications as the foundation for a test you were going to develop, which you choose and why
   - In addition to gathering evidence of validity based on test content, the other types of evidence you would gather to ensure the interpretations or inferences made from the test scores are likely to be correct
   - What, if anything, you would do to enhance the face validity of your test

## Project 2

### BACKGROUND

As you learned in Chapter 6 of the textbook, there are different strategies we can use to gather evidence of validity. We can gather evidence of validity based on (a) test content, (b) response processes, (c) internal structure, (d) relations with other variables, and (e) the consequences of testing. While the more evidence of validity the better, it is not always possible to gather all the different sources of evidence because the most appropriate strategies depend on the purpose of the test. Gathering evidence of validity is critical for a variety of reasons. One reason is that important decisions are made using test scores. If tests are not accurate or do not predict what they are believed to predict, then bad decisions might be made. Another reason is to ensure tests are used in a way that complies with federal law. Civil rights laws prohibit using tests to make employment decisions that result in discrimination based on characteristics such as race, religion, sexual orientation, and gender. To help those who use tests to make employment decisions better comply with the law, in 1978, The U.S. Civil Service Commission, the Department of Labor, the Department of Justice, and the EEOC jointly adopted the *Uniform Guidelines on Employee Selection Procedures*.

### YOUR TASK

1. **Review the following information:**
   - Review Chapter 6 of your textbook to refresh your memory of the different methods for gathering evidence of validity.
   - Search the Internet to find the EEOC's *Uniform Guidelines on Employee Selection Procedures*. Read through the *Guidelines* to learn about the standards for those who use tests to make employment decisions.

2. **Research a legal challenge/lawsuit against an organization.** Search the Internet or library to find a legal challenge/lawsuit that involved an organization using a hiring tool (a test or an interview) to make an employment decision. Thoroughly review existing literature to learn as much as you can about the legal challenge. Document the facts related to the case, beginning with the charge/complaint against the organization.

3. **Apply your learning to the specific legal challenge.** Identify what source(s) of validity evidence existed to support validity of the hiring tool used by the organization. Based on what you learned in Chapter 6 of your textbook and by reading the EEOC's *Uniform Guidelines on Employee Selection Procedures*, what could the organization have done differently to minimize liability risk?

# Project 3

**BACKGROUND**

Imagine you were in graduate school serving as the teaching assistant for a psychology instructor. Because some of the students in the course are struggling with the concepts in Chapter 6, the instructor has asked you to spend 1 hour with these students to help increase their understanding of the Chapter 6 material. In addition to meeting with the students, the instructor requested that you create a visual learning aid you can use not only as an instructional tool when meeting with the students, but that students can take with them and use as a study tool for future exams.

**YOUR TASK**

1. **Search the Internet to learn more about visual learning aids.** Conduct a search of the Internet to learn more about the value of visual learning aids and the different types of learning aids. When searching, consider using key terms such as *visual learning aids, graphic organizer, concept maps, cognitive organizer, concept diagrams,* and *story maps*.

2. **Create a visual learning aid of the Chapter 6 material.** Review the learning objectives at the beginning of Chapter 6. Create a well-thought-out visual learning aid to enhance student understanding of the important concepts associated with each learning objective. Your visual learning aid should be professional-looking and include visual symbols and words to express Chapter 6 concepts, as well as the connections between them. Creativity is encouraged.

## Practice Questions

### Multiple Choice

1. A valid test
   a. consistently measures whatever it measures.
   b. consistently measures multiple constructs.
   c. measures only one construct.
   d. allows one to make correct inferences about the meaning of the scores.

2. The current *Standards* (AERA, APA, & NCME, 2014) include discussion of five sources of evidence of validity. Which of the following is one of those sources?
   a. Construct validity
   b. Criterion-related validity
   c. Test content
   d. Face validity

3. Which one of the following is NOT considered a traditional type of validity?
   a. Content
   b. Criterion related
   c. Construct
   d. Alternate forms

4. Demonstrating evidence of validity is often logical rather than statistical for which one of the following?
   a. Face validity and validity evidence based on a test's relationships with a criterion
   b. Face validity and validity evidence based on a test's content
   c. Construct validity and validity evidence based on a test's relationships with a criterion
   d. Validity evidence based on a test's content and based on a test's relationships with a criterion

5. If we demonstrate that a test allows us to identify individuals who are likely to become depressed, we have demonstrated evidence of validity based on the test's
   a. content.
   b. relationship with a criterion.
   c. relationship with a construct.
   d. appearance to the test taker.

6. What type of evidence of validity exists if you took an algebra test that required you to perform a representative sample of algebraic calculations?
   a. Validity based on its content
   b. Validity based on its relationship with a criterion
   c. Validity based on its relationship with a construct
   d. Face validity

7. What type of evidence of validity exists if a test developer finds that scores on a new employment test, designed to predict success on the job, correlate with employees' performance appraisal ratings?
   a. Validity based on the test's relationship with a criterion
   b. Validity based on the test's relationship with a construct
   c. Validity based on the test's content
   d. Face validity

8. What type of attribute does a test measures if the attribute can be described in terms of specific behaviors?
   a. Abstract
   b. Nonspecific
   c. Concrete
   d. Specific

9. Which one of the following types of attribute is most difficult to describe in terms of behaviors?

   a. Abstract

   b. Concrete

   c. Nonspecific

   d. Specific

10. Evidence of validity based on a test's content is easiest for tests such as mathematical achievement tests that measure _____ attributes and more difficult for tests such as personality tests that measure _____ attributes.

    a. abstract; concrete

    b. concrete; abstract

    c. nonspecific; specific

    d. specific; nonspecific

11. If test takers perceive a test as appropriate, they are referencing evidence of what?

    a. Face validity

    b. Reliability

    c. Validity based on content

    d. Validity based on relationship with a construct

12. What evidence exists for a writing test that requires a test taker to perform a representative sample of writing activities (for example, writing a poem, writing an essay, writing a term paper)?

    a. Validity based on the test's relationship with a construct

    b. Validity based on the test's relationship with a criterion

    c. Validity based on the test's content

    d. Face validity

13. What is the first step to ensuring that a test demonstrates evidence of validity based on its content?

    a. Develop test specifications

    b. Define the testing universe

    c. Determine the content areas

    d. Determine the instructional objectives

14. The content validity ratio for a test item can range from what to what?

    a. −1.00 to 0

    b. 0 to 1.00

    c. −1.00 to 1.00

    d. 0 to 10.00

## Short Answer

**Remembering**

1. How are the traditional concepts of content, criterion-related, and construct validity similar? How are they different?

2. Discuss the five sources of evidence of validity described in the 2014 *Standards* (AERA, APA, & NCME, 2014).

3. What are test specifications, and what is typically included in test specifications?

4. What are the four steps test developers use to administer a competency exam? Describe one in detail.

**Applying**

5. How does the 1999 and 2014 treatment of validity in the *Standards* differ from the treatment of validity prior to 1999?

6. What is the difference between abstract and contract attributes and what are some examples of each?

**Evaluating**

7. In what situations is it appropriate to demonstrate evidence of validity based on test content, relationships with a criterion, and relationships with a construct? When would it be appropriate to collect evidence of more than one type of validity?

8. What does it mean when we say that validity should be viewed as a unitary concept?

9. What might happen if the testing universe and content areas for a written test was not well defined prior to test development?

## Multiple-Choice and Short-Answer Practice Question Answer Key

### Multiple Choice

| Question | Answer | Textbook Page | Explanation |
|---|---|---|---|
| 1. | d | 165 | A test in and of itself is neither valid nor invalid. Instead, validity concerns the inferences that are made from test scores. Hence, validity is not a property of the test. Rather, validity refers to the consequences and interpretation of test scores for their intended purpose. Furthermore, to establish validity, we have to collect different types of evidence to show that the inferences are appropriate. |
| 2. | c | 164–165 | 1. Evidence based on test content<br>2. Evidence based on response processes<br>3. Evidence based on internal structure<br>4. Evidence based on relations with other variables<br>5. Evidence based on the consequences of testing |
| 3. | d | 164–165 | Before the 1999 *Standards*, validity was viewed in three distinct categories: content validity, construct validity, and criterion (related) validity. In contrast, alternative forms is a method for assessing a test's reliability and is not directly related to validity. |
| 4. | b | 179 | Face validity concerns whether test takers and others view the test as measuring what it is supposed to measure. This is a subjective process, and it focuses on whether the test "looks" valid to the test taker or others. Also, evidence of validity based on test content involves logically and systematically showing that the test's content is representative of the construct being measured. As a result, neither forms of validity generally involve statistical analyses. However, criterion and construct evidence for validity almost always involve such analyses. |
| 5. | b | 165 | A criterion is an outcome that a test user is interested in predicting. For example, companies are interested in predicting the future performance of applicants, thus the criterion in this example is job performance. Therefore, criterion-related validity evidence seeks to determine the relationship between the test and job performance. |

*(Continued)*

(Continued)

| Question | Answer | Textbook Page | Explanation |
|---|---|---|---|
| 6. | a | 164 | Because the items on the test (i.e., the test content) are representative of the algebraic calculations, we would say that the test has evidence of validity based on its content. While content valid tests are often face valid, remember that face validity refers to if the test "looks valid" and does not refer to what the test actually measures or its content. Thus, in this case, the best answer is evidence based on its content. |
| 7. | a | 165 | When a test score predicts a future outcome (often called a *criterion*), we say the test demonstrates evidence of validity based on its relationship with a criterion. This question describes a specific type of evidence called *predictive evidence of validity* because the test scores are significantly related to an important *future* outcome of employee performance, thereby making the test a valid selection tool. |
| 8. | c | 166 | Some tests measure attributes that are relatively easy to observe and are highly specific. In these cases, we say the test is measuring a concrete attribute. These types of attributes are easier to measure, and it is easier to collect evidence for their validity. |
| 9. | a | 166 | The textbook defines two types of attributes: concrete and abstract. Concrete attributes are easier to observe. Abstract attributes are much more difficult to describe or measure because it might not be clear exactly what behaviors are most important to be measured. For example, what is leadership? What are the specific behaviors that demonstrate leadership and how will we measure them? Obviously, leadership is a vague and abstract concept. Because of this, it is much harder to collect validity evidence for such an abstract attribute. |
| 10. | b | 166 | Both mathematics and achievement are well understood and are easier to define attributes. Therefore, they are concrete in nature. In contrast, personality is much more ambiguous and vague, and therefore, it is best described as an abstract attribute. |
| 11. | a | 179 | Face validity refers to whether test takers think that the test is measuring what it is supposed to be measuring. While face validity is often an important consideration when choosing a test, it is not a type of psychometric validity. There are many tests that may have significant evidence of validity for intended use, but do not appear face valid to the test takers. |

| Question | Answer | Textbook Page | Explanation |
|---|---|---|---|
| 12. | c | 167 | Evidence of validity based on test content requires that the test cover all major aspects of the testing universe (of the construct) in the correct proportion. Thus, if the test taker is performing representative samples of writing activities, then the test content does sample from the construct of writing. |
| 13. | b | 168 | The first step in gathering evidence based on test content is to carefully define the body of knowledge or behaviors that a test represents, which is the testing universe. Defining the testing universe often involves reviewing other instruments that measure the same construct, interviewing experts who are familiar with the construct, and researching the construct by locating theoretical or empirical research on the construct. The purpose is to ensure that the test developer clearly understands and can clearly define the construct that he or she will be measuring. Evidence of validity based on test content requires that the test cover all major aspects of the testing universe (the construct[s] being measured) in the correct proportion. |
| 14. | c | 178 | Content validity ratios are sometimes used to demonstrate content-based evidence of validity and are based on a survey of subject matter experts. They can range from between −1.00 and 1.00, where a value of 0.00 means that 50% of the experts believe a test item to be essential. |

## Short Answer

| Question | Explanation |
|---|---|
| 1. | Prior to the 1999 *Standards for Educational and Psychological Testing* (AERA, APA, & NCME, 2014), experts talked about three types of validity: content validity, criterion-related validity, and construct validity. These three approaches to validity are similar in that they all focus on the appropriateness, meaningfulness, and usefulness of a test and the inferences being drawn from the test scores. They are all slightly different types of evidence, however. Content validity refers to the representativeness between the test and the domain it is intended to measure. Criterion-related evidence refers to the extent to which the scores on the test are related to one or more outcomes. Finally, construct validity indicates the degree to which the test measures the concept or characteristic it is designed to measure. |
| 2. | The 2014 *Standards* refers to five sources of validity evidence. The first type is *evidence based on test content*, which examines if the content of a test is representative of the concepts it is intended to measure. The second type is *evidence based on the response process*. This type of evidence involves observing test takers to ensure that the mental processes used to answer questions matches the expected processes required of the test. The third type is *evidence based on the internal structure* of the test. This type of evidence ensures the psychometric structure of the test matches the intended structure. The fourth type is *evidence based on relationships with other variables*, and it determines if the test scores are related to other outcomes that we would expect them to be related to. The fifth and final type is *evidence based on the consequences of testing* and looks at both intended and unintended consequences of testing to ensure unbiased results. |
| 3. | Test specifications include the detailed plans that are prepared during the test development process to document the details about a test's content. Test specifications include a clearly defined testing universe, the content areas (subject matter that a test will measure), and the number of questions that will be included to assess each content area. Test specifications may also include information such as the purpose and intended use of the test; the format and length of the test; and how the test is to be delivered, administered, and scored. |
| 4. | Test developers typically follow four steps when developing a competency exam. First, they determine the learning objectives of the training program. To determine the learning objectives of the training program, developers often conduct a job analysis to determine the knowledge, skills, and abilities required for a particular job. Second, they outline the content areas of the exam to ensure that relevant subject matter is neither omitted nor emphasized inappropriately on the exam. Third, they establish the format for the exam, carefully deciding whether the exam will be a practical exam or a written exam and the types of items to include on the exam. Last, they write the exam items to measure the content areas identified during the second step and meet the learning objectives identified in the first step. |

| Question | Explanation |
|---|---|
| 5. | The 1999 and 2014 *Standards* differed from previous standards in that the 1999 and 2014 *Standards* strongly supported a unitary view of test validity that characterized validity as the degree to which evidence supports the interpretations of test scores as entailed by the proposed uses of the test. In contrast, older versions of the *Standards* divided the validity into three types of validity: content, criterion, and construct validity. |
| 6. | Tests can measure either concrete attributes or abstract attributes. Concrete attributes can be described in terms of specific, observable, and measurable behaviors. A few examples of tests that measures concrete attributes might be a test that measures a person's ability to ride a bicycle or drive a car. We can observe specific behaviors that are associated with these two abilities.<br><br>Abstract attributes are more difficult to describe in terms of observable behaviors than concrete attributes. A few examples of tests that measure abstract attributes might be a test that measures intelligence or personality. |
| 7. | It is always sound practice to collect as much evidence of validity as required to support the assertions that are or will be based on test scores. This often means collecting a variety of types of evidence. Given that the classical views of content, criterion-related, and construct validity closely align to three of the types of validity evidence that are discussed within the most recent *Standards*, it would be appropriate to collect this type of evidence in many situations when it is practical or feasible to do so. |
| 8. | Modern views of validity concern the meaning that is placed on test scores. Put another way, a test with evidence of validity is one in which the interpretation of test scores is consistent with the intended purpose. As a result, validity is a single or unitary concept; there are no different types of validity as inferred by older views of validity. |
| 9. | By defining the testing universe and identifying the content areas to include on a test, test developers are able to define the body of knowledge or behaviors that a test represents. Having a well-defined testing universe and well-defined content area are critical to demonstrating evidence of validity based on test content. If the testing universe and content areas are not well defined, a test may include items that are not measuring what the test developer intends the test to measure. Therefore, decisions made based on a test score may not be good decisions. |

# 7 How Do We Gather Evidence of Validity Based on Test–Criterion Relationships?

## Overview

In Chapter 7 of the textbook, you were introduced to evidence of validity based on test–criterion relationships. Hopefully, after reading the chapter, you have a clearer understanding of how to gather evidence of validity based on test–criterion relationships, how to read and interpret validity studies, and different methods to obtain this evidence. While Chapter 7 of the textbook included foundational information about the concept of gathering validity based on test–criterion relationships, Chapter 7 of the workbook provides you with the opportunity to demonstrate your understanding of material presented in the textbook and apply your learning by completing some practical and critical-thinking exercises linked to specific learning objectives. Chapter 7 of the workbook will also allow you to complete chapter-level projects to demonstrate your understanding of multiple topics within the chapter. Chapter 7 of the workbook ends with some multiple-choice and short-answer questions you can use to self-assess your understanding of the material.

# Practical and Critical-Thinking Exercises

## Purpose

This section contains five exercises you can complete to demonstrate your understanding and apply your learning (Exercises 7.1–7.5) and one exercise you can complete to reflect on your learning (Exercise 7.6). The exercises, linked to learning objectives, are displayed below.

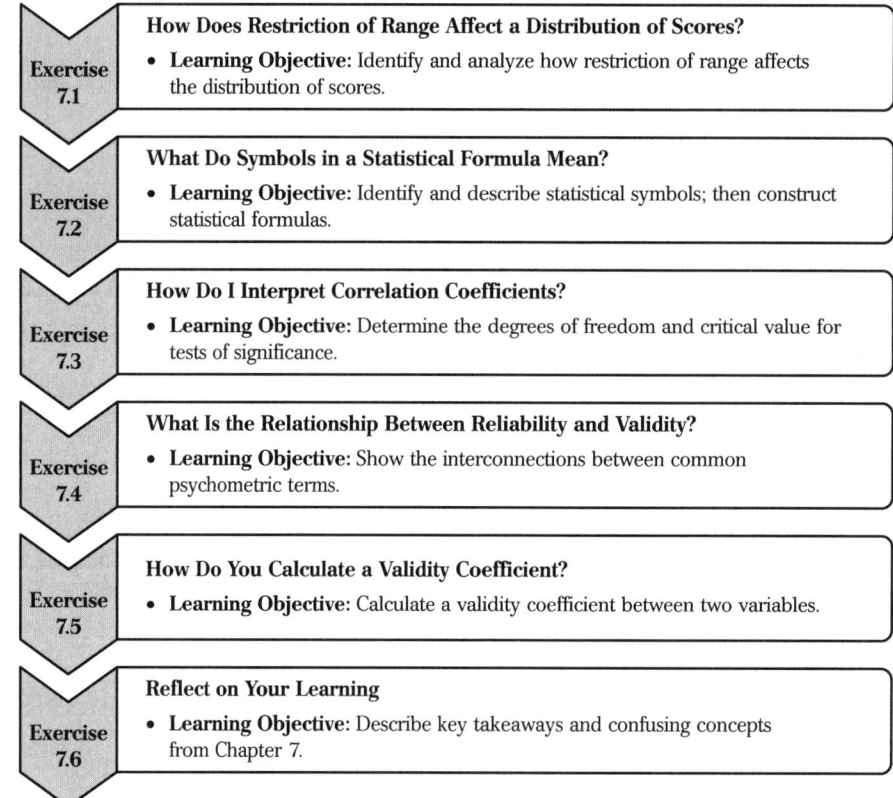

**Exercise 7.1** — How Does Restriction of Range Affect a Distribution of Scores?
- **Learning Objective:** Identify and analyze how restriction of range affects the distribution of scores.

**Exercise 7.2** — What Do Symbols in a Statistical Formula Mean?
- **Learning Objective:** Identify and describe statistical symbols; then construct statistical formulas.

**Exercise 7.3** — How Do I Interpret Correlation Coefficients?
- **Learning Objective:** Determine the degrees of freedom and critical value for tests of significance.

**Exercise 7.4** — What Is the Relationship Between Reliability and Validity?
- **Learning Objective:** Show the interconnections between common psychometric terms.

**Exercise 7.5** — How Do You Calculate a Validity Coefficient?
- **Learning Objective:** Calculate a validity coefficient between two variables.

**Exercise 7.6** — Reflect on Your Learning
- **Learning Objective:** Describe key takeaways and confusing concepts from Chapter 7.

## Exercise 7.1: How Does Restriction of Range Affect a Distribution of Scores?

**OBJECTIVE**

Identify and analyze how restriction of range affects the distribution of scores.

**BACKGROUND**

When a need exists to show a relationship between test scores and some future behavior, researchers often use the predictive method to establish evidence of validity. The predictive method involves administering the test to a large group of people and then some point later in time collect scores on some other measure of behavior for each person who took the test. The scores on the test are then correlated with the scores on the other measure of behavior to see if there is a strong relationship between the test scores, as determined by the validity coefficient. Gathering evidence of validity using the predictive method can be difficult due to the potential for restriction of range. A restriction of range occurs when a test developer does not have access to the full distribution of scores because of some artifact in how the data were collected. Ideally, test developers like to have the full range of scores available, but unfortunately, this is not possible in many situations, such as in the example in For Your Information Box 7.2 in your textbook. Restriction of range is important to understand so that any inference made from a test is accurate. For Exercise 7.1, you will identify potential sources of restriction of range from different examples and then discuss the effects the restriction of range has on the inference.

**YOUR TASK**

1. **Identify the restriction of range.** Review "The Predictive Method" section of Chapter 7 of your textbook, including For Your Information Box 7.2, to learn more about a validity study that used the predictive method and how restriction of range can affect validation study results. Identify the restriction of range for the scenario provided in the chart below. Then, for each scenario below, describe three or more possible sources that might explain why a researcher might experience a restriction of range when gathering evidence of validity via the predictive method. Document your findings in the chart below.

| Scenario | Describe three or more possible sources that might cause a restriction of range to occur given each scenario. |
|---|---|
| [EXAMPLE] | [EXAMPLE] |
| At the beginning of the school year, admission counselors at XYZ University administered the Self-Perceptions of Adults test to accepted college students identified as at risk. At-risk status is determined during the registration process, where all students receive an academic success code generated from multiple factors. Students with low (but acceptable) scores on the SAT/ACT, average high school grades, self-identified as first-generation college students, and other factors associated with poor academic success are provided an academic success code indicating they are at-risk students. To gather evidence of predictive validity of the Self-Perceptions of Adults test, at the end of both the Fall and Spring semesters, administration compared student GPAs to student scores on the Self-Perceptions of Adults test. | 1. No access to students not accepted to the college<br><br>2. Only administered to students identified as at risk<br><br>3. Missing descriptions for additional factors |

*(Continued)*

(Continued)

| Scenario | Describe three or more possible sources that might cause a restriction of range to occur given each scenario. |
|---|---|
| 1. A marketing firm administered a newly developed leadership skills assessment to all employees working within the organization. Those who scored high on the test were enrolled in a leadership training program, and those who did well in the program were offered a manager position. To gather evidence of validity using the predictive method, 6 months later, the test scores of those hired into the manager position were correlated with supervisory ratings of leadership skills. | 1.<br><br>2.<br><br>3. |
| 2. Students at a local elementary school take an intelligence test at the beginning of each school year for placement in an advanced STEM (science, technology, engineering, and math) program. Students who score in the top 5th percentile have the option to participate in the program, and those who score in the top 10th percentile have the option to participate as a guest student. To gather evidence of validity using the predictive method, at the end of the school year, student grades from students who scored in the top 5th percentile are compared to grades from students who scored in the top 10th percentile. | 1.<br><br>2.<br><br>3. |
| 3. The human resources director for a call center wants to know if conditional employees who complete new hire training have the customer service knowledge they need to perform successfully on the job. She creates a knowledge test and administers the test to all new hires upon completing the new hire training. To be hired fulltime, individuals must score a 70 or higher on the test. Six months after the new hire training, the customer service scores of all individuals who passed the test are collected. To gather evidence of validity using the predictive method, test scores from the new hire training are correlated with customer service scores. | 1.<br><br>2.<br><br>3. |

2. **Deconstruct the effects restriction of range may cause.** Analyze how each possible reason for restriction of range you identified above might affect the distribution of test scores from the validity study. Document the results of your analysis in the chart below.

| Scenario | Possible Reasons for Restriction of Range | Describe how each possible source for a restriction of range might influence the validity coefficient from the validity study. |
|---|---|---|
| 1 | 1 | |
| | 2 | |
| | 3 | |
| 2 | 1 | |
| | 2 | |
| | 3 | |
| 3 | 1 | |
| | 2 | |
| | 3 | |

# Exercise 7.2: What Do Symbols in a Statistical Formula Mean?

**OBJECTIVE**

Identify and describe statistical symbols; then construct statistical formulas.

**BACKGROUND**

One method for determining if a test is performing properly is to gather evidence of validity based on test–criterion relationships. This method involves examining if test scores are related to other variables. For example, we may develop a test to predict a sales person's performance on the job. To provide evidence that the test actually does predict sales performance, we might administer the test to a large group of sales people and then correlate their test scores with manager ratings of performance on the job. The result would be a validity coefficient (a linear quantitative estimate of the relationship between the test scores and manager ratings). To increase your understanding of the symbols used when conducting validity studies, for Exercise 7.2, you will identify and define different statistical symbols, arrange the symbols to create formulas, and explain the intended use of the formula.

**YOUR TASK**

1. **Identify and define statistical symbols.** Review Chapter 7 of the textbook and locate the statistical symbols used in formulas. After identifying the symbol listed in the chart below, explain when the symbol is used and what the symbol means. Document your findings in the chart below.

| Statistic | When to Use | What It Means |
|---|---|---|
| $R$ | | |
| $r^2$ | | |
| $R^2$ | | |
| $Y'$ | | |
| $b$ | | |

| Statistic | When to Use | What It Means |
|---|---|---|
| $X$ | | |
| $p$ | | |
| $df$ | | |

2. **Construct and describe three statistical formulas.** Construct three formulas using all the statistical symbols identified in the chart above and using each symbol at least one time. Include at least three symbols in each formula. You may use the symbols more than once, and you can include symbols not identified in the chart above. Then describe the intended use for each formula you identified.

| | Formula | Intended Use |
|---|---|---|
| 1 | | |
| 2 | | |
| 3 | | |

3. **Write a brief scenario.** Choose one of the formulas you constructed and described above. Based on what you found out about the applicability of the formula, create a scenario to make the formula applicable.

# Exercise 7.3: How Do I Interpret Correlation Coefficients?

**OBJECTIVE**

Determine the degrees of freedom and critical value for tests of significance.

**BACKGROUND**

When gathering evidence of validity based on test–criterion relationships, test developers correlate the scores on their test with the scores on another measure of interest to see if there is a strong relationship between the two sets of scores. The resulting validity coefficient then is evaluated to determine whether it is large enough (i.e., statistically significant) to claim that the test effectively predicts the criterion. But, before conducting the validity study, the researcher must first set a standard of comparison against which the statistical results of the study will be evaluated. This standard of comparison is referred to as the alpha level. To increase your understanding of how to interpret correlation coefficients, for Exercise 7.3, you will determine if correlation coefficients are statistically significant using a table of critical values for the Pearson product–moment correlation coefficients.

**YOUR TASK**

1. **Read the following.**

   The alpha level establishes the maximum level of probability the researcher is willing to accept that the results of the study were due simply to chance. After conducting the study, the actual statistical results (called the *p*-value) is compared to the alpha level that the researcher previously chose. This comparison will determine if the results of the study are strong enough for the researcher to be willing to declare that observed results were due to the true relationship between the test and the criterion, and not simply due to chance. Both the alpha level and the *p*-value are necessary to make this determination. The lower we set the alpha level, the more stringent the study will be. For instance, if we set the alpha level to be .05, we are saying that for us to consider our study to have produced statistically significant results, there can only be a 5% probability that our results were due to chance. In this case, the resulting *p*-value of our study would have to be less than or equal to .05. The lower the *p*-value, the lower the likelihood that the relationship from analyzing the results of the study found was due to chance. For example, study results that found a *p*-value of .10 mean that there was a 10% chance that the results were due to chance; a *p*-value of .01 means that there was only a 1% chance. To declare the results of a study as statistically significant, the researcher will compare the *p*-value to the alpha level set at the beginning of the study. Researchers most typically set their alpha levels at .05. Therefore, for the researcher to declare the study to be statistically significant, the resulting *p*-value must be equal to or less than .05. If the researcher had set the alpha level to .01, then to be declared significant, the *p*-value from the study would have been less than or equal to .01—a much more stringent standard.

2. **Determine whether the correlation coefficients are significant.** Read the "Calculating and Evaluating Validity Coefficients" section of Chapter 7 of your textbook. Then, determine if each of the 10 validity coefficients below is significant, showing the degrees of freedom and critical value you used to make your determination, and provide a rationale for your decision. Document your findings in the chart below.

|  | N | Tail | Validity Coefficient | Alpha Set | df = N − 2 | Critical Value | Is the correlation significant? | Rationale |
|---|---|---|---|---|---|---|---|---|
| 1. | 47 | One | .3814 | .05 | 45 | .2429 | Yes | Validity coefficient exceeds critical value |
| 2. | 72 | One | .2959 | .05 | 70 | .1954 | Yes | Validity coefficient exceeds critical value |
| 3. | 16 | One | .5104 | .005 | 14 | .6226 | No | Validity coefficient is less than critical value |
| 4. | 92 | One | .2627 | .01 | 90 | .2418 | Yes | Validity coefficient exceeds critical value |
| 5. | 27 | One | .3417 | .005 | 25 | .4869 | No | Validity coefficient is less than critical value |
| 6. | 42 | One | .5176 | .025 | 40 | .3044 | Yes | Validity coefficient exceeds critical value |
| 7. | 15 | One | .5417 | .05 | 13 | .4409 | Yes | Validity coefficient exceeds critical value |
| 8. | 38 | One | .2897 | .05 | 36 | .2709 | Yes | Validity coefficient exceeds critical value |
| 9. | 102 | One | .2714 | .01 | 100 | .2301 | Yes | Validity coefficient exceeds critical value |
| 10. | 32 | One | .2798 | .05 | 30 | .2960 | No | Validity coefficient is less than critical value |

3. **Answer the questions below.**

Why are tests of significance important when examining evidence of validity?

_____
_____
_____

What happens if a small change to the critical value or degrees of freedom (*df*) is made, and how could the changes affect the data and the results?

_____
_____
_____

What would happen if you changed the alpha level? How would the change affect the validity of the test based on test–criterion relationships?

_____
_____
_____

# Exercise 7.4: What Is the Relationship Between Reliability and Validity?

**OBJECTIVE**

Show the interconnections between common psychometric terms.

**BACKGROUND**

A test's reliability can affect the validity coefficient we calculate when gathering evidence of validity. According to classical test theory, a person's observed test score is the sum of the individual's true score on the construct and random measurement error. Random error always reduces the reliability of a test. The more that random error affects a test score, the less that score can correlate with any other measurement—even itself. One way we provide evidence of validity is to correlate test scores with some criterion measure to calculate a validity coefficient. We can quantify the degree to which a test's unreliability can affect (attenuate or reduce) the validity coefficient calculated when gathering evidence of validity. To increase your understanding of the relationship between reliability and validity, for Exercise 7.4, you will define key terms from the chapter and demonstrate their relationship with a mind map.

**YOUR TASK**

1. **Define key terms used to describe the relationship between reliability and validity.** Read the "Relationship Between Reliability and Validity" section in Chapter 7 of your textbook. While reading, pay particular attention to the terms in the chart below. Provide a five- to seven-word definition of each term listed. Then explain why understanding each of the terms listed in the chart is important. In crafting your response, think about what the consequences of inadequate or incorrect knowledge of the term might be. Document your definitions and list of terms in the chart below.

| Term | Five- to Seven-Word Definition | Why is the term important to understand in the context of psychological testing? |
|---|---|---|
| True score | | |
| Attenuation due to unreliability | | |
| Reliability coefficient | | |
| Validity coefficient | | |

*(Continued)*

(Continued)

| Term | Five- to Seven-Word Definition | Why is the term important to understand in the context of psychological testing? |
|---|---|---|
| Operational validity | | |
| Predictor construct | | |
| Construct | | |
| Criterion measure | | |
| Random error | | |
| Observed measures | | |
| Predictive validity | | |
| Observed validity coefficient | | |
| Measurement error | | |
| Observed criterion measure | | |
| Correction for attenuation | | |
| Relationship | | |
| Criterion construct | | |

2. **Design a visual representation of the interconnections of psychometric concepts.**
   Design a visual to display how each of the psychometric concepts in Task 1 are interrelated. For instance, you could create a mind map to connect the concepts. Draw your visual in the space provided below.

   | **Visual Representation** |
   |---|
   |  |

## Exercise 7.5: How Do You Calculate a Validity Coefficient?

**OBJECTIVE**

Calculate a validity coefficient between two variables.

**BACKGROUND**

One method for obtaining evidence of validity is to investigate how well scores on a test correlate with specific behaviors, attitudes, or events. We refer to this as evidence of validity based on test–criterion relationships. When the scores do correlate, we can confirm that there is evidence of validity, and the test scores may be used to predict those specific behaviors, attitudes, or events. There are two methods for demonstrating evidence of validity based on test–criterion relationships: the predictive method and the concurrent method. With both methods, we perform tests of significance and then conclude whether the validity coefficient does or does not provide sufficient evidence of validity. For Exercise 7.5, you will calculate a validity coefficient based on simulated data from a study to gather evidence of validity based on test–criterion relationships and then answer some questions.

**YOUR TASK**

1. **Read the following text.**

    Imagine an organization had recently decided to integrate a commercially available employment test into the selection process for sales managers. The developers of the test claimed the test was very predictive of success of retail store managers; however, no evidence of validity based on test–criterion relationships existed for use with sales managers. Therefore, before formally integrating the test into the selection system, the organization decided to conduct a validity study. The organization administered the test to 10 individuals who applied and were selected into sales manager positions. They did not use the test scores to make any employment decisions. After 6 months, the organization had each sales manager's supervisor rate him or her on a scale from 1 to 5. The simulated data for each of the 10 sales managers is below.

| Candidate | Employment Test Score | Supervisor Rating (1–5) |
|---|---|---|
| Abel | 80 | 2 |
| Bartmann | 98 | 3 |
| Cardoza | 95 | 5 |
| Dixon | 55 | 3 |
| Everett | 70 | 2 |
| Friedman | 75 | 4 |
| Grass | 50 | 2 |
| Hart | 55 | 1 |
| Isaacs | 90 | 2 |
| Jensen | 60 | 1 |

2. **Calculate the validity coefficient**. Calculate the validity coefficient for the provided data. Show your work below.

3. **Answer the following questions.**

   Which method was used for demonstrating evidence of validity based on test–criteria relations? How do you know?

   _____

   _____

   _____

   _____

   What would have to be changed if the other method of demonstrating evidence of validity based on test–criteria relationships were chosen instead? What would be the pros and cons of each method?

   _____

   _____

   _____

   _____

   Does the validity coefficient provide sufficient evidence of validity? Why or why not? How would the alpha level affect your answer to this question?

   _____

   _____

   _____

   _____

   Suppose the company had not hired those who scored 60 or below on the employment test. What would the validity coefficient be for the six employees only? Why did the validity coefficient change?

   _____

   _____

   _____

   _____

## Exercise 7.6: Reflect on Your Learning

**OBJECTIVE**

Describe key takeaways and confusing concepts from Chapter 7.

**BACKGROUND**

In Chapter 7 of the textbook, you were introduced to evidence of validity based on test–criterion relationships. You read about how to gather evidence of validity, how to interpret validity studies, and how to apply different methods to obtain evidence. You were introduced to restriction of range, how to conduct a test of significance, and validity coefficients. Last, you learned about how to interpret and to make sense of the results. For Exercise 7.6, you will reflect on your learning from Chapter 7 of the textbook and identify key takeaways from the chapter.

**YOUR TASK**

1. **Identify your "Aha!" moments from Chapter 7.**
   - Identify 3 to 4 new insights or realizations you had after reading Chapter 7, referred to as "Aha!" moments.
   - Consider things that made you look at a concept, your life, or an issue in a completely different way than you had in the past.
   - Document your insights and realizations below, providing details of your learning.

2. **Identify some muddy moment discussion questions.**
   - Identify 2 to 3 concepts that are still "muddy" for you from the chapter.
   - Consider concepts you still don't understand, concepts you need clarified, and/or questions you want to ask.
   - Develop 1 to 3 questions to initiate a discussion in class to further your understanding of the concepts and get your questions answered.

| **Insights and Realizations** | 1. _____ |
| --- | --- |
| | 2. _____ |
| | 3. _____ |
| | 4. _____ |
| **Muddy Moments Discussion Questions** | |
| | 1. _____ |
| | 2. _____ |
| | 3. _____ |

# Chapter-Level Projects

## Project 1

**BACKGROUND**

When gathering evidence of validity based on test–criterion relationships, inexperienced test developers tend to only focus on the test and pay less attention to the criterion measure. This can be a costly mistake because a criterion-based approach to test validation involves examining the correlation between *the test and the criterion*. Poorly developed criteria can cause just as many problems as poorly developed tests. Two concerns when developing criteria are criterion contamination and criterion insufficiency. Criterion contamination is present when the criterion measures more dimensions than those measured by the test. Criterion insufficiency occurs when the criterion does not represent all of the relevant dimensions in the behavior, attitude, or event being measured. When this happens, the criterion has decreased evidence of validity based on its content because it has underrepresented some important characteristics.

**YOUR TASK**

1. **Read the situation below.**

   Imagine you were a test developer who had recently completed your development of a test designed to predict something. You were in the final phase of test development, gathering evidence of validity based on test–criterion relationships.

2. **Answer the following questions.**

   a. What is your test designed to predict?

   b. What criterion would you use? Why?

   c. Is your criterion objective or subjective? Why?

   d. How would you know your criterion measures what it is supposed to measure?

   e. What would you do to avoid criterion contamination and criterion insufficiency?

   f. Would you use a predictive method or a concurrent method for demonstrating evidence of validity based on test–criterion relationships? Why?

   g. What steps would you take to gather your evidence of validity based on test–criterion relationships given your answer above?

3. **Develop an awareness pamphlet.** Develop an awareness pamphlet where you educate novice test developers on the most critical issues when gathering evidence of validity based on test–criterion relationships. Include condensed/modified answers to the questions above in your awareness pamphlet.

# Project 2

## BACKGROUND

"Did you ever build a model airplane that flew?" This single question was an excellent predictor of success in flight school in World War II. In fact, this item alone predicted success as well as the entire Air Force Battery (Casio & Aguinis, 2011). Items like this are called *biodata* and are often used in organizational settings. Biodata are based on the idea of behavioral consistency. For example, if a person had built a model plane that flew, this would likely suggest an interest in planes, an understanding of aerodynamics, and so on. Those applicants who built planes that flew would have a better basic understanding entering flight school and would probably show more interest during flight school, which would lead to greater success.

## YOUR TASK

1. **Read the following scenario.**

    The term *biodata* is a broad term, and therefore there are a lot of variations and an exact definition is difficult. However, Meal (1991) described 10 dimensions of biodata items.[1] 'One of them is job relevance. Interestingly, biodata items do not always need to be directly related to the job. Below are three questions that vary along this dimension. Suppose that these questions were used as part of a selection system for salespeople.

    - *Job relevant: How many units of cereal did you sell during the last calendar year?*
    - *Less job relevant: Are you proficient at crossword puzzles?*
    - *Less job relevant: How many books have you read in the last month?*

    The first question is clearly directly related to a sales job. The other two questions are less relevant, and unless the job is a crossword puzzle maker or book reviewer, they do not seem very job relevant. However, just because they are not directly related to the job does not always mean they will be bad predictors of job success.

    Although there are many ways to develop biodata items, one traditional approach is to construct a large number of items that might predict job performance. These items are then administered to a sample of individuals for whom you can obtain job performance data. Using statistical analyses, the questions with the strongest observed correlations to the job performance criterion would be kept, and the other items would be discarded.[2]

---

[1] Meal, M. A. (1991). A conceptual rationale for the domain and attribute of biodata items. *Personnel Psychology, 44*, 763–792. Retrieved from http://onlinelibrary.wiley.com/journal/10.1111/%28ISSN%291744-6570

[2] Casio, W. F., & Aguinis, H. (2011). *Applied psychology in human resource management* (7th Ed.). Boston: Prentice Hall.

2. **Create your own 10-item biodata measure to predict success in a job.** Identify a job of interest to you. Be creative, exploring different types of jobs by searching the Internet. For example, your assessment may be used to predict success of police officers, snake milkers, avalanche forecasters, or bounty hunters. Then, create a 10-item biodata assessment to predict success in the job.

3. **Write a 2-page paper describing how you would conduct a study to collect validation evidence for your biodata measure.** After reflecting on your learnings from Chapter 7 of the textbook, write a 2-page paper describing how you would conduct a study to collect validation evidence for your biodata measure. Integrate as many concepts as possible from Chapter 7 of your textbook.

## Project 3

**BACKGROUND**

Imagine you were in graduate school serving as the teaching assistant for a psychology instructor. Because some of the students in the course are struggling with the concepts in Chapter 7, the instructor has asked you to spend 1 hour with these students to help increase their understanding of the Chapter 7 material. In addition to meeting with the students, the instructor requested that you create a visual learning aid you can use not only as an instructional tool when meeting with the students, but that students can take with them and use as a study tool for future exams.

**YOUR TASK**

1. **Search the Internet to learn more about visual learning aids.** Conduct a search of the Internet to learn more about the value of visual learning aids and the different types of learning aids. When searching, consider using key terms such as *visual learning aids, graphic organizer, concept maps, cognitive organizer, concept diagrams,* and *story maps*.

2. **Create a visual learning aid of Chapter 7 material.** Review the learning objectives at the beginning of Chapter 7. Create a well-thought-out visual learning aid to enhance student understanding of the important concepts associated with each learning objective. Your visual learning aid should be professional-looking and include visual symbols and words to express Chapter 7 concepts, as well as the connections between them. Creativity is encouraged.

## Practice Questions

### Multiple Choice

1. When a test is used to predict future performance, there must be evidence of validity
   a. based on test takers' perceptions.
   b. based on test relationship with a criteria.
   c. using the predictive method.
   d. using the concurrent method.

2. Sarah conducted a study in which she correlated students' scores on the SAT taken in high school with students' grade point averages at the end of the first year of college. Her study was designed to find evidence of what type of validity?
   a. Validity based on test content
   b. Validity using the concurrent method
   c. Validity based on test takers' perceptions
   d. Validity using the predictive method

3. In the study at Brigham Young University, researchers correlated scores on the PREParation for Marriage Questionnaire with measures of marital satisfaction and marital stability. In this study, what were the measures of marital satisfaction and marital stability?
   a. Predictors
   b. Tests
   c. Criteria
   d. Coefficients

4. One problem with studies of validity using the predictive method is that there may be
   a. no evidence of validity based on test content.
   b. no criterion measure.
   c. restriction of range.
   d. low reliability.

5. Both the predictive method and the concurrent method are ways to establish evidence of what?
   a. Validity based on test–criterion relationships
   b. Validity based on test content
   c. Validity based on the perceptions of the test takers
   d. Both validity and reliability

6. What is a major difference between the predictive method and the concurrent method?
   a. The place where the criterion is measured
   b. The people for whom the criterion is measured
   c. The time when the criterion is measured
   d. The format in which the criterion is measured

7. Sharon wanted to show evidence of validity for a test that was designed to predict reading readiness for kindergarten children. She chose as her criterion the overall score on a published standardized test of academic performance that was administered to the children after they completed first grade. When she completed her study, she was dismayed that the validity was much lower than she expected. Which one of the following was most likely responsible for the low validity?
   a. Reliability contamination
   b. Validity contamination
   c. Face validity contamination
   d. Criterion contamination

8. When we ask, "What is the probability that our study would have yielded the validity coefficient we found by chance alone?" we are conducting a

a. validation study.
   b. reliability study.
   c. test of significance.
   d. linear regression.

9. Which one of the following helps us interpret a validity coefficient by telling us how much variance the predictor and the criterion share?
   a. Reliability coefficient
   b. Test of significance
   c. Content validity ratio
   d. Coefficient of determination

10. The difference between linear regression and multiple regression is the number of
    a. predictors.
    b. criteria.
    c. coefficients of determination.
    d. participants.

11. What does the linear regression formula ($Y' = a + bX$) allow us to do?
    a. Predict the value of the criterion measure associated with any test score
    b. Calculate the predictive validity of a test
    c. Provide evidence of validity based on test content
    d. Estimate the accuracy of any test score

12. Which one of the following is used to indicate the incremental validity of a predictor?
    a. $R^2\Delta$
    b. $R^2$
    c. $r$
    d. $b$

## Short Answer

**Remembering**

1. What is meant by evidence of validity based on test–criteria relationships? What are two research methods for obtaining such evidence?

2. Why do we conduct tests of significance and calculate the coefficient of determination?

3. What is the coefficient of multiple determination?

4. How would you describe a restriction of range?

**Applying**

5. What is the difference between evidence of validity based on test content and evidence of validity based on test–criteria relationships?

6. What is the difference between reliability and validity? Give an example.

7. Discuss the difference between objective criteria and subjective criteria. Give examples of each.

8. Why is it important to evaluate the quality of the criterion when gathering evidence of validity of a test using the concurrent method?

**Evaluating**

9. What are some challenges that organizations face when seeking to obtain predictive evidence of validity for a test?

10. What is the relation between correlation and linear regression? How does the process of linear regression help us make predictions?

11. How would you devise procedures on the use of multiple regression to determine incremental validity for two predictors?

# Multiple-Choice and Short-Answer Practice Question Answer Key

## Multiple Choice

| Question | Answer | Textbook Page | Explanation |
|---|---|---|---|
| 1. | c | 184, 186 | When it is important to show a relationship between test scores and a future behavior, researchers use the predictive method to establish evidence of validity. This method requires that a group of people take the test (the predictor), and their scores are held for a predetermined time period, such as 6 months. Later researchers collect information on the criterion. If the test scores and the criterion scores are significantly correlated, then the test has demonstrated predictive evidence of validity. |
| 2. | d | 184 | Because Sarah collected test scores (SAT) at one point in time and then at a later point in time collected data on her criterion (first year college grade point average), she used the predictive method. This approach requires a lag time between testing and collection of the criterion measure. |
| 3. | c | 185 | Marital satisfaction and marital stability were measures that were external to the test and were expected to be related to test scores. Therefore, they are criteria. We would use the word *criterion* if there was a single measure. For example, marital satisfaction is a criterion, and marital stability is a criterion, but when we talk about both of them together, they are criteria, which is plural. |
| 4. | c | 187 | The concurrent method requires that you collect information on the criterion at the same time as the test scores. Often only those who scored well on the test will be hired, admitted, and so on, and will be the only ones on which the criterion measure can be collected. Given that those selected are expected to be the best performers, the lower end of performance on the criterion is likely to be cut off. Thus, there is likely to be range restriction, which can lower the validity coefficient. |
| 5. | a | 184 | The textbook describes two methods that can be used to establish evidence of validity based on test–criteria relationships. The first method is the predictive method, which collects criteria data after the test was given (e.g., 6 months later). The second method is the concurrent method, which collects information on the criteria at approximately the same time as the test is given. |
| 6. | c | 184, 186, 188 | The difference between the predictive method and the concurrent method is the time when the criterion is measured. Otherwise they are the same, and both are used to establish evidence validity based on the relationship between a test and a criterion. |

| Question | Answer | Textbook Page | Explanation |
|---|---|---|---|
| 7. | d | 190 | If the criterion measures more dimensions than the test, we say that criterion contamination is present. In the question, the test measures reading readiness, but the criterion measures the broader construct of academic performance. |
| 8. | c | 192 | Tests of statistical significance evaluate if the relationship between the test and the criterion could have happened simply by chance or sampling error. The statistical test will determine the probability that the relationship is significantly different from zero. |
| 9. | d | 195 | The coefficient of determination is obtained by squaring the validity coefficient and is often called $r^2$. It indicates the amount of variance that is shared by the variables. For example, if the correlation between two variables is .50, then $.50 \times .50 = .25$. This means that 25% of the variance is shared between the two variables, and 75% of each variable's variance is unique and not shared with the other variable. This is important because greater amounts of shared variance indicate stronger relationships. A perfect correlation of 1.00 or −1.00 indicates the variables share 100% of their variance, and a correlation of 0.00 means the variables are completely unrelated and share 0% of their variance. |
| 10. | a | 201 | Linear and multiple regression are essentially the same statistical technique. The difference is that multiple regression is more general in the sense that it allows for more than one predictor variable. |
| 11. | a | 200 | In the formula for linear regression, $Y'$ is the score on the criterion, and $X$ is the score on the test. Therefore, evaluating data based on this formula allows us to predict the value on the criterion based on any test score. |
| 12. | a | 205 | In linear regression, the symbol $R^2$ is the coefficient of multiple determination showing the amount of shared variance between all the predictors and the criterion. When there is only one predictor in the regression equation, $R^2$ is the validity for that one predictor. Incremental validity is the increase in validity ($R^2$) when a second predictor is added to the regression model. Because the symbol $\Delta$ is used in statistics to indicate change, when the two symbols are combined, the result is $R^2\Delta$, indicating the change in validity or the incremental validity of the second predictor over and above that of the first predictor. |

## Short Answer

| Question | Explanation |
|---|---|
| 1. | Validity evidence based on test–criteria relationships has traditionally been referred to as *criterion-related validity*. This type of validity evidence is obtained by examining the relationship between the test scores and some outcome that is external to the test. For example, test developers may examine the relationship between SAT scores and later college academic performance. If individuals with higher test scores tend to have higher academic performance, then that is an indication of validity. There are two approaches to collecting criterion-related validity evidence. The first is the predictive method. This method requires that the test developer obtain test scores and then at a later point in time collect the criterion measure. The example of using SAT scores to predict later academic performance is an example of the predictive method. The concurrent method is the second way to collect the data. Using this approach, the test developer collects both the test scores and the criterion measure at the same time. For example, to show evidence of validity, the test developer might give an employment test to current employees and correlate the test scores with their performance appraisal data collected at the same time. |
| 2. | Because tests scores are used to make important decisions, it is essential to know if the obtained relationship between test score and criterion is statistically significant. While tests of significance are judged in a yes or no manner, they also provide information on the probability that the validity coefficient is greater than zero. In contrast, the coefficient of determination lets the test developer know the strength of the relationship between the test and the criterion. It is calculated by squaring the correlation coefficient between the test and the criterion ($r$), which is then interpreted as the degree of shared variance between the two. The coefficient of multiple determination is a statistic obtained through multiple regression analysis, and the variance is accounted for by all the predictors in the equation. The greater the amount of shared variance, the stronger the relationship and the more useful the test is in predicting the criterion. When a reduction in the range of scores occurs, such as when some people are dropped from the validity study, the validity coefficient may be lower than it would be if all the person were included in the study. |
| 3. | The coefficient of multiple determination is a statistic obtained through multiple regression analysis, which is interpreted as the total proportion of variance in the criterion variable that is accounted for by all the predictors in the multiple regression equation. It is the square of the multiple correlation coefficient, $R$. |
| 4. | A restriction of range refers to the reduction in the range of scores that occurs when some people are dropped from a validity study. An example would be when low performers are not hired, causing the validity coefficient to be lower than it would be if all persons were included in the study. |
| 5. | Evidence of validity based on test content is concerned with demonstrating that the items in the test are representative of the content domain that is being tested. In contrast, evidence of validity based on test–criteria relationships only concerns itself with whether the test predicts external criteria and does not look at the content of the test. |

| Question | Explanation |
|---|---|
| 6. | Reliability/precision and validity are related concepts and are both important to ensure that test scores are fair, unbiased, and useful. Reliability/precision refers to the consistency of measurement. In contrast, validity refers to the appropriateness and accuracy of the inferences test users make based on test scores. The two concepts are related. Consider a target where all of the shots are left of the bull's-eye. The shots are consistent (reliability), but they are not accurate (validity). Now consider a target where all of the shots are centered right on the bull's-eye. Now all of the shots are consistent (reliability) and accurate (validity). Hence reliability/precision is a necessary, but not a sufficient condition for validity. |
| 7. | There are two types of criteria. The first is objective criteria, which are observable. Examples are the number of sick days or total sales. The second type is subjective criteria, which are based on a person's judgment. For example, a peer rating of leadership skills or a teacher's rating of a student's sociability would be subjective criteria. |
| 8. | Selection of an appropriate criterion is an important consideration when using the concurrent method for collecting evidence of validity. A common concern is criterion contamination, which occurs when the criterion measures things that are not related to the test. For example, total sales could be used as a criterion when performing a concurrent study for sales ability. However, total sales are affected by many other factors than the sales ability. In some circumstances, the sales region may play a bigger role in total sales than sales ability. |
| 9. | Collecting the criterion measure using a predictive method can be difficult for organizations. This is because when the predictive method is used, there is a time period between test administration and the collection of the criterion measure. For example, an organization could give a test to a large group of potential hires, put them through a training program, and then examine their success in the training program. The problem with this approach is that few organizations would like to go through the time and expense of training people who are unlikely to be successful. Therefore, an organization is likely to only train people who score high on the test. As a result, this will likely decrease the amount of variance in the criterion measure by removing people who would likely have been less successful in the training. Statistically, this is called *criterion range restriction* and usually results in a lower validity coefficient. |
| 10. | Correlation and regression are similar in that both indicate the degree of relationship between variables and both use the same statistical model. The difference is that linear regression can be used to predict the criterion score based on test score, whereas correlation does not allow this direct prediction. |
| 11. | Researchers use multiple regression when they want to predict a criterion using more than one predictor variable. First the researchers run a regression analysis using only one of the variables, and they examine the resulting $R^2$ to determine the validity for that variable. Next, they run a second regression analysis using both predictors and examine the $R^2$ once again. The difference between the two indicates the validity of the second predictor over and above the first predictor variable and is referred to as incremental validity. The usefulness of this procedure is that it will allow the researcher to make a decision about whether adding a second predictor will significantly contribute to the prediction of the criteria. |

# 8 How Do We Gather Evidence of Validity Based on a Test's Relation to Constructs?

## Overview

In Chapter 8 of the textbook, you were introduced to evidence of validity based on a test's relation to constructs. Hopefully, after reading the chapter, you have a clearer understanding of what we mean by construct, the steps for defining or explaining a psychological construct, the processes we use for establishing evidence of validity based on a test's relationship with other constructs, and the role of exploratory and confirmatory factor analysis in establishing validity. While Chapter 8 of the textbook included information important to understanding how we gather evidence of validity based on a test's relation to constructs, Chapter 8 of the workbook provides you with the opportunity to demonstrate your understanding of material presented in the textbook and apply your learning by completing some practical and critical-thinking exercises linked to specific learning objectives. Chapter 8 of the workbook will also allow you to complete chapter-level projects to demonstrate your understanding of multiple topics within the chapter. Chapter 8 of the workbook ends with some multiple-choice and short-answer questions you can use to self-assess your understanding of the material.

# Practical and Critical-Thinking Exercises

## Purpose

This section contains five exercises you can complete to demonstrate your understanding and apply your learning (Exercises 8.1–8.5) and one exercise you can complete to reflect on your learning (Exercise 8.6). The exercises, linked to learning objectives, are displayed below.

**Exercise 8.1** — **How Would You Describe Construct Explication?**
- **Learning Objective:** Explain construct explication steps and their importance.

**Exercise 8.2** — **What Is the Foundational Element of Construct Explication, and Why Is It Needed?**
- **Learning Objective:** Experience the first step of the construct explication process.

**Exercise 8.3** — **How Do I Behaviorally Define Abstract Constructs?**
- **Learning Objective:** Identify other constructs that relate to a theoretical construct.

**Exercise 8.4** — **How Do I Differentiate Between Exploratory and Confirmatory Factor Analysis?**
- **Learning Objective:** Determine when to conduct either exploratory or confirmatory factor analysis.

**Exercise 8.5** — **How Do I Interpret a Multitrait-Multimethod Correlation Matrix?**
- **Learning Objective:** Interpret a multitrait-multimethod correlation matrix.

**Exercise 8.6** — **Reflect on Your Learning**
- **Learning Objective:** Describe key takeaways and confusing concepts from Chapter 8.

# Exercise 8.1: How Would You Describe Construct Explication?

**OBJECTIVE**

Explain construct explication steps and their importance.

**BACKGROUND**

Some tests are designed to measure abstract constructs that we cannot observe or measure directly. Because we cannot measure psychological constructs directly, theoretical explanations help us to define the construct. Theoretical explanations help us define behaviors that will show evidence of the construct we are interested in measuring. We can create a theoretical explanation using a process called construct explication. To increase your understanding of the construction explication process, in Exercise 8.1, you will define the construct explication steps and their importance, and then answer some questions.

**YOUR TASK**

1. **Reflect on the steps and importance of construct explication.** Review the "Construct Explication" section in Chapter 8 of your textbook to learn more about the three steps we often use to define or explain a psychological construct. After identifying each step, in your own words, craft a definition for each step, and explain why each step is important. Then, search the Internet to find two additional resources to increase your understanding of the construct explication process. Identify additional insights from the Internet resources. Document your answers in the chart below.

| From Miller and Lovler Textbook | | Two Internet Resources |
|---|---|---|
| **Identify and Define Each Step** | **Why the Step Is Important** | **Additional Insights** |
| Step 1: | | |
| Step 2: | | |
| Step 3: | | |

2. **Answer the following questions.**

What are 10 examples, not mentioned in your textbook, of psychological constructs?

_____
_____
_____
_____
_____
_____
_____
_____
_____
_____
_____
_____
_____

Why is defining a psychological construct necessary?

_____
_____
_____
_____

What challenges might we face with defining a psychological construct?

_____
_____
_____
_____

What would happen if a construct is not well defined prior to designing a test to measure the construct?

_____
_____
_____
_____

# Exercise 8.2: What Is the Foundational Element of Construct Explication, and Why Is It Needed?

**OBJECTIVE**

Experience the first step of the construct explication process.

**BACKGROUND**

A well-defined construct will help later in the process when gathering evidence of validity based on a test's relation to constructs. A well-thought-out definition provides the framework of the construct and clarifies future expectations during the validation process. The construct definition is the framework that provides the structure required during the validation process comprised by a careful review of empirical studies and theoretical observations. The definition represents the constructs scope that includes relevant and detailed information as a guide for the creation of the test, the evaluation, and other processes. For Exercise 8.2, you will apply the first step of construct explication.

1. **Apply the first step of construct explication.** Research a theory that includes four or more constructs. For example, the theory of planned behavior is divided into six psychological constructs that represent a person's ability to exert self-control. While there is no one place you can go to find a list of all theories you might consider, if you search the Internet for "ChangingMinds.org Psychological Theories," you will find a number of psychological theories to select from. After you locate a theory with at least four constructs, complete the chart below. If the theory you choose has more than four constructs, choose any four constructs to use for this activity. Provide a definition of each psychological construct identified within the theory and then describe one way to observe or measure the behavior. Document your findings in the chart below.

| Theory: | |
|---|---|
| **Psychological Construct Definitions** | **Observation or Measure of the Construct** |
| 1. | |
| 2. | |

*(Continued)*

(Continued)

| Theory: | |
|---|---|
| **Psychological Construct Definitions** | **Observation or Measure of the Construct** |
| 3. | |
| 4. | |

2. **Answer the following questions.**

   What is the result if a construct is well defined and grounded in theory, but the tool used to measure the attribute or attitude is not well defined or aligned to the construct? Think of what you need to find during the first step to complete Steps 2 and 3.

   _____
   _____
   _____
   _____
   _____
   _____
   _____

   What additional information, beyond defining the construct, would you need to gather in Step 1 of the construct explication process to help you with Steps 2 and 3?

   _____
   _____
   _____
   _____
   _____
   _____
   _____

# Exercise 8.3: How Do I Behaviorally Define Abstract Constructs?

**OBJECTIVE**

Identify other constructs that relate to a theoretical construct.

**BACKGROUND**

Many psychological tests are designed to measure abstract constructs. Abstract constructs are not directly observable, but rather they exist in our imagination. Examples of abstract constructs are love, self-esteem, intelligence, and personality. We cannot "see" constructs like self-esteem, but rather, these constructs exist in theory. Because we cannot observe or measure them directly, to design a test to measure them, we must identify behaviors that show evidence of these constructs. To increase your understanding of the process we use to explain a psychological construct, in Exercise 8.3, after distinguishing between concrete and abstract constructs, you will find theories that define five abstract constructs and then identify observable behaviors that might show evidence of each construct.

**YOUR TASK**

1. **Determine type of construct.** Review the "Notion of Construct Validity" section in Chapter 8 of your textbook. For each construct below, indicate if the construct is a concrete or an abstract construct. Document your answer and rationale in the table below.

| Construct | Type of Construct | Rationale |
|---|---|---|
| Conscientiousness | | |
| Aggressiveness | | |
| Temperature | | |
| Enthusiasm | | |
| Love | | |

*(Continued)*

(Continued)

| Construct | Type of Construct | Rationale |
|---|---|---|
| Motivation | | |
| Distance | | |
| Jealousy | | |
| Height | | |
| Arithmetic knowledge | | |
| Critical thinking | | |

2. **Define the construct.** Identify five abstract constructs not included in the previous table, including a theory where the construct is clearly defined. Document each abstract construct, the name of the theory, and the definition of the construct in the table below.

| Abstract Construct | Theory | Definition of Construct |
|---|---|---|
| 1. | | |
| 2. | | |

| Abstract Construct | Theory | Definition of Construct |
|---|---|---|
| 3. | | |
| 4. | | |
| 5. | | |

3. **Behaviorally define each abstract construct.** Identify three to five observable behaviors that might show evidence of each construct based on the definition of the construct above. Document the construct and behaviors in the table that follows.

| Construct | Observable Behaviors Based on Construct Definition |
|---|---|
| 1. | |
| 2. | |
| 3. | |
| 4. | |
| 5. | |

# Exercise 8.4: How Do I Differentiate Between Exploratory and Confirmatory Factor Analysis?

**OBJECTIVE**

Determine when to conduct either exploratory or confirmatory factor analysis.

**BACKGROUND**

Psychological tests are designed to measure constructs. For example, we may design a test to measure a concrete construct such as knowledge of arithmetic. However, the construct may have underlying constructs (or factors), such as addition, subtraction, multiplication, and division. While not all tests have underlying constructs—that is, they are homogeneous or unidimensional—others do have underlying constructs. These tests are referred to as heterogeneous or multidimensional. The statistical procedures of factor analysis allows us to identify whether the pattern of correlations among all items on a test can be more simply explained by a smaller number of underlying constructs, or factors. To increase your understanding of the different types of factor analysis, for Exercise 8.4, you will describe your understanding of factor analysis and then determine which type of factor analysis would be appropriate for provided scenarios.

**YOUR TASK**

1. **Ground yourself in foundational information regarding factor analysis.** Read the "Factor Analysis" section of Chapter 8 of your textbook to refresh your memory of why we use factor analysis, the two types of factor analysis, and the unique elements of both types. In your own words, document your insights in the chart below.

| | Why We Use Factor Analysis | |
|---|---|---|
| | **Definition** | **Unique Elements** |
| **Confirmatory Factor Analysis** | | |
| **Exploratory Factor Analysis** | | |

Chapter 8 ■ How Do We Gather Evidence of Validity Based on a Test's Relation to Constructs?    205

2. **Differentiate between exploratory and confirmatory factor analysis.** In the following chart is a scenario where an explanatory factor analysis would be appropriate. Come up with four additional scenarios, two where exploratory factor analysis would be appropriate and two where confirmatory factor analysis would be appropriate. Explain your rationale for each. Document your findings in the chart below.

| Scenario | Exploratory or Confirmatory | Rationale |
|---|---|---|
| A biology instructor recently designed a test. He would like to gather evidence of internal consistency reliability but is unsure if he can do so using one test for internal consistency. He knows that using one test for internal consistency would be appropriate only if the test measured one factor or construct. He decides to conduct a factor analysis to determine if there are any underlying factors or constructs that would lead to the need to run multiple tests to check for evidence of internal consistency reliability. | Exploratory | |
| | Exploratory | |
| | Exploratory | |
| | Confirmatory | |
| | Confirmatory | |

# Exercise 8.5: How Do I Interpret a Multitrait-Multimethod Correlation Matrix?

## OBJECTIVE

Interpret a multitrait-multimethod correlation matrix.

## BACKGROUND

One way to identify evidence of validity is to use the multitrait-multimethod approach. With this approach, we look for evidence of convergent and discriminant validity, both of which are needed to claim a measure has evidence of validity based on a test's relation to constructs. First, we look for convergence—the degree to which concepts that should be theoretically related actually are related. Second, we look for divergence—the degree to which concepts that should not be theoretically related are actually not related. We arrange the results in a matrix to show the correlations between the test we are gathering validity evidence for and the other measures. To increase your understanding of how to interpret a multitrait-multimethod correlation matrix, for Exercise 8.5, you will review a multitrait-multimethod correlation matrix and then answer some questions.

## YOUR TASK

1. **Review the information below.**

    Seligson and colleagues (2003)[1] conducted a validation study of the Brief Multidimensional Student's Life Satisfaction Scale (BMSLSS). In addition to using data from students in Grades 6–8, the researchers conducted another study with 46 high school students from a different school. The table below contains the multitrait-multimethod correlation matrix from the second study.

| | MTMM Matrix for High School Students | | | | | | | | | |
|---|---|---|---|---|---|---|---|---|---|---|
| | MSLSS | | | | | BMSLSS | | | | |
| | A1 | B1 | C1 | D1 | E1 | A2 | B2 | C2 | D2 | E2 |
| A1 | | | | | | | | | | |
| B1 | 0.26 | | | | | | | | | |
| C1 | 0.36 | 0.36 | | | | | | | | |
| D1 | 0.62 | 0.56 | 0.46 | | | | | | | |
| E1 | 0.64 | 0.55 | 0.54 | 0.70 | | | | | | |
| A2 | 0.70 | *0.34* | *0.31* | *0.56* | *0.66* | | | | | |
| B2 | *0.32* | 0.67 | *0.31* | *0.50* | *0.57* | <u>0.52</u> | | | | |
| C2 | *0.23* | *0.26* | 0.63 | *0.35* | *0.37* | <u>0.28</u> | <u>0.33</u> | | | |
| D2 | *0.47* | *0.33* | *0.31* | 0.61 | *0.42* | <u>0.55</u> | <u>0.25</u> | <u>0.40</u> | | |
| E2 | *0.40* | *0.44* | *0.17* | *0.46* | 0.57 | <u>0.35</u> | <u>0.61</u> | <u>0.12</u> | <u>0.20</u> | |

*Note:* A = family, B = friends, C = school, D = living environment, E = self. The numbers set in bold are the validity coefficients. The heterotrait–monomethod correlations are underlined. The heterotrait–heteromethod correlations are set in italics.

*Source:* Reprinted by permission from Springer Nature: Springer Nature, Social Indicators Research. "Preliminary Validation of the Brief Multidimensional Students' Life Satisfaction Scale (BMSLSS)", Julie L. Seligson, E. Scott Huebner, Robert F. Valois, 2003.

---

[1] Seligson, J. L., Huebner, S., & Valois, R. F. (2003). Preliminary validation of the Brief Multidimensional Students' Life Satisfaction Scale (BMSLSS). *Social Indicators Research, 61,* 121–145. doi:10.1023/A: 1021326822957

2. **Answer the following questions.**

Which figures represent convergent evidence of validity? Which pair had the greatest convergent evidence? Which pair had the least?

Which figures represent discriminant evidence of validity? How do the discriminant coefficients compare with the convergent coefficients?

Do these data indicate evidence of construct validity for the BMSLSS? Explain your answer.

## Exercise 8.6: Reflect on Your Learning

**OBJECTIVE**

Describe key takeaways and confusing concepts from Chapter 8.

**BACKGROUND**

In Chapter 8 of the textbook, you were introduced to the constructs of explication and factor analysis. You read about the steps required to conduct construct explication. You were also introduced to factor analysis as a statistical analysis to help identify constructs, or factors, for a test. Last, you learned about the two ways to conduct factor analysis by exploring or confirming different test constructs. For Exercise 8.6, you will reflect on your learning from Chapter 8 of the textbook and identify key takeaways from the chapter.

**YOUR TASK**

1. **Identify your "Aha!" moments from Chapter 8.**
   - Identify 3 to 4 new insights or realizations you had after reading Chapter 8, referred to as "Aha!" moments.
   - Consider things that made you look at a concept, your life, or an issue in a completely different way than you had in the past.
   - Document your insights and realizations below, providing details of your learning.

2. **Identify some muddy moment discussion questions.**
   - Identify 2 to 3 concepts that are still "muddy" for you from the chapter.
   - Consider concepts you still don't understand, concepts you need clarified, and/or questions you want to ask.
   - Develop 1 to 3 questions to initiate a discussion in class to further your understanding of the concepts and get your questions answered.

| | |
|---|---|
| **Insights and Realizations** | 1. _____ <br> 2. _____ <br> 3. _____ <br> 4. _____ |
| **Muddy Moments Discussion Questions** | 1. _____ <br> 2. _____ <br> 3. _____ |

# Chapter-Level Projects

## Project 1

**BACKGROUND**

Validation studies are necessary to gather evidence of validity and make an informed inference based on the results of a test. Gathering evidence of construct validity includes gathering theoretical and psychometric evidence. There are multiple ways of gathering psychometric evidence of construct validity depending on the type of construct being measured. Because establishing evidence of construct validity involves accumulating and relating all of the psychometric information known about a test, we show how familiar concepts—such as reliability/precision, evidence of validity based on test content, and evidence of validity based on a test's relationships with other variables—are linked together.

**YOUR TASK**

1. **Design a validation study for a test that measures self-esteem in preadolescents**. Review the "Gathering Evidence of Construct Validity" section in Chapter 8 of your textbook. Now, imagine you have been asked to gather evidence of construct validity for a test that includes 30 statements to which a test taker responds *true of me* or *not true of me*. Also imagine the test measures test takers' feelings/perceptions about their academic and athletic skills, physical attractiveness, and relationships with friends and family. Describe your validation study below:

   _____

   _____

   _____

   _____

   _____

   _____

   _____

   _____

   _____

2. **Write a 1- to 2-page description of your validation study.** Write a 1- to 2-page description of your validation study. In your descriptions, address the following questions:

   a. What psychometric information would you need about a test to gather evidence of its validity?

*(Continued)*

(Continued)

    b. Would you need to administer measures other than the test you are validating? If so, what other measures would you like to administer?

    c. Can you gather all of the information you need in one administration? Explain why or why not.

    d. What statistical procedures would you use to analyze your data?

    e. What specific types of judgments or decisions will your study allow you to make? What types of judgments or decisions will you not be able to make?

    f. What follow-up studies will your validation study potentially require?

# Project 2

**BACKGROUND**

One of the most important aspects of test development is defining, in behavioral terms, the construct you intend to measure by the test. This process is called construct explication, and it is one of the necessary first steps in the development process. Construct explication is a process and often consists of three steps: (a) identifying the behaviors that relate to the construct, (b) identifying other constructs that may be related to the construct being explained, and (c) identifying behaviors related to similar constructs and determining whether these behaviors are related to the original construct.

**YOUR TASK**

1. **Explicate five constructs.** Make a list of five people you know well. For each person, identify one abstract construct that you think would best describe the person. The constructs you chose should not be concrete or easily observable physical characteristics. Rather, the constructs you choose should be characteristics like "funny," "warm," or "practical" (Don't use these!). For each of the five constructs that you named, explicate the construct by identifying at least three behaviors that you have observed the person perform and that make you think that the construct you used to describe the person is appropriate. Next, list three behaviors that you don't believe that the person would do if the construct you are using to describe the person is accurate. In effect, you are checking on the discriminate validity of your construct.

2. **Identify five people to interview.** Identify five people you can interview. Tell each person that you are going to present them with five terms that are often used to describe people. Ask them to think of at least five behaviors that would lead them to believe that the term used to describe that person was correct.

3. **Compare your behaviors.** Compare the three behaviors that you identified in Step 1 with the five behaviors that your interviewees identified in Step 2 for each construct.

4. **Create a PPT or Prezi presentation.** Create a presentation where you include a table with each of your five constructs and a side-by-side comparison that displays your five behaviors and the behaviors your interviewees identified. Address the following in your presentation:

   - What are the biggest differences between the way in which you explicated the construct and the way in which your interviewees did? How can you account for these differences?

*(Continued)*

(Continued)

- Examine the list of all behaviors that you gathered from your interviewees. Group the ones that are most similar to each other together. Looking at the groupings you made, name the constructs that seem to best represent the behaviors. Are the construct names the same as the construct names you started with? If not, why do you think there are differences?
- Would the constructs you just named above still describe the people that you identified at the beginning of this exercise? Why, or why not?

## Project 3

**BACKGROUND**

Imagine you were in graduate school serving as the teaching assistant for a psychology instructor. Because some of the students in the course are struggling with the concepts in Chapter 8, the instructor has asked you to spend 1 hour with these students to help increase their understanding of the Chapter 8 material. In addition to meeting with the students, the instructor requested that you create a visual learning aid you can use not only as an instructional tool when meeting with the students, but that students can take with them and use as a study tool for future exams.

**YOUR TASK**

1. **Search the Internet to learn more about visual learning aids.** Conduct a search of the Internet to learn more about the value of visual learning aids and the different types of learning aids. When searching, consider using key terms such as *visual learning aids, graphic organizer, concept maps, cognitive organizer, concept diagrams,* and *story maps*.

2. **Create a visual learning aid of Chapter 8 material**. Review the learning objectives at the beginning of Chapter 8. Create a well-thought-out visual learning aid to enhance student understanding of the important concepts associated with each learning objective. Your visual learning aid should be professional-looking and include visual symbols and words to express Chapter 8 concepts, as well as the connections between them. Creativity is encouraged.

## Practice Questions

### Multiple Choice

1. Why have a number of theorists challenged the strategies of developing evidence of test validity based on content or relationships with other criteria?
   a. Theorists did not believe they got good results.
   b. Strategies were difficult to understand and implement.
   c. Strategies failed to link the testing instrument to a theory.
   d. Strategies were seldom used by test developers.

2. For his senior thesis, Mohammed identified the behaviors that relate to self-esteem. He then identified other constructs that may be related to self-esteem. And finally, he identified behaviors related to similar constructs, such as self-efficacy, and determined whether these behaviors were related to self-esteem. In his thesis, Mohammed was carrying out the process of construct
   a. investigation.
   b. experimentation.
   c. remuneration.
   d. explication.

3. According to the example in your textbook, gravity is a(n)
   a. subjective criterion.
   b. objective criterion.
   c. theoretical construct.
   d. physical construct.

4. When Susan included a number of educated guesses or predictions in her thesis about aggression, what was she providing?
   a. Traits
   b. Constructs
   c. Factors
   d. Hypotheses

5. Self-efficacy is an example of a(n)
   a. subjective criterion.
   b. objective criterion.
   c. theoretical construct.
   d. physical construct.

6. Which one of the following does NOT provide evidence of construct validity?
   a. Reliability
   b. Convergent correlations
   c. Dragnet empiricism
   d. Evidence based on test content

7. The theory underlying psychological testing suggests that a test
   a. cannot have a stronger correlation with any other variable than it does with itself.
   b. cannot have a stronger correlation with itself than it does with an outside criterion.
   c. must have an equally strong correlation with a criterion as it does with itself.
   d. must have a stronger correlation with a criterion than it does with itself.

8. Which one of the following is NOT provided by the multitrait-multimethod design?
   a. Reliability or precision
   b. Predictive evidence of validity
   c. Convergent evidence of validity
   d. Discriminant evidence of validity

9. If test scores correlate with constructs that the underlying theory says are

related, which one of the following types of evidence of validity is being demonstrated?

a. Predictive

b. Concurrent

c. Discriminant

d. Convergent

10. Hiroshi conducted a study where he delivered a training program designed to raise self-efficacy. He measured training participant self-efficacy before and after the training and found that self-efficacy increased after the training. Which one of the following methods was he using for establishing evidence of construct validity?

a. Multitrait-multimethod design

b. Experimental intervention

c. Nomological network

d. Construct explication

11. Sherer and colleagues (1982) administered their measure of self-efficacy and a measure of interpersonal competency to 376 students and found a moderate correlation between the two tests. What type of evidence of validity is indicated by the correlation?

a. Predictive

b. Face

c. Convergent

d. Content

12. John developed a math test for his thesis. He administered the math test with a test of reading ability and was happy when he found that the scores on the two tests were not correlated. What type of evidence of validity does the correlation that John found provide?

a. Face

b. Concurrent

c. Discriminant

d. Convergent

13. For his senior thesis, Ricardo proposed a set of underlying factors for the construct of altruism. He then administered a test of altruism and used an advanced statistical technique based on correlation to analyze these data. Which one of the following did Ricardo use?

a. Confirmatory factor analysis

b. Linear regression

c. Multitrait-multimethod design

d. Exploratory factor analysis

14. Yassi carried out a factor analysis in which she broadly looked for underlying theoretical structures in her construct. Which one of the following designs did Yassi use?

a. Confirmatory factor analysis

b. Linear regression

c. Multitrait-multimethod design

d. Exploratory factor analysis

## Short Answer

| | |
|---|---|
| **Remembering** | 1. What is construct validity? |
| | 2. What is a nomological network, and what is an example? |
| | 3. What are the steps and activities involved in construct explication? |
| | 4. What is the purpose of factor analysis? |
| **Applying** | 5. Is construct validity really a different type of validity? Why, or why not? |
| | 6. What information would you need to provide evidence of validity for a personality test? |
| | 7. What is the difference between convergent and discriminant evidence of validity? |
| | 8. What are two things that would demonstrate evidence of validity based on the test's relation to the construct? |
| **Evaluating** | 9. How do you evaluate information on reliability, convergent evidence of validity, and discriminant evidence of validity with a multitrait-multimethod matrix? |
| | 10. How do test developers interpret evidence of construct validity, and what type of data do they need to gather to demonstrate evidence of construct validity? |
| | 11. What information would a test developer need to defend the concepts of confirmatory factor analysis and exploratory factor analysis if the validity of a test is questioned? |

# Multiple-Choice and Short-Answer Practice Question Answer Key

## Multiple Choice

| Question | Answer | Textbook Page | Explanation |
|---|---|---|---|
| 1. | c | 213 | Using the content and criterion approach for evidence of validity neglected the construct a test was designed to measure. Psychologists, as a group, are very concerned about theory and constructs. Focusing attention on the theories of psychological behavior and linking this to the underlying construct refocuses attention on the basic ideas concerning measurement. |
| 2. | d | 214 | Construct explication is the process of relating a construct to a psychological theory and proposing a nomological network of the constructs and behaviors to which the construct is related. This process has three steps. First, identify behaviors that relate to the construct. Second, identify other constructs that may be related to the construct being explained. Third, identify behaviors related to similar constructs and determine whether these behaviors are related to the original construct. |
| 3. | c | 212 | The textbook used the well-known example of gravity being a theoretical construct. Before Newton, the theory of gravity did not exist. Newton created the theory and then tested his theory by making observations, such as an apple falling to earth. The observations over time have supported this theory, and over time, enough evidence has accumulated to strongly support the theory of gravity. |
| 4. | d | 215 | Hypotheses are educated guesses or predictions about how variables may be related. For example, based on theory or previous empirical work, Susan may have good reason to hypothesize specific patterns of relations between aggression and other constructs. She can then test this to provide validity evidence based on a test's relationship to other constructs. |
| 5. | c | 212 | The textbook uses self-efficacy as an example of a theoretical construct. It cannot be directly measured. Instead, evidence can be obtained by measuring other observable behaviors. |
| 6. | c | 217 | Dragnet empiricism is not an acceptable way to provide evidence of construct validity. Construct validity should be based on testable hypotheses within the nomological network. Dragnet empiricism, instead, simply involves collecting evidence based on convenience. |
| 7. | a | 217 | A correlation ranges from −1.00 to 1.00, where 1.00 indicates a perfect positive correlation. When a variable is correlated with itself, the result is a correlation of 1.00. For all practical purposes, this can only occur when a variable is correlated with itself. Thus, when a test is correlated with any other variable, it will be less than 1.00 and necessarily less than its correlation with itself. |

*(Continued)*

(Continued)

| Question | Answer | Textbook Page | Explanation |
|---|---|---|---|
| 8. | b | 218 | The multitrait-multimethod design is used for investigating construct validity. Therefore, predictive evidence of validity, which is traditionally called *criterion-related validity*, is not provided by the method. The other three answer options are forms of evidence that can be provided by the multitrait-multimethod design. |
| 9. | d | 218 | Convergent evidence of validity is a form of evidence that shows the test scores are correlated with scores from similar tests (measuring similar constructs). In contrast, when test scores do not correlate with test scores from unrelated constructs, this is called discriminant evidence of validity. |
| 10. | b | 221 | Experimental interventions in which the test is used as a dependent variable make a substantial contribution to the argument for evidence of construct validity. If the underlying theory predicts that a course of treatment or training will increase or decrease the psychological construct, a significant difference between pretest scores and posttest scores would be evidence of construct validity for the test. |
| 11. | c | 217–218 | Convergent evidence of validity occurs when test scores measuring similar constructs are correlated. Thus, in this case, with self-efficacy and interpersonal competency being similar constructs, a correlation was expected and was found. |
| 12. | c | 218 | John should be happy because one would not expect test scores for dissimilar constructs (such as reading and math ability) to be correlated. By finding that they were not related, he had obtained discriminant evidence of validity, which examines if constructs or measurements that are supposed to be unrelated are, in fact, unrelated. |
| 13. | a | 225 | Confirmatory factor analysis is a statistical procedure where the researcher considers the theory associated with the test and proposes a set of underlying factors or relationships that he or she expects to see. The researcher then conducts a confirmatory factor analysis to determine if those relationships actually exist. |
| 14. | d | 224 | Exploratory factor analysis is a statistical technique that does not propose a formal hypothesis, but instead uses the procedure to broadly identify underlying constructs. The key difference between the confirmatory and exploratory approaches to factor analysis is that with confirmatory, the researcher specifies the structure beforehand that he or she expects to see, and with exploratory, the researcher does not propose a structure. |

## Short Answer

| Question | Explanation |
|---|---|
| 1. | The 2014 *Standards* do not use the traditional term of construct validity. The newest *Standards* view validity as a unitary concept that addresses the accuracy and appropriateness of the inferences based on test scores. |
| 2. | A nomological network is a technique we use for defining a psychological construct. We define the psychological construct by showing how the construct is related to as many other constructs and behaviors as possible. |
| 3. | Measurement of an abstract construct depends on our ability to observe and measure behavior that is related to the construct. There are three steps for accomplishing this, and the process is referred to as *construct explication*. The steps and activities are (1) identify the behaviors that are related to the construct, (2) identify other constructs that may be related to the construct being explained, and (3) identify behaviors related to similar constructs and determine whether these behaviors are related to the original construct. |
| 4. | Factor analysis is an advanced statistical procedure based on the concept of correlation that helps us identify the underlying constructs or factors being measured. We use exploratory factor analysis when we are not clear on the factors that underlie a set of test scores and when we want to identify the underlying factors. We use confirmatory factor analysis when we know in advance what we believe the underlying factors are in a set of test scores and desire to confirm those factors. |
| 5. | Construct validity cannot be a different "type" of validity. However, the more traditional view of construct validity sees it as the test's accuracy of measurement of the underlying theoretical construct the test was designed to measure. |
| 6. | Answers should include a definition of personality and the identification of the different constructs, such as agreeableness or conscientiousness, or traits, such as cheerfulness or stubbornness. The focus on the answer should include an evaluation of the construct and any associated behaviors that demonstrate the construct, the type of tests typically used, and the definition of the construct. That type of measurement would best support the construct, and students should identify if the construct is theoretical or practical. |
| 7. | Convergent evidence of validity indicates the correlations of one test to another when the constructs are similar. Discriminant evidence of validity occurs when two tests do not correlate because the constructs are unrelated. |
| 8. | The answers for this question will vary, but most should include a discussion on the correlations of the knowledge required for the position and the math skills. Students should discuss a definition of the math constructs in their answer along with the factors the questions should include, along with one statistical analysis, such as factor analysis or multitrait-multimethod correlations. |

*(Continued)*

(Continued)

| Question | Explanation |
|---|---|
| 9. | Refer to Figure 8.4 in your textbook to see the types of evidence that can be found in a multitrait-multimethod matrix. Reliability is found along the main diagonal in parentheses. For example, the reliability of $A_1$ (extraversion measured by a self-report) is .89. Convergent validity evidence is found along the diagonals between the broken-line triangles. For example, construct A (extraversion) is measured by three methods, and the convergent validity evidence between Method 1 (self-report) and Method 3 (objective test) is .56. Evidence of discriminant validity is found in the dashed triangles. The values found in these triangles represent the measurement of different constructs by different methods. Thus, one would expect these values to be the lowest of the matrix, and they provide the best evidence of discriminant validity. |
| 10. | There are two main approaches to gathering evidence of construct validity. They are gathering theoretical evidence and psychometric evidence. The first step is to gather evidence based on theoretical grounds by reviewing as many studies as possible involving the construct and its relations with other observable and measurable behaviors. The next step is to gather quantitative or psychometric evidence. There are several methods to gather this type of evidence. Reliability is a necessary component of construct validity evidence; if the construct cannot be consistently measured, then it cannot be measured accurately. Convergent and discriminant validity evidence is another approach. Convergent evidence of validity occurs when measures of similar constructs are related. Discriminant evidence of validity occurs when measures of different types of constructs are unrelated. For example, you would expect reading scores from two different tests to be related, but you would not expect them to be related to scores on a math test. There is also the multitrait-multimethod design that collects reliability, convergent, and discriminant evidence at the same time. The underlying theory of a construct can be examined experimentally, where the test is used as a dependent variable. Evidence based on content can also provide evidence of construct validity showing that the test content and construct domain overlap. Finally, construct validity evidence can be based on the test's relationship with external criteria that the test should be related to. |
| 11. | Factor analysis is an advanced statistical procedure that looks at how items on a test interrelate, and it is based on their correlations with each other. Using this technique, test developers can examine the underlying concepts or constructs that a test measures. Confirmatory factor analysis is used to determine if a test actually aligns with the underlying hypothesized constructs that the test is supposed to measure. Using this technique, test developers would state what the hypothesized underlying factors and constructs are and statistically test these against the empirically observed relationships found in the test data. If the hypothesized structure aligns with the observed structure, then this is considered convergent evidence of validity. In contrast, exploratory factor analysis is just that—exploratory. The test developer does not specify any expected structure. Instead, he or she uses the technique to explore and uncover the underlying structure found in the observed test data. |

# 9 How Do We Construct and Administer Surveys and Use Survey Data?

## Overview

In Chapter 9 of the textbook, you were introduced to how we construct, administer, and use survey data. Hopefully, after reading the chapter, you have a clearer understanding of the similarities and differences between a survey and a psychological test; the five-phase scientific approach we use to construct, administer, and use survey data; and how we gather evidence of survey reliability/precision and validity. While Chapter 9 of the textbook included foundational information about constructing, administering, and using survey data, Chapter 9 of the workbook provides you with the opportunity to demonstrate your understanding of material presented in the textbook and apply your learning by completing some practical and critical-thinking exercises linked to specific learning objectives. Chapter 9 of the workbook will also allow you to complete chapter-level projects to demonstrate your understanding of multiple topics within the chapter. Chapter 9 of the workbook ends with some multiple-choice and short-answer questions you can use to self-assess your understanding of the material.

# Practical and Critical-Thinking Exercises

## Purpose

This section contains five exercises you can complete to demonstrate your understanding and apply your learning (Exercises 9.1–9.5) and one exercise you can complete to reflect on your learning (Exercise 9.6). The exercises, linked to learning objectives, are displayed below.

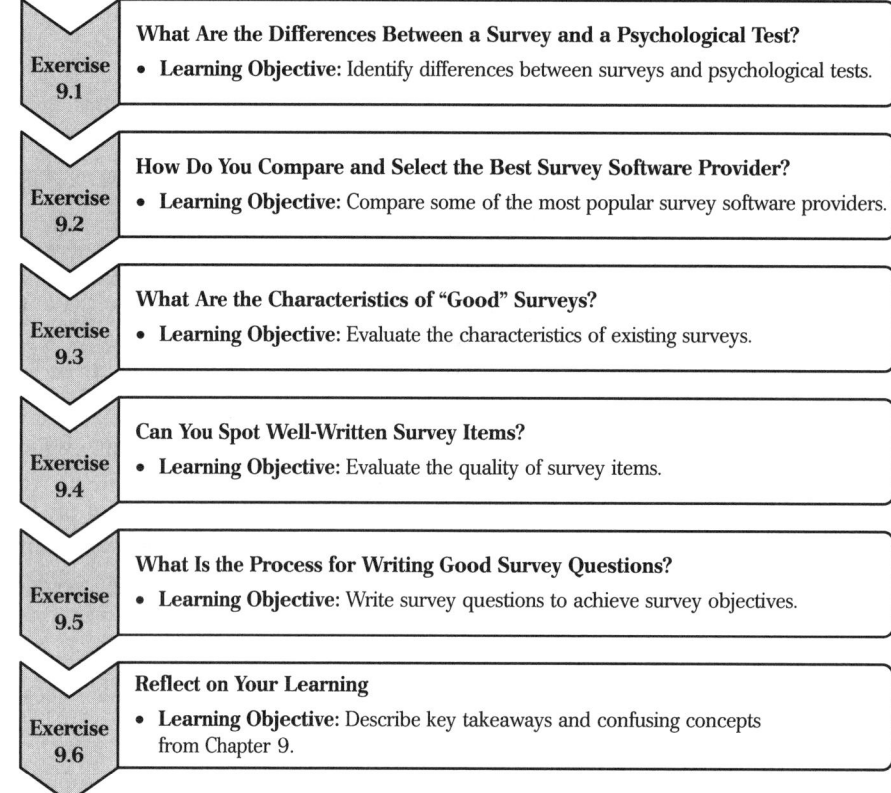

**Exercise 9.1** — What Are the Differences Between a Survey and a Psychological Test?
- **Learning Objective:** Identify differences between surveys and psychological tests.

**Exercise 9.2** — How Do You Compare and Select the Best Survey Software Provider?
- **Learning Objective:** Compare some of the most popular survey software providers.

**Exercise 9.3** — What Are the Characteristics of "Good" Surveys?
- **Learning Objective:** Evaluate the characteristics of existing surveys.

**Exercise 9.4** — Can You Spot Well-Written Survey Items?
- **Learning Objective:** Evaluate the quality of survey items.

**Exercise 9.5** — What Is the Process for Writing Good Survey Questions?
- **Learning Objective:** Write survey questions to achieve survey objectives.

**Exercise 9.6** — Reflect on Your Learning
- **Learning Objective:** Describe key takeaways and confusing concepts from Chapter 9.

# Exercise 9.1: What Are the Differences Between a Survey and a Psychological Test?

**OBJECTIVE**

Identify differences between surveys and psychological tests.

**BACKGROUND**

As you learned in Chapter 9 of the textbook, while we administer both surveys and psychological tests to gather important information from individuals, surveys differ from psychological tests in two ways. First, surveys focus on group outcomes, while tests focus on individual outcomes. Second, survey results are typically reported at the question level, while test results are typically reported at the individual level. It is important to understand that surveys are not the same as psychological tests and that they are used for different purposes. To increase your understanding of the similarities and differences between surveys and psychological tests, in Exercise 9.1, you will locate and compare two examples of surveys and two examples of psychological tests.

**YOUR TASK**

1. **Provide examples of surveys and psychological tests to compare.** Conduct an Internet search to locate two examples of surveys and two examples of psychological tests. In the table below, document the purpose of each survey and psychological test, and then describe the characteristics you identified that classify each as a survey or a psychological test.

| Survey | Purpose | Characteristics |
|---|---|---|
|  |  |  |
|  |  |  |

| Psychological Test | Purpose | Characteristics |
|---|---|---|
|  |  |  |
|  |  |  |

2. **Answer the following questions.**

What are the similarities and differences between the two surveys you located? Do you feel that one better meets the criteria of a survey? Why or why not?

_____

_____

_____

_____

_____

What are the similarities and differences between the two psychological tests you located? Do you feel that one better meets the criteria for a psychological test? Why or why not?

_____

_____

_____

_____

_____

Compare one of the surveys with one of the psychological tests. How are they similar? How are they different?

_____

_____

_____

_____

_____

# Exercise 9.2: How Do You Compare and Select the Best Survey Software Provider?

**OBJECTIVE**

Compare some of the most popular survey software providers.

**BACKGROUND**

Before technological advancements, surveys were created by hand, distributed in a paper form, and results were analyzed manually. Today, much of the survey development, administration, and analysis process is automated. A significant number of survey software companies exist that allow survey researchers to design, collect, analyze, and report survey results using automated processes. Many of the software packages share similarities but also have distinct differences. There is not just one best survey software provider; rather, individuals should research and select the survey software provider that best suits their needs. In Exercise 9.2, you will compare some popular survey software providers and select the best provider given a hypothetical situation.

**YOUR TASK**

1. **Compare the capabilities/offerings of popular survey software providers.** Thoroughly review the websites in On the Web Box 9.3 in Chapter 9 of your textbook. Document the capabilities/offerings of each, including the cost and any thoughts you have, in the table below.

| Survey Software Provider | Capabilities/Services Offered | Cost | Overall Thoughts |
|---|---|---|---|
| #1 | | | |
| #2 | | | |
| #3 | | | |
| #4 | | | |
| #5 | | | |
| #6 | | | |
| #7 | | | |
| #8 | | | |
| #9 | | | |
| #10 | | | |
| #11 | | | |

2. **Select the best survey software provider(s).** Based on your research of popular survey software providers above, select the one or two best providers for each of the scenarios below. Document the best survey software provider(s) and your rationale in the table that follows.

| Scenario | Survey Software Provider(s) | Rationale |
|---|---|---|
| You need to create a simple survey with 50–75 items that you need to be able to distribute only one time to at least 300 individuals. You will need to have access to the software for at least 3 months to complete your analysis of the data and report your findings. | | |
| You need to create a rather complex survey with 30–50 items of various types (multiple choice, Likert-type, short answer). The survey will be distributed to a minimum of 100 individuals more than once. You will need access to the software for at least 1 year to complete your analysis of the data and report your findings. | | |
| You need to create several surveys of varying length that you can administer to between 50–150 individuals per round, over multiple rounds. You need to be able to analyze the data and report the findings. | | |

3. **Identify your own scenarios.** Select one survey software provider not included in the table above. Create a detailed scenario where you would need to create a survey that would involve leveraging most of the features of the survey software provider. Document the scenario below. Include enough detail to demonstrate your deep understanding of the survey software's capabilities.

_____

_____

_____

_____

## Exercise 9.3: What Are the Characteristics of "Good" Surveys?

**OBJECTIVE**

Evaluate the characteristics of existing surveys.

**BACKGROUND**

When watching television, reading the newspaper, or even listening to the radio, you've probably heard or read about survey results. For example, you might hear that, based on a recent survey, a majority of high school students do not feel they are adequately prepared for college or that over 15% of adults have experienced a mental illness. The believability of these results depends on the quality of the survey from which the results were obtained. Constructing and administering a good survey takes time. Constructing a good survey is as much of a science as it is an art. Science is a process—and to construct good surveys, we must follow a scientific process (method). As an art, developing good surveys takes years of practice. Being able to identify the characteristics of a good survey is important because doing so can help you not only evaluate the credibility of claims made based on survey results, but to create and implement good surveys yourself. In Exercise 9.3, you will evaluate the characteristics of five surveys referencing the list of seven characteristics listed in the textbook.

**YOUR TASK**

1. **Review and list the characteristics of good surveys.** Review "The Scientific Approach to Constructing, Administering, and Using Survey Data" and the "Survey Reliability/Precision and Validity" section in Chapter 9 of your textbook.

2. **List the seven characteristics that "good" surveys share.**

    1. _____

    2. _____

    3. _____

    4. _____

    5. _____

    6. _____

    7. _____

3. **Locate a survey.** Locate two research articles or dissertations where the author had to design a survey as their data collection tool. Ensure one article or dissertation includes a survey that you believe does meet the seven characteristics and one article or dissertation where you believe the survey meets few, if any, of the seven characteristics. For each survey, provide the rationale for why you believe the survey does or does not meet each characteristic.

| Characteristic | Survey 1 (Good Example) | Survey 2 (Poor Example) |
|---|---|---|
| #1 | | |
| #2 | | |
| #3 | | |
| #4 | | |
| #5 | | |
| #6 | | |
| #7 | | |

# Exercise 9.4: Can You Spot Well-Written Survey Items?

**OBJECTIVE**

Evaluate the quality of survey items.

**BACKGROUND**

To answer a survey question, individuals go through a complex four-step cognitive process. They must first comprehend the question. Then, they must retrieve the answer from their memory. Next, they must make a judgment about whether what they have retrieved meets the objectives of the question. Last, they must communicate their response. By following some of the best practices when writing survey questions, we make the cognitive process easier for respondents and increase the chances of obtaining accurate information. In Exercise 9.4, you will find and evaluate a commercially available survey to determine if the items are written following best practices.

**YOUR TASK**

1. **Read about best practices when writing survey questions.** Read the "Writing Survey Questions" section of "The Scientific Approach to Constructing, Administering and Using Survey Data" in Chapter 9 of your textbook.

2. **Evaluate the survey items for a commercially available survey.** Locate a commercially available survey. Carefully review and evaluate the questions on the survey against the best practices below. Provide an example of an item, and if the answer is yes, describe how the item exemplifies the best practice. If your answer is no for any one best practice, provide an example of how you would revise the item to better exemplify the best practice.

| | Yes | No | Provide example of one item. | If yes, describe how item demonstrates best practice. | If no, how would you revise the item? |
|---|---|---|---|---|---|
| Are all questions purposeful and straightforward? | | | | | |
| Are all questions unambiguous? | | | | | |

*(Continued)*

(Continued)

| | Yes | No | Provide example of one item. | If yes, describe how item demonstrates best practice. | If no, how would you revise the item? |
|---|---|---|---|---|---|
| Are all questions written in correct syntax? | | | | | |
| Are the appropriate rating scales and response options used? | | | | | |
| Do all questions have the appropriate categorical alternatives? | | | | | |
| Do all questions ask one and only one question? | | | | | |
| Are all questions written at a comfortable reading level? | | | | | |

# Exercise 9.5: What Is the Process for Writing Good Survey Questions?

**OBJECTIVE**

Write survey questions to achieve survey objectives.

**BACKGROUND**

Chapter 9 of your textbook includes a comprehensive discussion of a five-phase scientific approach to constructing and administering surveys and analyzing the resulting data. The five phases are preparing for the survey; constructing the survey; administering the survey; coding, entering, and analyzing the survey data; and presenting the findings. For Exercise 9.5, you will follow the process for completing the first two phases.

**YOUR TASK**

1. **Read about the five-phase scientific approach.** Read "The Scientific Approach to Constructing, Administering, and Using Survey Data" section in Chapter 9 of your textbook. Pay particular attention to the steps involved in preparing for the survey and constructing the survey. Use the space below to capture any themes or notes from your research.

2. **Identify four survey objectives.** Imagine you were asked to create a survey to assess public opinion regarding a new product or service. Identify and write four specific survey objectives. Operationally define each objective, including two operational definitions per objective. Document the information in the table below.

| Objective | Operational Definition |
|---|---|
| #1 | 1.<br><br>2. |
| #2 | 1.<br><br>2. |
| #3 | 1.<br><br>2. |
| #4 | 1.<br><br>2. |

3. **Determine the most appropriate type of survey item.** For each objective, determine the most appropriate item type. Document the item type and provide your rationale in the table below.

| Objective | Item Type | Rationale |
|---|---|---|
| 1 | | |
| 2 | | |
| 3 | | |
| 4 | | |

4. **Write your survey questions.** In the following table, write your survey questions for each of your survey objectives following best practices.

| Survey Questions |
|---|
| 1. |
| 2. |
| 3. |
| 4. |
| 5. |

*(Continued)*

(Continued)

| Survey Questions |
|---|
| 6. |
| 7. |
| 8. |

5. **Answer the questions below.**

   What process did you use to identify your survey objectives and operational definitions?

   _____
   _____
   _____
   _____
   _____

   How did you decide what type of survey item to write for each objective (e.g., multiple choice, ranking, rating)?

   _____
   _____
   _____
   _____
   _____

   Describe which survey item type was the easiest to write and which survey item type was the most difficult to write. Explain why you selected each.

   _____
   _____
   _____
   _____
   _____

## Exercise 9.6: Reflect on Your Learning

**OBJECTIVE**

Describe key takeaways and confusing concepts from Chapter 9.

**BACKGROUND**

In Chapter 9 of the textbook, you were introduced to surveys. You read about what surveys are, how they differ from psychological tests, and how to construct and administer surveys. You were introduced to survey software providers and how to apply the five-phase scientific approach to creating and administering surveys. Lastly, you learned about how to gather evidence of reliability/precision and validity for surveys. For Exercise 9.6, you will reflect on your learning from Chapter 9 of the textbook and identify key takeaways from the chapter.

**YOUR TASK**

1. **Identify your "Aha!" moments from Chapter 9.**
   - Identify 3 to 4 new insights or realizations you had after reading Chapter 9, referred to as "Aha!" moments.
   - Consider things that made you look at a concept, your life, or an issue in a completely different way than you had in the past.
   - Document your insights and realizations below, providing details of your learning.

2. **Identify some muddy moment discussion questions.**
   - Identify 2 to 3 concepts that are still "muddy" for you from the chapter.
   - Consider concepts you still don't understand, concepts you need clarified, and/or questions you want to ask.
   - Develop 1 to 3 questions to initiate a discussion in class to further your understanding of the concepts and get your questions answered.

| | |
|---|---|
| **Insights and Realizations** | 1. _____<br>2. _____<br>3. _____<br>4. _____ |
| **Muddy Moments Discussion Questions** | 1. _____<br>2. _____<br>3. _____ |

# Chapter-Level Projects

## Project 1

**BACKGROUND**

Surveys are instruments we use to gather important information from individuals. Just like psychological tests, surveys need to be well designed. Well-designed surveys produce valid, meaningful data that can be used to make good decisions. Poorly designed surveys result in inaccurate data, which then results in misleading interpretations and bad decisions.

**YOUR TASK**

1. **Learn about the purpose of course evaluation surveys.** Imagine you are a graduate student who has been asked by a faculty member to find a course evaluation survey she can administer to students at the end of all of her courses. Begin by searching the Internet to learn more about course evaluation surveys. For example, learn as much as you can about the purpose of course evaluation surveys, including the objectives and types of questions included in well-designed course evaluation surveys.

2. **Locate and critically evaluate four existing course evaluation surveys.** Conduct research to locate four course evaluation surveys you might recommend to the faculty member. Critically evaluate each of the four surveys using the information presented in Chapter 9 of your textbook and what you learned from your Internet research.

3. **Create a presentation.** Create a presentation where you recommend a specific course evaluation survey to the instructor. Include in your presentation the criteria you used to evaluate each survey, the extent to which each survey met the criteria, and your rationale for recommending one specific course evaluation survey.

# Project 2

**BACKGROUND**

Constructing a good survey is not as simple as it may seem at first. There are many steps involved in designing a good survey. For example, we need to think carefully about the objectives or purpose of the survey. We then need to carefully construct the survey items to ensure the items clearly link with the objectives. Further, we need to carefully think through the survey format to ensure the instructions are clear and the survey is formatted in a way that it is easy to complete and score. And, ideally, we want to pretest the survey to ensure those who will be taking the survey clearly understand the survey instructions and survey items.

**YOUR TASK**

1. **Read the information below.**

    Imagine you are tasked with the responsibility of giving a formal presentation to your peers. This is the first time you have prepared and delivered a presentation, and you want to make it a positive learning experience. So, in addition to making the presentation, you decide to collect audience feedback, requiring that you create an audience feedback survey.

2. **Develop your audience feedback survey.** Prepare for and design a 5- to 10-item audience feedback survey following the best practices described in Chapter 9 of your textbook.

3. **Create a presentation.** Create a PowerPoint or Prezi presentation to explain the following:

    - Your survey purpose and objectives, including operational definitions
    - The best practices you followed when writing your survey items and formatting your survey
    - The process you would recommend for pretesting your survey, providing rationale for your process
    - Your reflections on the survey development process, including such things as how much time it took you to develop the survey, what was most difficult, what was least difficult, and what challenges you experienced

## Project 3

**BACKGROUND**

Imagine you were in graduate school serving as the teaching assistant for a psychology instructor. Because some of the students in the course are struggling with the concepts in Chapter 9, the instructor has asked you to spend 1 hour with these students to help increase their understanding of the Chapter 9 material. In addition to meeting with the students, the instructor requested that you create a visual learning aid you can use not only as an instructional tool when meeting with the students, but that students can take with them and use as a study tool for future exams.

**YOUR TASK**

1. **Search the Internet to learn more about visual learning aids.** Conduct a search of the Internet to learn more about the value of visual learning aids and the different types of learning aids. When searching, consider using key terms such as *visual learning aids, graphic organizer, concept maps, cognitive organizer, concept diagrams,* and *story maps.*

2. **Create a visual learning aid of Chapter 9 material.** Review the learning objectives at the beginning of Chapter 9. Create a well-thought-out visual learning aid to enhance student understanding of the important concepts associated with each learning objective. Your visual learning aid should be professional-looking and include visual symbols and words to express Chapter 9 concepts, as well as the connections between them. Creativity is encouraged.

## Practice Questions

### Multiple Choice

1. Psychological tests focus on _____ outcomes, and surveys focus on _____ outcomes.
   a. individual; group
   b. group; individual
   c. individual; individual
   d. group; group

2. The results of psychological tests are usually reported _____, and the results of surveys are often reported _____.
   a. as an overall score; as an overall score
   b. as an overall score; at the question level
   c. at the question level; as an overall score
   d. at the question level; at the question level

3. Surveys are research tools for collecting information to describe and compare which of the following?
   a. People's attitudes
   b. People's attitudes and knowledge
   c. People's attitudes, knowledge, and behaviors
   d. People's attitudes, knowledge, behaviors, and motives

4. If we asked parents to complete a survey to find out how they feel about their children wearing school uniforms, we would be asking them about their
   a. knowledge.
   b. attitude(s).
   c. behavior(s).
   d. motive(s).

5. If we come to believe that Friday the 13th is an unlucky day because of a superstition, we have acquired this knowledge through
   a. intuition.
   b. authority.
   c. tenacity.
   d. rationalism.

6. According to Helmstadter (1970), which one of the following methods of acquiring knowledge is the best for gathering accurate information?
   a. Intuition
   b. Tenacity
   c. Authority
   d. Scientific method

7. How many steps are associated with the scientific method?
   a. Three
   b. Five
   c. Seven
   d. Nine

8. Which one of the following statements is FALSE about surveys?
   a. Constructing surveys is as much a science as it is an art.
   b. In most cases, surveys are experimental research techniques.
   c. Surveys are used to collect important information from individuals.
   d. Surveys gather information about attitudes, knowledge, and behaviors.

9. When constructing a survey, the developer must have knowledge of all of the following EXCEPT
   a. different types of surveys.
   b. different types of survey questions.

c. selecting the appropriate respondents.

d. how to assemble questions into a survey instrument.

10. Research suggests that when people answer survey questions, they go through what stages?

    a. Comprehension, retrieval, and response communication
    b. Comprehension, retrieval, judgment, and response communication
    c. Comprehension, judgment, and response communication
    d. Comprehension, judgment, retrieval, and response communication

11. Which one of the following would you NOT recommend when assembling a survey?

    a. Using shading to prevent respondents from writing in specific sections
    b. Integrating white space so that the survey looks inviting and is easy to complete
    c. Printing on one side of the paper so respondents can use the other side for taking notes
    d. Spiral binding surveys that are very long

12. Nonsampling errors are errors associated with all of the following EXCEPT the

    a. choice of the individuals to be included in the survey.
    b. design and administration of the survey.
    c. quality of the survey questions.
    d. consistency of the way in which the survey administrators ask follow-up questions.

13. Which one of the following is NOT a purpose of pretesting a survey?

    a. Identifying sources of sampling measurement errors
    b. Examining the effectiveness of question revisions
    c. Indicating the effect of alternative versions of a question or survey
    d. Assessing the final version of a survey for ease of completion

14. Which one of the following is TRUE about simple random sampling?

    a. Every member of a population has an equal chance of being chosen.
    b. Every $n$th (for example, every fifth) person in a population is chosen.
    c. A population is divided into subgroups or strata.
    d. Clusters are selected, and participants are selected from each cluster.

15. When should you use cluster sampling?

    a. When the population is very small
    b. When it is not feasible to list all individuals who belong to a population
    c. When it is impossible to select a random sample from the population
    d. When the population is very homogeneous

16. Which one of the following is FALSE about sample size?

    a. The sample size should be equal to or greater than 30% of the population size.
    b. The sample size can be calculated by knowing the confidence interval and level.
    c. The more dissimilar the members of the population, the larger the sample that is necessary.
    d. The smaller the sample size, the more error the survey results are likely to include.

17. Which one of the following would we NOT use to describe or summarize responses to individual survey question?

a. Descriptive statistics

b. Frequency distributions

c. Univariate analyses

d. Bivariate analyses

18. Univariate analyses include all of the following EXCEPT

    a. frequency counts.

    b. percentages.

    c. means, modes, and medians.

    d. correlations.

19. Bivariate analyses include all of the following EXCEPT

    a. correlation coefficients.

    b. cross-tabulations.

    c. chi-square comparisons.

    d. percentages.

## Short Answer

**Remembering**

1. Describe the similarities and differences between surveys and psychological tests. Provide examples of each.
2. What steps do we follow when using the scientific method?
3. List four different types of survey questions. Give an example of each.
4. Define reliability and validity as they apply to surveys.

**Applying**

5. How does the scientific method differ from other methods of acquiring knowledge?
6. What factors should someone consider when selecting a survey software provider or product?

**Evaluating**

7. Compare the methods for acquiring knowledge according to Helmstadter (1970). Give an example of each.
8. Describe each step in the scientific method in terms of survey research.
9. Explain the importance of reliability and validity when collecting data using surveys.

# Multiple-Choice and Short-Answer Practice Question Answer Key

## Multiple Choice

| Question | Answer | Textbook Page | Explanation |
|---|---|---|---|
| 1. | a | 240 | Both psychological tests and surveys are used to make important decisions and collect information about individuals. However, surveys are generally used at the group level, while psychological tests are used at the individual level. For example, an organization may give a survey to employees to determine their level of job satisfaction. The organization typically does not examine individual responses, but it examines the job satisfaction for groups of employees. |
| 2. | b | 241 | The results of a psychological test are often reported in terms of an overall derived score or scaled scores. On the other hand, the results of surveys are often reported at the question level by providing the percentage of respondents who selected each answer alternative. The distinction between surveys and tests is not always clear, however. |
| 3. | c | 241 | As the textbook describes, surveys allow us to collect information to describe and compare how people feel about things (attitudes), what they know (knowledge), and what they do (behaviors). |
| 4. | b | 241 | The key word in the question stem is *feel*. This word suggests that the survey is interested in measuring the parents' attitudes about school uniforms. It would be entirely possible, however, to construct a survey that measures their knowledge or behavior as well. |
| 5. | c | 250 | Table 9.1 describes Helmstadter's six methods by which knowledge is obtained. Information acquired through tenacity is based on superstition or habit, leading people to continue believing something we have always believed. For example, people may come to believe that a certain brand is better than others simply because they have always used it. |
| 6. | d | 251 | The scientific method often leads to the most accurate information because it is more systematic and objective than the other methods of acquiring information. |
| 7. | b | 251 | While there may be some minor disagreement among researchers concerning the exact five steps of the scientific method, they are generally considered to be the following:<br>1. Identify the question and form a hypothesis<br>2. Design a study to test the hypothesis |

*(Continued)*

(Continued)

| Question | Answer | Textbook Page | Explanation |
|---|---|---|---|
| | | | 3. Conduct the study |
| | | | 4. Analyze and interpret the data collected during the study |
| | | | 5. Communicate the results |
| 8. | b | 253 | The correct answer, which is an incorrect statement about surveys, is that surveys are in most cases experimental research techniques. Experimental methods allow us to determine cause and effect and surveys generally do not allow us to do this. Instead surveys are primarily used in a descriptive manner. |
| 9. | c | 254 | Selecting appropriate respondents is not part of constructing a survey. It is a part of the survey process although, as appropriate, respondents must be identified before the survey can be administered. All of the other answer options are important to know about when constructing a survey. |
| 10. | b | 257 | Cognitive psychologists and survey researchers have studied how respondents answer survey questions. The research shows that it can be a difficult and complex cognitive task. The research suggests that when people answer survey questions, they go through at least four stages: Comprehension → Retrieval → Judgment → Response Communication. First respondents must comprehend or understand the question, which involves things like having the required vocabulary capabilities and the ability to attend to the entire question. Once they understand the question, they have to retrieve the appropriate information from their memory. After they retrieve the information, they need to determine or judge that the information meets the criteria of the question. Finally, respondents must correctly communicate their response. |
| 11. | c | 266 | Surveys do not require respondents to take notes, so there is no need to print surveys on one side to allow for note taking. All of the other answer options are important considerations when preparing a survey instrument, and they are more fully described in the textbook section "Preparing the Survey Instrument." |
| 12. | a | 266 | Pretesting the survey will allow the developer to identify nonsampling measurement errors that may occur. These are errors that are associated with the design and administration of the survey and not the choice of the survey respondents. All of the choices except "a" are nonsampling errors. |

## Chapter 9 ■ How Do We Construct and Administer Surveys and Use Survey Data?

| Question | Answer | Textbook Page | Explanation |
|---|---|---|---|
| 13. | a | 271 | Sampling errors do not come into play when pretesting a survey. They occur when the test is actually administered and are a result of selecting an inappropriate sample, not selecting a large enough sample, or incorrect distribution of the survey. |
| 14. | a | 270 | When a simple random sampling approach is used, every member of the population has an equal chance of being chosen as part of the sample. Because of this characteristic, it is often assumed that the sample will be representative of the population. However, this is not always the case, and it is always possible that the sample will vary in key ways from the population. |
| 15. | b | 270 | Cluster sampling is used when it is not possible to list all of the members who belong to a particular population. It is also often used when the target population is large and has relatively homogeneous groups of individuals within the population. Each one of the homogeneous groups becomes a cluster. Then clusters can be randomly sampled. |
| 16. | a | 271 | There is no set percentage of the population that the sample should be. Instead, determining sample size is a complex science that considers many factors, such as desired level of confidence and the homogeneity of the respondent population. |
| 17. | d | 276 | Descriptive statistics, frequency distributions, and univariate analyses all help us to describe or summarize the main characteristics of the data that are collected by survey questions. However, we use bivariate analyses to provide information on two variables or groups. For instance, a correlation coefficient is a bivariate statistic because it enables us to describe the relationship between two variables. |
| 18. | d | 276 | Univariate analysis only examines one variable or question at a time. In contrast, a correlation requires two variables and examines the relationship between the two variables. Thus, the correlation is considered a bivariate analysis. |
| 19. | d | 276 | The first three answer options—correlation coefficients, cross tabulations, and chi-square comparisons—require two variables and are therefore considered bivariate analyses. The only answer option that is not a bivariate analysis is "percentages," which only requires a single variable and is therefore considered a univariate analysis. |

## Short Answer

| Question | Explanation |
|---|---|
| 1. | Surveys allow researchers to collect information, so they can understand people and compare people's attitudes, knowledge, and behaviors. The words *survey* and *test* are often confused, but there are differences (and similarities) between the two. First the similarities. Both surveys and tests are used to collect data and make decisions. These decisions can be relatively low stakes and have little impact, or they can be high stakes that have important impact on the lives of individuals or groups of people. For example, a supervisor could survey her employees to determine if they would prefer pepperoni or cheese pizza at a work function, or a government could conduct a survey to determine the unemployment rate, which has broad economic and political impacts. Surveys and tests are different in that tests generally focus on individual outcomes, and surveys focus on group outcomes. For example, tests are used to make a decision about a single person, such as whether a college admits a student. Surveys focus on groups, such as how satisfied the owners are with the performance of a certain type of car. Another difference is that surveys often report their results at the individual item level focusing on the percentage of respondents choosing each answer option. Tests, on the other hand, tend to focus on an overall score. |
| 2. | Generally, the process involves stating a hypothesis, planning a study, conducting the study and collecting data, analyzing the data, and communicating the findings. Each step is further elaborated below.<br><br>1. *Identify a problem and state a hypothesis.* In terms of survey research, this requires the researcher to conduct a literature review, gather people who are knowledgeable about the survey topic, and conduct focus groups.<br><br>2. *Design a study to test the hypothesis.* At this step, the survey researcher should know about different types of surveys and questions; should know how to write questions, how to assemble the survey, and how to pretest surveys; and should be able to devise a data analysis plan.<br><br>3. *Conduct the study.* Here the survey researcher should understand how to sample respondents and be able to handle all the logistics of survey administration.<br><br>4. *Analyze the data.* At this step, the researcher should know how to enter and code data and be able to conduct appropriate statistical analyses.<br><br>5. *Communicate the research findings.* For the final stage, the researcher should be able to write reports, prepare presentation materials, and present the results to groups of people. |
| 3. | There are many different types of survey questions. Below are some of the most popular types that were described in the textbook.<br><br>a. Open-ended<br>b. Closed-ended<br>c. Yes/no questions<br>d. Fill in the blank<br>e. Implied no choice<br>f. Single-item choice |

| Question | Explanation |
|---|---|
| | g. Enfolded |
| | h. Free choice |
| | i. Multiple choice |
| | j. Ranking |
| | k. Rating |
| | l. Guttman format |
| | m. Likert and other intensity scale formats |
| | n. Semantic differential |
| | o. Paired comparisons and constant referent comparisons |
| | Perhaps the most popular type of survey question is the Likert format. This type of question requires that respondents indicate their amount of agreement or disagreement on a symmetric scale. For example, respondent may be asked to indicate their level of agreement with the statement "Overall I am satisfied with my job" using the following response options 1 = Strongly Disagree, 2 = Disagree, 3 = Neither Disagree Nor Agree, 4 = Agree, 5 = Strongly Agree. |
| | Opened-ended questions are a popular type of survey question. While easy to construct, the answers they elicit can be difficult to code and interpret. An example of an open-ended prompt is, "Describe your level of satisfaction with your job." |
| | Another popular survey question type is the multiple-choice format. An example is "What is the biggest driver of you overall job satisfaction?" With the response options of (a) pay, (b) co-workers, (c) type of work, (d) supervisor. When developing written multiple-choice questions, it can be difficult for the researcher anticipate all of the possible response options. As a result, sometimes a catch-all options such as other will be used with an opportunity to write in additional information. While useful, this can introduce the same coding and interpretation issues found with open-ended questions. |
| | A less used type of survey question is the semantic differential. For this type of question, the respondents are asked to choose their position along two bi-polar adjectives. An example is "Circle the number representing your overall job satisfaction." |
| | Dissatisfied 1 2 3 4 5 6 7 8 9 10 Satisfied |
| 4. | A survey must measure what it is intended to measure consistently (reliability) and accurately (validity) if we are to make good decisions with the obtained information. Remember that reliability is a necessary, but not sufficient, condition for a valid test. For example, an unreliable survey cannot be valid because the measurements would be "scattered" all over, which necessarily means there is no accuracy. However, a highly reliable survey still can be inaccurate as it can consistently give you erroneous information. All of the previously discussed approaches to reliability that are used with tests, such as test–retest, alternate forms, and split-half reliability can be applied to surveys. |
| 5. | The scientific method tends to be more systematic and objective than the other methods. All attempts are explicitly made to remove personal beliefs, perceptions, biases, values, attitudes, and emotions. |

*(Continued)*

(Continued)

| Question | Explanation |
|---|---|
| 6. | As technology has advanced, many aspects of surveying have been automated. Third-party providers and specialists have emerged to assist survey researchers. There are many firms dedicated to providing survey software so that individuals and companies can design, collect, analyze, and report their own data quickly and easily. While there are many different survey software products available, there are similarities and differences among them. There is no single best survey software, and the choice of software depends on the researcher's specific needs, desires, and constraints. For example, one researcher may need quick, simple software that provides easy-to-design and implement templates. Another researcher may need to design and implement complex surveys on an ongoing basis. Some individuals may have limited or no funds available, while others may have funding to help support their survey needs. Thus, SurveyMonkey, which allows users to create up to 10 surveys and 100 respondents for free, may be quite sufficient. However, researchers who need to create many surveys and collect data on thousands of individuals may need different software. In this case, the researcher might select one of SurveyMonkey's paid plans (Select, Gold, Platinum, and Enterprise), which have increasing levels of features and support. <br><br> Another factor researchers may consider is access to respondents. Some survey software providers help identify and survey respondents who are within the researchers' identified population. One more feature survey researchers might want to consider is the extent of reporting support that is provided. Some software only provides basic reports, while other software allows highly powerful report design and analyses. Finally, some software allows for complex survey administration schemes, such as 360° or multirater surveys. This is a popular survey approach where a focal individual (a supervisor for example) will be rated on important job performance dimensions by subordinates, peers, managers, and even possibly customers. |
| 7. | Helmstadter in 1970 identified six methods people use to obtain knowledge. They are tenacity, intuition, authority, rationalism, empiricism, and scientific method. The first three place few demands on information processing and are easy to perform. The last three require more effort. <br><br> Below is a brief description of each with an example. <br><br> 1. Tenacity—Knowledge is accepted because we have accepted it for so long. For example, we use a certain type of toilet paper because we have used it for so long, so it must be the best. And conversely because it is the best, we have used it for so long. <br><br> 2. Intuition—Knowledge is accepted based on a gut feeling or because it appears self-evident; thus, there is no process of assessment. For example, the Earth appears to us to be flat, so we assume it is flat. <br><br> 3. Authority—Knowledge is accepted based on the status of the source. For example, we believe that the Earth is the center of the universe because religious authorities say it is at the center. <br><br> 4. Rationalism—Knowledge is gained by reaching a conclusion through logical analysis. Logical syllogisms are an example: All men are mortal, Socrates is a man, therefore, Socrates is mortal. |

| Question | Explanation |
|---|---|
| | 5. Empiricism—Knowledge is gained by reaching a conclusion based on observation and gathering of data. For example, we take a specific type of pill and our headache goes away. Therefore, it must have been the pill that made the headache go away. |
| | 6. Scientific method—Knowledge is gained by reaching a conclusion based on a systematic and objective process. Generally, the process involves stating a hypothesis, planning a study, conducting the study and collecting data, analyzing the data, and communicating the findings. An example of the scientific method is the process that is used by most articles published in peer-reviewed psychological journals on measurement and testing. |
| 8. | The scientific method tends to be more systematic and objective than the other methods. All attempts are explicitly made to remove personal beliefs, perceptions, biases, values, attitudes, and emotions. |
| 9. | The psychometric concepts of reliability and validity apply to surveys as well as to tests. When applied to testing, validity refers to whether there is evidence to support the inferences based on tests scores. This same approach applies to surveys. However, for surveys, it is common to focus more heavily on evidence related to construct validity as it is important to know that the survey actually measures the concepts or constructs the researcher is intending to measure. |

# 10 How Do We Develop a Test?

## Overview

In Chapter 10 of the textbook, you were introduced to the steps for developing a test. After reading the chapter you have a clearer understanding of the process for constructing a test plan, the various formats and process for writing test questions, the importance of the instructions that accompany a test, and why it is important to conduct a pilot test before a test is ready for administration. While Chapter 10 of the textbook included foundational information about psychological test development, Chapter 10 of the workbook provides you with the opportunity to demonstrate your understanding of material presented in the textbook and apply your learnings by completing some practical and critical thinking exercises linked to specific learning objectives. Chapter 10 of the workbook will also allow you to complete chapter-level projects to demonstrate your understanding of multiple topics within the chapter. Chapter 10 of the workbook ends with some multiple-choice and short-answer questions you can use to self-assess your understanding of the material.

# Practical and Critical-Thinking Exercises

## Purpose

This section contains five exercises you can complete to demonstrate your understanding and apply your learning (Exercises 10.1–10.5) and one exercise you can complete to reflect on your learning (Exercise 10.6). The exercises, linked to learning objectives, are displayed below.

**Exercise 10.1**
**What Is It Like to Develop Test Plans?**
- **Learning Objective:** Create test plans to measure a concrete and an abstract attribute.

**Exercise 10.2**
**What Is It Like to Compose Test Items?**
- **Learning Objective:** Compose test items from existing test specifications.

**Exercise 10.3**
**What Is the Difference Between Objective and Subjective Test Questions?**
- **Learning Objective:** Distinguish between objective and subjective test questions, including their strengths and weaknesses.

**Exercise 10.4**
**Can You Identify Good Test-Taker Instructions?**
- **Learning Objective:** Identify good test-taker instructions.

**Exercise 10.5**
**How Do You Write Test Instructions?**
- **Learning Objective:** Write three sets of test instructions.

**Exercise 10.6**
**Reflect on Your Learning**
- **Learning Objective:** Describe key takeaways and confusing concepts from Chapter 10.

# Exercise 10.1: What Is It Like to Develop Test Plans?

**OBJECTIVE**

Create test plans to measure a concrete and an abstract attribute.

**BACKGROUND**

When developing a test, the first step is to define the testing universe, the target audience, and test purpose. The testing universe is identified by operationally defining the construct the test will measure. The target audience is defined by identifying the characteristics of the persons who will take the test. The test purpose includes not only what the test will measure, but also how the test users will use the test scores. The second step when developing a test is to develop a test plan. The test plan typically includes a concise definition of the testing construct the test will measure, the content to be measured (the testing universe), and the types of questions the test will contain (the test format). To increase your understanding of what it's like to develop a test plan, in Exercise 10.1, you will consider two hypothetical situations, create test plans for both situations, and then reflect on the process.

**YOUR TASK**

1. **Read the two scenarios below.** Use the space below to capture any themes or notes necessary to complete the exercise.

    **Scenario 1:** Imagine you are a psychology professor preparing to develop a quiz to measure student knowledge of one chapter within your textbook.

    **Scenario 2:** Imagine you are a counseling psychologist and you want to create your own test to measure marital satisfaction.

2. **For each scenario, answer the questions in the table below.** First, review the following two sections in Chapter 10 of your textbook: "Defining the Testing Universe, Audience, and Purpose" and "Developing a Test Plan." Also review the "Demonstrating Evidence of Validity Based on Test Content During Test Development" section of Chapter 6. Then, document your questions for each scenario in the table below. Keep in mind that Scenario 1 involves developing a test to measure a concrete attribute, while Scenario 2 involves developing a test to measure an abstract attribute.

|  | Scenario 1 | Scenario 2 |
| --- | --- | --- |
| What questions do you need to ask to define the testing universe, the target audience, and the test purpose? |  |  |
| What questions do you need to ask to create a test plan? |  |  |

3. **Create two test plans/test specification tables.** After obtaining answers to the questions above, on a separate sheet of paper, create two test plans/test specification tables. Create one test plan to achieve the objective in Scenario 1 and another test plan to achieve the objective in Scenario 2. Include all the information you think would be necessary for another person to design the test.

4. **Answer the questions below.**

   How did you feel as you were developing the test plans/test specification tables? What was the experience like?

   _____
   _____
   _____
   _____
   _____
   _____

   Which test plan/test specification table was easier to create? Why?

   _____
   _____
   _____
   _____
   _____
   _____

   What did you struggle most with?

   _____
   _____
   _____
   _____
   _____

# Exercise 10.2: What Is It Like to Compose Test Items?

**OBJECTIVE**

Compose test items from existing test specifications.

**BACKGROUND**

Prior to building a house, architects will create a detailed blueprint. The blueprint consists of drawings to show the specifications of a house. For example, the blueprint might include the layout of the rooms, the dimensions of each room, and the materials to be used. The blueprint provides all the information builders need to build a sturdy house that meets homebuilding guidelines, and it meets the needs of the entity or person building the house. Like well-designed homes, well-designed tests need blueprints also, although we often refer to these blueprints as a test plan or test specification table. With well-designed test specifications, test-item writers have all the information they need to write test items. However, writing test items is not easy. To increase your understanding of what it is like to compose test items, in Exercise 10.2, you will write knowledge-test questions based on an existing test specification.

**YOUR TASK**

1. **Review the information below.**

    Imagine you are a graduate assistant for a psychology professor. The professor is currently in the process of designing a new Tests and Measurements class. The professor shares that your role will be to design the quizzes to be administered throughout the class, but she has already created the test specifications for each quiz. She shares with you the test specifications she has created for the first quiz, indicating she'd like the quiz items to be primarily multiple-choice questions, but that she'd also like to include one or two essay questions.

2. **Review the test specifications below.**

| **Class:** Tests and Measurements | **Item Format:** Multiple choice | **Desired Test Length:** Approximately 10 items |
|---|---|---|
| **Testing Universe:** This exam is intended to measure Test and Measurement student knowledge of terms and concepts, as well as their ability to apply the terms and concepts, from Chapter 5 of the textbook ("What Is Test Reliability/Precision?"). ||||

| Chapter Learning Objective | Weight | Knowledge of Terms and Concepts (# of Qs) | Application of Learning (# of Qs) |
|---|---|---|---|
| 1. Define reliability/precision and describe three methods for estimating the reliability/precision of a psychological test and its scores. | 40% | 2 | 2 |
| 2. Describe how an observed test score is made up of the true score and random error, and describe the difference between random error and systematic error. | 10% | 1 | |

| Chapter Learning Objective | Weight | Knowledge of Terms and Concepts (# of Qs) | Application of Learning (# of Qs) |
|---|---|---|---|
| 3. Calculate and interpret a reliability coefficient, including adjusting a reliability coefficient obtained using the split-half method. | 20% | 1 | 1 |
| 4. Identify four sources of test error and six factors related to these sources of error that are particularly important to consider. | 30% | 2 | 1 |
| **TOTAL** | **100%** | **6** | **4** |

3. **Compose the 10 test items.** On a separate sheet of paper, compose the 10 test items for this quiz, using the test specifications above.

4. **Take another student's test.** Exchange your quiz with another classmate's, using the process identified by your instructor.

5. **Discuss the following questions with your partner.**
   - What was the experience of writing multiple-choice test questions like?
   - How did you go about identifying the content from which to write multiple-choice and essay questions?
   - What is the primary difference, if any, in what is being measured by the multiple-choice and essay questions?
   - What did you struggle most with?
   - How are your quizzes similar and different? Why are there differences?
   - Do each of the questions really measure what you think they measure? Why or why not?
   - Is one quiz better than the other? If so, why?
   - How did you decide what content to write the items on?
   - If you had designed the test specifications, what would you have done differently than the faculty member?

# Exercise 10.3: What Is the Difference Between Objective and Subjective Test Questions?

**OBJECTIVE**

Distinguish between objective and subjective test questions, including their strengths and weaknesses.

**BACKGROUND**

When writing test questions, we can choose to write objective or subjective test items. Each of these item types has advantages and drawbacks related to: (a) opportunities to sample the testing universe, (b) difficulty and time it takes to construct the test items, (c) ease of scoring, and (d) response sets that may influence scores. To increase your understanding of objective and subjective test questions, in Exercise 10.3, you will differentiate between objective and subjective test questions.

**YOUR TASK**

1. **Differentiate between objective and subjective item formats.** Review the "A Comparison of Objective and Subjective Formats" section of Chapter 10 in your textbook. Then, define each item format in your own words, providing three unique examples of each item format. Ensure the examples you provide are not ones contained in the textbook. Summarize the strengths and weaknesses of each format. Document the information in the table below.

|  | **Objective Item Format** | **Subjective Item Format** |
|---|---|---|
| Definition |  |  |
| Examples |  |  |
| Strengths |  |  |
| Weaknesses |  |  |

## Exercise 10.4: Can You Identify Good Test-Taker Instructions?

**OBJECTIVE**

Identify good test-taker instructions.

**BACKGROUND**

Consider the countless number of tests you have taken in your lifetime. Were the test-taker instructions always well written and clearly understood? You probably needed to ask clarifying questions at least a few times. It is important for the test taker to have instructions provided that are clear, leaving little to nothing to question. Having clear instructions will help to ensure that the test taker knows what is being asked so they are able to provide the most accurate response to the best of their ability. To increase your understanding of the importance of good test-taker instructions, in Exercise 10.4, you will identify, review, and rate the test-taker instructions for three tests.

**YOUR TASK**

1. **Locate three tests online**. Conduct an Internet search of free tests using key words such as free tests, free practice tests, online practice tests, etc. Select three to further review.

2. **Read and compare the test-taker instructions**. Review *Writing the Administration Instructions* section in Chapter 10 of the textbook, paying particular attention to the characteristics that make up good test-taker instructions. Read the test-taker instructions for each of the three tests you selected online and complete the test. Take note of what was clear in the instructions and what questions you had before, during, and after completing the test. Complete the chart below.

| Test | Characteristics Met | What Was Good | What Could Be Improved |
|---|---|---|---|
| 1 | | | |
| 2 | | | |
| 3 | | | |

3. **Rate the test-taker instructions**. Rate each of the test-taker instructions using the Likert-type scale below. Provide a rationale for your rating.

   1 = Very poorly written

   2 = Somewhat poorly written

   3 = Neither well written or poorly written

   4 = Somewhat well written

   5 = Very well written

| Test | Rating | Rationale |
|---|---|---|
| 1 | | |
| 2 | | |
| 3 | | |

# Exercise 10.5: How Do You Write Test Instructions?

**OBJECTIVE**

Write three sets of test instructions.

**BACKGROUND**

Even with well-constructed test items, if there are no instructions or there are poorly written instructions, the test may be administered, taken, or scored improperly. Therefore, it is important for test developers, especially those who develop commercially available tests, to ensure the tests they develop have well-written instructions. To increase your understanding of how to write good test instructions, in Exercise 10.5, you will write three sets of test instructions a test developer should write when developing a test.

**YOUR TASK**

1. **Read the information below.**

   Imagine you work for a large organization that offers services related to developing, administering, and scoring psychological tests. You are in the process of developing a new test psychologists can use to measure kindergarten children's ability to process what they hear. Before pilot testing the newly designed test, you must write the test instructions.

2. **Answer the questions below.**

   What are the three sets of instructions a test developer should write?

   - _____
   - _____
   - _____

   What are the issues the test developer should consider when writing the administrator instructions?

   _____
   _____
   _____
   _____
   _____

   What are the issues the test developer should consider when writing the test-taker instructions?

   _____
   _____
   _____
   _____
   _____

What are the issues the test developer should consider when writing the test-scoring instructions?

_____

_____

_____

_____

_____

3. **Write administration instructions.** Write administration instructions for the above-referenced scenario. Be sure to write all three sets of instructions and include the necessary details for each.

| Type of Instruction | Instructions |
| --- | --- |
|  |  |
|  |  |
|  |  |

# Exercise 10.6: Reflect on Your Learning

### OBJECTIVE

Describe key takeaways and confusing concepts from Chapter 10.

### BACKGROUND

In Chapter 10 of the textbook, you were introduced to the initial steps for developing psychological tests. You learned about how to define the testing universe, the target audience, and the purpose of the test. Additionally, you learned how to develop a test plan and conduct a pilot test. For Exercise 10.6, you will reflect on your learning from Chapter 10 of the textbook and identify key takeaways from the chapter.

### YOUR TASK

1. **Identify your "Aha!" moments from Chapter 10.**
    - Identify 3 to 4 new insights or realizations you had after reading Chapter 10, referred to as "Aha!" moments.
    - Consider things that made you look at a concept, your life, or an issue in a completely different way than you had in the past.
    - Document your insights and realizations below, providing details of your learning.

2. **Identify some muddy moment discussion questions.**
    - Identify 2 to 3 concepts that are still "muddy" for you from the chapter.
    - Consider concepts you still don't understand, concepts you need clarified, and/or questions you want to ask.
    - Develop 1 to 3 questions to initiate a discussion in class to further your understanding of the concepts and get your questions answered.

| | |
|---|---|
| **Insights and Realizations** | 1. _____ <br> 2. _____ <br> 3. _____ <br> 4. _____ |
| **Muddy Moments Discussion Questions** | 1. _____ <br> 2. _____ <br> 3. _____ |

# Chapter-Level Projects

## Project 1

**BACKGROUND**

Test development is a complex process that is both a science and an art. As a science, there are common steps we follow when designing a test. The first step includes the process of constructing a test plan. From this test plan, items are developed. Next, the test developer must write the instructions for the test user and test taker. Last, the test is piloted to see how well it performs. As an art, writing good test items and instructions comes with practice.

**YOUR TASK**

1. **Create an interview script with a partner.** Find a partner to work with. Together, prepare a written interview script that includes interview questions that will elicit detailed responses on best practices when designing a test. Also include written responses to each question. Build into your script a discussion of a minimum of 10 best practices from Chapter 10 of the textbook, beginning with creating a test plan and ending with piloting of a test.

2. **Conduct and video record the interview.** Decide who will be the interviewer and who will be the interviewee. Be creative in your interview and have fun! Use your smartphone, a digital camera, or the webcam on your laptop to record the interview. We suggest that you hold your camera in landscape position while you record. Landscape videos display a little better. The next step is uploading the interview to a video-sharing website. A bunch of free platforms, like YouTube and Vimeo, are available. Search the Internet to find a video-sharing platform *you* like. Follow your instructor's directions for how to share your video link.

# Project 2

**BACKGROUND**

When designing a test, we follow a scientific process. First, we construct a test plan. Then, using the test plan as a guide, we construct the test items following best practices in item development. Then, in addition to writing test-taker instructions, for commercially available tests, we write administrator instructions and instructions for scoring the test.

**YOUR TASK**

1. **Team up with other students.** Form a group of three or four students, as directed by your instructor. As a team, you will work cooperatively to create your own test of college adjustment following the steps below.

2. **Create a test plan.** Create a test plan for your college adjustment test using the constructs, definitions, and behaviors in For Your Information Box 10.1 in your textbook.

3. **Compose your test items.** Compose your test items following your test plan.

4. **Write your test instructions.** Write your administrator instructions, test-taker instructions, and scoring instructions.

5. **Compare your test plans, test items, and test instructions**. As directed by your instructor, engage in discussion with other teams to discuss (a) what the experience was like, (b) what was easy and what was most difficult, and (c) the similarities and differences in your test plans, test items, and test instructions.

# Project 3

**BACKGROUND**

Imagine you were in graduate school serving as the teaching assistant for a psychology instructor. Because some of the students in the course are struggling with the concepts in Chapter 10, the instructor has asked you to spend 1 hour with these students to help increase their understanding of the Chapter 10 material. In addition to meeting with the students, the instructor requested that you create a visual learning aid you can use not only as an instructional tool when meeting with the students, but that students can take with them and use as a study tool for future exams.

**YOUR TASK**

1. **Search the Internet to learn more about visual learning aids.** Conduct a search of the Internet to learn more about the value of visual learning aids and the different types of learning aids. When searching, consider using key terms such as *visual learning aids, graphic organizer, concept maps, cognitive organizer, concept diagrams,* and *story maps*.

2. **Create a visual learning aid of Chapter 10 material.** Review the learning objectives at the beginning of Chapter 10. Create a well-thought-out visual learning aid to enhance student understanding of the important concepts associated with each learning objective. Your visual learning aid should be professional-looking and include visual symbols and words to express Chapter 10 concepts, as well as the connections between them. Creativity is encouraged.

# Practice Questions

## Multiple Choice

1. What is the first step in developing a new test?
   a. Creating a test plan
   b. Examining the suitability of the test format
   c. Adequately sampling behaviors from a specific test domain
   d. Defining the testing universe, audience, and purpose

2. Making a list of the characteristics of persons who will take a test is which part of the test-development process?
   a. Defining the purpose
   b. Defining the target audience
   c. Defining the test universe
   d. Developing the test plan

3. A job analysis provides the basis for a test plan in
   a. organizations.
   b. clinical settings.
   c. educational settings.
   d. No Child Left Behind.

4. What do we call the type of questions that a test contains?
   a. Construct explication
   b. Construct operationalization
   c. Behavioral definition
   d. Test format

5. Which one of the following is an objective test format?
   a. Multiple choice
   b. Sentence completion
   c. Interview
   d. Essay

6. Which one of the following models assumes that the more the test taker responds in a particular fashion, the more the test taker exhibits the attribute being measured?
   a. Categorical model of scoring
   b. Ipsative model of scoring
   c. Cumulative model of scoring
   d. Validity model of scoring

7. In a test Alice developed, the test user assigned a diagnosis to the test taker based on the test taker's score. Which one of the following models of scoring was she using?
   a. Categorical
   b. Cumulative
   c. Ipsative
   d. Validity

8. Which one of the following item types is characterized by a question that has a stem that is followed by a number of distracters?
   a. Forced choice
   b. True/false
   c. Essay
   d. Multiple choice

9. For which one of the following formats is scoring easiest?
   a. Essay
   b. Interview
   c. Multiple choice
   d. Sentence completion

10. Eric developed a test that instructed test takers to choose one of two words that appeared to be unrelated but equally acceptable. Which one of the following formats was he using?
    a. Multiple choice
    b. Forced choice
    c. Sentence completion
    d. True/false

11. What one of the following is considered the most often used subjective test in organizations?
    a. Essay
    b. Multiple choice
    c. Interview
    d. Projective drawing

12. Felicia was concerned that the target audience for her test would be more likely to choose the most acceptable answer instead of the truest answer. What was she concerned about?
    a. Acquiescence
    b. Social desirability
    c. Faking
    d. Projection

13. Test developers use reverse scoring to offset the effects of
    a. social desirability.
    b. acquiescence.
    c. faking.
    d. random responding.

14. Random responding is most likely to occur when test takers
    a. lack the necessary skills to take a test or do not wish to be evaluated.
    b. wish to make themselves appear favorably to the test user.
    c. wish to make themselves appear mentally ill or incompetent.
    d. have the tendency to agree with any ideas or behaviors presented.

15. As a rule of thumb, how many more items than called for within the test plan should test developers write?
    a. Three times as many items
    b. Two and one half times as many items
    c. Two times as many items
    d. The same amount of items

16. What does the suggestion in the textbook to "make all test items independent" mean?
    a. Ensure all items are independent of the test universe.
    b. Ensure all items are heterogeneous.
    c. Ensure one item does not provide the answer to another item.
    d. Ensure that all items are reliable and valid.

17. Which one of the following is defined as "Behaviors which are culturally sanctioned and approved but which are improbable of occurrence"?
    a. Social desirability
    b. Items on the Marlowe–Crowne Social Desirability Scale
    c. Response sets
    d. Acquiescence

18. What instrument do test developers use to identify test responses that appeal to people who wish to show themselves in a favorable light?
    a. College Adjustment Scales
    b. Computer-adapted test
    c. Marlowe–Crowne Social Desirability Scale
    d. Multiple-choice test

19. Which one of the following item formats is likely to be used to assess perform capabilities when hiring a commercial airline pilot?
    a. Performance assessment
    b. Simulation
    c. Portfolio
    d. Interview

20. Marie designed a self-esteem test for preschool children. Her instructions to the administrator required that the test questions be read orally. The children were instructed to circle a printed face on the answer sheet (variations of a face smiling or frowning) to indicate their answers. Because Marie could not find any preschoolers to use in her pilot study, she administered the test to fifth graders instead. What is wrong with what Marie did?
    a. Preschoolers' self-esteem cannot be measured.
    b. Tests should not be administered orally to preschoolers.
    c. The test takers in her pilot study were not the same as her target audience.
    d. Nothing was wrong with what Marie did.

## Short Answer

| | |
|---|---|
| **Remembering** | 1. Identify the first four steps of developing a test.<br>2. Recall the activities involved in each of the four steps of developing a test.<br>3. Describe the multiple-choice format. What are its advantages and disadvantages?<br>4. Describe the essay format. What are its advantages and disadvantages? |
| **Applying** | 5. Identify the benefits and drawbacks of using an objective test format. Give three examples.<br>6. Identify the benefits and drawbacks of using a subjective test format. Give three examples.<br>7. Show how multiple-choice tests are scored.<br>8. Show how essay tests are scored. |
| **Evaluating** | 9. Explain why it is important to follow the test-development process.<br>10. Assess what you risk by not following the test-development process.<br>11. Describe three models of scoring tests. Which one is the best format?<br>12. Describe the three types of complex item formats included in the Standards for Psychological Testing that can be used in specialized testing situations. |

## Multiple-Choice and Short-Answer Practice Question Answer Key

### Multiple Choice

| Question | Answer | Textbook Page | Explanation |
|---|---|---|---|
| 1. | d | 284 | The first step is to define the testing universe, audience, and purpose. The other options listed in the question are part of the development process, but they are not the first step. This passage from *Alice's Adventures in Wonderland* shows why it is so important to take the time to define these aspects of the test first.<br><br>"Would you tell me, please, which way I ought to go from here?"<br><br>"That depends a good deal on where you want to get to," said the Cat.<br><br>"I don't much care where—" said Alice.<br><br>"Then it doesn't matter which way you go," said the Cat.<br><br>"—so long as I get somewhere," Alice added as an explanation.<br><br>"Oh, you're sure to do that," said the Cat, "if you only walk long enough."<br><br>Testing is not a haphazard adventure that one does for fun. It is a structured process and the developer must know where he or she is going right from the start. |
| 2. | b | 286 | Knowing who the test takers will be is critical to developing a successful test. This must be determined from the start as it will guide and influence the rest of the process. Consider a selection test for administrative law judges and entry-level security guards. These two groups will have vastly different levels of reading ability, and the test should be written accordingly. Or consider a test that will be used in occupational rehabilitation. This is a population that could require a lot of test administration accommodations. |
| 3. | a | 288 | A job analysis is most likely to be conducted when developing an employee selection test for an organization. A job analysis is a structured process that identifies the knowledge, skills, abilities, and other characteristics (KSA&Os) required to perform a job. For test-development purposes and because of legal guidelines, it is also common to identify tasks and behaviors that occur on the job. The job analyst then clearly demonstrates that the KSA&Os that have been identified are required to perform one or more job tasks. The most important tasks and KSA&Os are identified, and these form the basis for a test blueprint ensuring that the test only covers content required for successful job performance. |

| Question | Answer | Textbook Page | Explanation |
|---|---|---|---|
| 4. | d | 288 | Test format refers to the type of questions being asked on the test. There are two broad types of questions: objective test questions and subjective test questions. Objective test questions have a single correct answer. Examples include multiple choice and true/false. Subjective tests differ from objective tests in that there is not a single correct answer. For example, an essay question has as many possible answers as there are examinees (if any two responses were identical, it would be attributed to cheating). Because there is no single correct answer, scoring requires judgment, and the scorers need to be trained to ensure interrater reliability. |
| 5. | a | 288 | A multiple-choice question requires that the test taker select a single answer that can be demonstrated to be true. This is the key feature of an objective test. In contrast, the other options listed can have more than one possible correct answer. Consider this example. After reading a paragraph of text, the test taker is asked, "Before finding the dollar, John was feeling _____." One possible correct answer might be sad. However, synonyms for sad are depressed, gloomy, and miserable—all of which would probably be acceptable answers as well. The characteristic of having more than one possible correct or acceptable answer is the defining characteristic of the subjective test format. |
| 6. | c | 290 | The cumulative model is the most common method of scoring, and it assumes that the more the test taker responds in a particular way, the more of the attribute he or she has. For example, if one examinee gets 98 out of 100 addition problems correct, and another examinee gets only 50 correct, we would assume that the first examinee has a greater knowledge of addition. It is typical to simply add one point for each correct answer. However, different scoring methods are possible. In contrast, ipsative scoring is a forced choice scale that has respondents select one of two equally attractive items. For example, which of the following two items best describe you? "I like to go to parties" or "I am hard working." This type of scoring is mainly used for personality tests. Categorical scoring is used to place individuals into a specific group and is often used for clinical diagnosis—either you have attention-deficit/hyperactivity disorder or you do not. It is important to note that both ipsative and categorical models can incorporate a cumulative scoring model. |

*(Continued)*

(Continued)

| Question | Answer | Textbook Page | Explanation |
|---|---|---|---|
| 7. | a | 290 | As described in Question 6, categorical models require that a test taker be placed into a specific category or group and are often used in clinical diagnosis. However, categorical models can also be used in many other settings, such as in certification testing. If the test taker surpasses a specific score, then he or she has demonstrated the required level of knowledge to be considered certified in the content domain the test was designed to measure. |
| 8. | d | 292 | A multiple-choice test question is probably the most commonly used question format and as a result is a familiar format to nearly all test takers. The multiple-choice question consists of a stem that states the question or the problem to be answered. The distracters are incorrect answer options. The distracters should be plausible to a person who does not know the correct answer (which is called the key). The other options listed have a question stem, but they do not have distracters. One might argue that true/false items have a key and one distractor. In a sense, this is correct. However, distracters should be plausible answers directly related to the question being asked. True/false items do not have this characteristic. |
| 9. | c | 292 | The multiple-choice format is extremely easy to score because there is a single correct answer. As a result, scoring can be done by computer or by untrained individuals. Because of this, scoring is fast and cheap. In contrast, the other options require more complex responses without a single easily identified correct answer. This means that scoring must be done by trained individuals, which takes more time and costs more money. |
| 10. | b | 293 | Forced-choice tests are most commonly used in personality assessment. Instead of either selecting the correct answer, constructing a response such as writing an essay, or using a rating scale, the test taker must choose between multiple statements that may appear to be equally appealing. Frequently, these statements describe behavior or personality. For example, test takers may be presented with the following statements and be asked to select the two that are most like them: "I can easily relax"; "I pay attention to details"; "I like to work in a group"; "I have high personal standards." |

Chapter 10 ■ How Do We Develop a Test? 273

| Question | Answer | Textbook Page | Explanation |
|---|---|---|---|
| 11. | c | 294 | Interviews are the most commonly used selection tool in organizations. They are considered to be subjective tests. Remember subjective tests do not have a single correct answer, and the test taker's response must be interpreted and scored. In a multiple-choice test, there is a single correct answer. Essay and projective drawing are both subjective tests but are not commonly used in organizational settings. |
| 12. | b | 296 | This question addresses types of response biases. It is well known that test takers can intentionally or unintentionally distort how they respond. The textbook covers three types of biases: social desirability, acquiescence, and random responding. Research has shown that some people have a response style or response set that leads them to choose answers that are the most socially acceptable even though their true beliefs might actually be different. This type of response set is called social desirability. Acquiescence is another type of response bias that occurs when individuals have a tendency to simply agree with all the statements presented in a test. Research has shown that people may have a natural tendency toward this response bias influenced by cultural norms. Random responding and faking are the third type of response biases. These types of biases occur when the test taker does not want to respond accurately. He or she may simply respond randomly without reading questions, or may intentionally try to present an inaccurate picture of himself or herself. One example would be faking insanity in response to a legal charge. |
| 13. | d | 297 | One way random responding can be detected is by employing a technique called reverse scoring. The test developer will ask more than one question that measures the same construct but ask these questions in opposite ways. For example, one item might be, "I am very satisfied with my job," and another item might be, "I am very dissatisfied with my job." If the test taker is consistently answering the questions, one would agree with one item and disagree with the other. |
| 14. | a | 297 | While random responding and faking are closely related types of response biases, they are different concepts. Random responding occurs when the test taker, for some reason, does not want to answer or is incapable of answering the test questions. In contrast, faking occurs when the test taker intentionally distorts answers to present an inaccurate image of himself or herself. |

*(Continued)*

(Continued)

| Question | Answer | Textbook Page | Explanation |
|---|---|---|---|
| 15. | c | 299 | Writing effective test items is both an art and a science, and not every question that is written will be of usable quality. In addition, pretesting or piloting items is a good practice. When the test developer examines the results of pretested items, he or she might find that some questions are too hard, some too easy, while others may display other psychometrically objectionable characteristics. Therefore, a general rule of thumb to follow is to develop twice as many test items as required by the test plan. This will allow the test developer to discard poor items and keep only the best-performing ones. |
| 16. | c | 300 | The textbook lists some suggestions for writing effective test items. One of these suggestions is to make all items independent. This means that one item should not tip off the answer of another item. For example, one item might ask, "Sigmund Freud, the father of psychoanalysis, stated..." Then another question on the same test might ask, "Who is the father of psychoanalysis?" Obviously, the astute test taker will find the correct answer to the first question in the second question. The result is that the second question will be ineffective in determining whether the test taker possesses the knowledge that the second question was designed to tap. |
| 17. | b | 297 | In the 1960s, two psychologists, Douglas Crowne and David Marlowe, developed a scale that measured the degree to which individuals tend to respond in socially desirable ways. They stated that the items on the test are culturally sanctioned, but highly improbable, behaviors. For example, one item asks if a person never hesitates to help someone in trouble. While most people would say this is a desirable characteristic, it is also extremely unlikely that someone would never hesitate to help someone in trouble. Stating that you never hesitate suggests that you chose that response because it was the most socially acceptable answer. Social desirability has been associated with a high need for approval. |
| 18. | c | 297 | Socially desirable responding has two key characteristics. First, the chosen answer is seen as being socially endorsed or sanctioned. The second characteristic is that test takers wish to present themselves in a highly positive manner. The Marlow–Crowne Social Desirability Scale was developed specifically to detect this type of responding by presenting items that are positive in nature but are unlikely to accurately describe a person. |

| Question | Answer | Textbook Page | Explanation |
|---|---|---|---|
| 19. | b | 295 | A simulation is similar to a performance assessment in that it requires test takers to demonstrate their skills and abilities to perform a complex task, such as piloting a plane. However, the tasks are not performed in the actual environment because of safety or cost-related concerns. In this case, it would be cheaper and safer to assess candidates with a simulation than place them in an actual plane. In addition, portfolios and interviews could be part of the selection process, but they are unlikely to be useful or collect much information about the performance capabilities of a pilot. |
| 20. | c | 306 | A pilot test is a scientific investigation of the evidence supporting the reliability and validity of test scores. Because validity concerns the inferences from test scores, it is important to pilot test using a sample similar to the target audience. If the pilot test sample and target audience sample are not similar, then it is difficult to conclude that the test is appropriate for the target audience. |

## Short Answer

| Question | Explanation |
|---|---|
| 1. | Step 1. Define test universe, target audience, and test purpose.<br><br>Step 2. Develop a test plan.<br><br>Step 3. Compose the test items.<br><br>Step 4. Write administration instructions. |
| 2. | **Step 1. Define test universe, target audience, and test purpose.**<br><br>This step is extremely important, and considerable time should be spent thinking about the universe, audience, and purpose of the test. First, the developer needs to create a working definition of what construct the test is being designed to measure. Second, the developer needs to determine who the audience is (the people who will be tested) because different audiences have different requirements. Next, the developer needs to understand how the scores will be used and for what purpose. All of these factors will greatly influence the rest of the test-development project.<br><br>**Step 2. Develop a test plan.**<br><br>In this step, the construct is operationalized with a more precise definition. Also, at this step, the developer chooses a test format or the type of questions that will be included (i.e., objective, subjective, projective). How the test will be administered and scored is determined as well. For example, will the test be using a cumulative, categorical, or ipsative model of scoring?<br><br>**Step 3. Compose the test items.**<br><br>Once Steps 1 and 2 are completed, the developer can begin constructing test items. The developer must make sure that the items developed correspond to the test plan or test blueprint. This includes determining the type of items that need to be developed. Will the items be objective (multiple choice, true/false, forced choice) or subjective (essay, interview, projective, sentence completion)? As a general rule, twice as many items as needed should be developed.<br><br>**Step 4. Write administration instructions.**<br><br>Developing instructions for administration is an important and often overlooked aspect of test development. Three sets of instructions need to be developed. The first set is for the test administrator covering such things as time limits, equipment needed, testing script to be read, and the required testing environment. The second set is for the test taker describing what he or she is to do and how to do it. The third set of instructions is for the test scorers. These instructions ensure that different scorers will evaluate answers in a similar manner. |
| 3. | Multiple choice is the most used item format and, as a result, it is more familiar to test takers. This type of question has a stem that presents the question or problem to be answered. It also has a key, which is the correct answer option, and distractors, which are incorrect answer options. Care must be taken when writing items to make sure that they are clear and concise. All distractors must be completely incorrect and should not provide any cues to the test taker that could increase the odds of guessing correctly. The major advantage of this type of item is that it is quick, easy, and inexpensive to score. |

| Question | Explanation |
|---|---|
| 4. | Essay questions are a popular type of subjective test item that are often found in educational settings. To answer these types of questions, the test taker needs to construct a response. Essay questions allow more freedom in responding than objective items. Because of this, some developers believe that it is easier to assess higher cognitive skills such as thinking, analysis, and evaluation using essay questions. Some students (and developers) like this type of item and believe that it also makes it possible for the test taker to demonstrate what they know more effectively than with objective tests. However, there are drawbacks to essay questions such as increased difficulty in scoring. |
| 5. | An objective test has several benefits. Because there is a single correct answer, they are easy to score, as no judgment is required to determine if the correct answer was given. They are also easier to align with a test plan or test blueprint. Both of these characteristics make it easier to evaluate and document the test. One disadvantage of an objective test format is that test takers may be able to more easily guess the correct answer than with a subjective test. Also, objective tests have been subject to the criticism that they only require recognition of facts and are not effective at evaluating deeper thinking. Another criticism of objective tests is that they stress recall and encourage rote memorization. However, well-developed objective items can overcome all these criticisms. |
| 6. | Subjective items allow for wider and more varied responses because the test taker must construct an answer. As a result, fewer cues are presented in the question itself. Proponents of subjective tests say that this format encourages more thinking and abstract reasoning than objective tests. However, because of the varied nature of responses, scoring of projective tests is more difficult and requires interpretation and judgment. This can introduce inconsistencies in scoring, which can lower the reliability and validity of the test. |
| 7. | Multiple-choice questions are generally inexpensive to score. However, because test takers have an opportunity to guess the correct answer, this must be taken into account when interpreting test scores. The effect of guessing on scores can be reduced by following good item-writing practices. |
| 8. | Essay questions are increasingly difficult to score. The increased flexibility in responding requires that scorers use judgment when interpreting and assigning scores to answers. The scoring also takes more time, and sometimes money, compared to objective tests. |
| 9. | Test development is a structured process that follows specific steps. Test formats are the types of questions that the test will contain. There are two broad types of formats: objective and subjective. Objective items include multiple choice, true/false, and forced choice. Types of subjective items include essay, interview, projective, and sentence completion. |
| 10. | When a test developer does not follow the test-development process, the test may perform poorly. Using a single format for a test helps to ensure that changes in format do not confuse test takers. This consistency also makes test development, administration, and scoring easier. |
| 11. | There is no single best model for scoring tests. The scoring model should be selected based on what has been defined as the testing universe, target audience, and test purpose. There are three basic models of scoring. The cumulative model of scoring is the most common and assumes that each "correct" answer is an indication of greater standing on the construct. The categorical model of scoring places each test taker into a distinct mutually exclusive group. Finally, the ipsative model of scoring requires the test taker to select among equally appealing options, and there is not necessarily a single correct answer. The ipsative scoring model shows the test taker's individual profile on the measured attribute(s) and does not enable comparisons of one test taker with another. It is important to note that the cumulative model can be used in conjunction with both the categorical and ipsative models of scoring. |

*(Continued)*

(Continued)

| Question | Explanation |
|---|---|
| 12. | The Standards for Educational and Psychological Testing include a discussion of three types of complex item formats: (1) performance assessments, (2) simulations, and (3) portfolios. The first is performance assessments, which require test takers to demonstrate their skills and abilities to perform complex behaviors and tasks in a setting that is as similar as possible to the conditions that will be found when the tasks are actually performed on the job. In an employment setting, performance assessments are often called work samples because they require the person to demonstrate his or her ability to perform tasks that have been identified as critical for successful job performance. The second specialized item format is a simulation. Simulations are similar to a performance assessment in that they require test takers to demonstrate their skills and abilities to perform a complex task. However, the tasks are not performed in the actual environment in which the real tasks will be performed, often because of safety or cost-related concerns. The third and final complex item format is a portfolio, which is a collection of work products that a person gathers over time to demonstrate his or her skills and abilities in a particular area. It is important to keep in mind that even though these item formats are complex in nature and may not appear to be tests as most people understand them, they are still evaluated using the same standards that are applied to any other test. |

# 11 How Do We Assess the Psychometric Quality of a Test?

## Overview

In Chapter 11 of the textbook, you were introduced to assessing the psychometric quality of a test. Hopefully, after reading the chapter you have a clearer understanding of how we quantitatively and qualitatively assess the psychometric quality of a test, the criteria we use to determine which test items to retain and which to drop, the process we then use for gathering evidence of reliability/precision and validity, and then compiling the test manual. While Chapter 11 of the textbook included foundational information about assessing the psychometric quality of a test, Chapter 11 of the workbook provides you with the opportunity to demonstrate your understanding of material presented in the textbook and apply your learning by completing some practical and critical-thinking exercises linked to specific learning objectives. Chapter 11 of the workbook will also allow you to complete chapter-level projects to demonstrate your understanding of multiple topics within the chapter. Chapter 11 of the workbook ends with some multiple-choice and short-answer questions you can use to self-assess your understanding of the material.

## Practical and Critical-Thinking Exercises

### Purpose

This section contains five exercises you can complete to demonstrate your understanding and apply your learning (Exercises 11.1–11.5) and one exercise you can complete to reflect on your learning (Exercise 11.6). The exercises, linked to learning objectives, are displayed below.

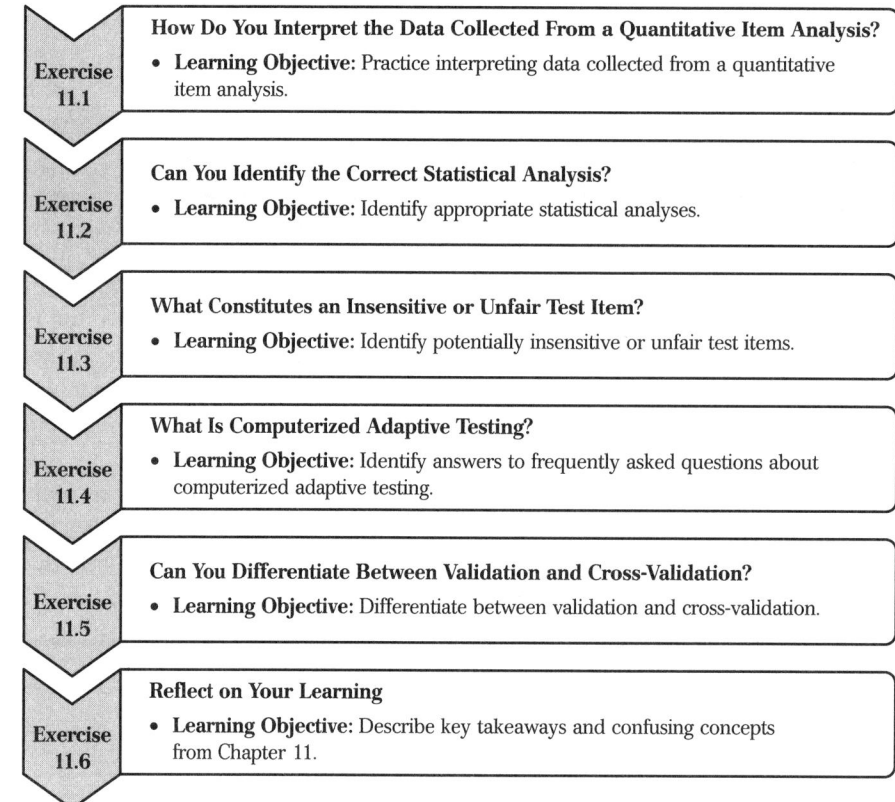

**Exercise 11.1** — How Do You Interpret the Data Collected From a Quantitative Item Analysis?
- **Learning Objective:** Practice interpreting data collected from a quantitative item analysis.

**Exercise 11.2** — Can You Identify the Correct Statistical Analysis?
- **Learning Objective:** Identify appropriate statistical analyses.

**Exercise 11.3** — What Constitutes an Insensitive or Unfair Test Item?
- **Learning Objective:** Identify potentially insensitive or unfair test items.

**Exercise 11.4** — What Is Computerized Adaptive Testing?
- **Learning Objective:** Identify answers to frequently asked questions about computerized adaptive testing.

**Exercise 11.5** — Can You Differentiate Between Validation and Cross-Validation?
- **Learning Objective:** Differentiate between validation and cross-validation.

**Exercise 11.6** — Reflect on Your Learning
- **Learning Objective:** Describe key takeaways and confusing concepts from Chapter 11.

# Exercise 11.1: How Do You Interpret the Data Collected From a Quantitative Item Analysis?

**OBJECTIVE**

Practice interpreting data collected from a quantitative item analysis.

**BACKGROUND**

After creating a test, it is not uncommon for the test developer to conduct a pilot test to examine the performance of test items to determine those that are performing well and not so well, and to revise those that could perform better. The pilot test often involves quantitatively analyzing the difficulty of each test item and each test item's ability to discriminate high from low performers. To increase your understanding of how to interpret quantitative item analysis results, in Exercise 11.1, you will interpret quantitative item analysis results and conduct your own item analysis.

**YOUR TASK**

1. **Identify what test items should be kept.** Imagine you conducted a quantitative item analysis for a newly designed test to measure student knowledge of math. Assume that the test is homogeneous, and your goal is to have a 10-item test. The results of the item analysis are displayed below. Following the directions in the "Conducting Quantitative Item Analysis" section of Chapter 11, interpret the data and circle the items you would retain to make a 10-item test. For each item retained, document your rationale for retaining the item in the table below.

| Item Number | Average Interitem Correlation | Difficulty | Discrimination Index | Rationale |
|---|---|---|---|---|
| 1 | .40 | .90 | 10 | |
| 2 | .38 | .50 | 60 | |
| 3 | .05 | .50 | 19 | |
| 4 | .30 | .48 | −2 | |
| 5 | .50 | .50 | 50 | |
| 6 | .01 | .98 | 0 | |

*(Continued)*

(Continued)

| Item Number | Average Interitem Correlation | Difficulty | Discrimination Index | Rationale |
|---|---|---|---|---|
| 7 | .60 | .60 | 48 | |
| 8 | .00 | .10 | 10 | |
| 9 | .55 | .49 | 40 | |
| 10 | .30 | .61 | −5 | |
| 11 | .44 | .51 | 80 | |
| 12 | −.10 | .66 | 7 | |
| 13 | .40 | .55 | 75 | |
| 14 | .77 | .43 | −10 | |
| 15 | .71 | .71 | 60 | |
| 16 | .33 | .56 | 40 | |
| 17 | .00 | .2 | 15 | |
| 18 | .22 | .35 | 60 | |
| 19 | .55 | .43 | 70 | |
| 20 | .04 | .40 | 16 | |

2. **Calculate the difficulty and discrimination index.** Imagine you conducted a quantitative item analysis for a newly designed 10-item test to measure student knowledge of statistics. You administered the test to 18 students, and the raw data from the item analysis are presented below. Correct answers are marked "1," and incorrect answers are marked "0." Following the directions in the "Conducting Quantitative Item Analysis" section of Chapter 11, calculate the item difficulty and item discrimination index for each test item. Document your answers in the bottom rows of the table below.

| Student | Item 1 | Item 2 | Item 3 | Item 4 | Item 5 | Item 6 | Item 7 | Item 8 | Item 9 | Item 10 | Score |
|---|---|---|---|---|---|---|---|---|---|---|---|
| 1 | 1 | 1 | 0 | 1 | 1 | 0 | 1 | 1 | 0 | 1 | |
| 2 | 0 | 0 | 0 | 1 | 0 | 0 | 0 | 0 | 1 | 1 | |
| 3 | 0 | 0 | 1 | 1 | 0 | 0 | 1 | 1 | 0 | 1 | |
| 4 | 0 | 0 | 0 | 0 | 0 | 0 | 1 | 0 | 0 | 1 | |
| 5 | 1 | 1 | 0 | 1 | 0 | 0 | 1 | 1 | 1 | 1 | |
| 6 | 1 | 1 | 1 | 1 | 1 | 1 | 1 | 1 | 1 | 1 | |
| 7 | 1 | 0 | 1 | 1 | 0 | 1 | 0 | 1 | 0 | 1 | |
| 8 | 1 | 1 | 1 | 1 | 1 | 1 | 1 | 1 | 0 | 1 | |
| 9 | 0 | 1 | 1 | 1 | 1 | 1 | 1 | 1 | 1 | 1 | |
| 10 | 0 | 0 | 0 | 1 | 0 | 1 | 1 | 1 | 1 | 1 | |
| 11 | 0 | 0 | 0 | 1 | 0 | 0 | 0 | 0 | 0 | 0 | |
| 12 | 0 | 1 | 1 | 1 | 1 | 1 | 1 | 1 | 1 | 1 | |
| 13 | 1 | 1 | 1 | 1 | 1 | 1 | 1 | 1 | 1 | 1 | |
| 14 | 0 | 1 | 0 | 1 | 0 | 1 | 1 | 1 | 1 | 1 | |
| 15 | 1 | 1 | 1 | 1 | 0 | 1 | 0 | 1 | 1 | 1 | |
| 16 | 0 | 1 | 0 | 1 | 0 | 0 | 0 | 0 | 0 | 0 | |
| 17 | 0 | 0 | 0 | 0 | 0 | 0 | 0 | 0 | 0 | 0 | |
| 18 | 1 | 1 | 1 | 0 | 0 | 1 | 1 | 1 | 0 | 0 | |
| p (item difficulty) | | | | | | | | | | | |
| D (item discrimination) | | | | | | | | | | | |

## Exercise 11.2: Can You Identify the Correct Statistical Analysis?

**OBJECTIVE**

Identify appropriate statistical analyses.

**BACKGROUND**

Because every item in a test contributes to a test's final score or outcome, test developers often conduct quantitative item analysis to determine the psychometric quality of the items and then determine which items to keep, which to modify, and which to delete. Quantitative item analysis requires test developers to conduct different types of statistical analyses of a group of test takers' responses to individual test items to calculate item difficulty, item discrimination index, item–total correlations, interitem correlations, item–criterion correlations, and item characteristic curves. To increase your understanding of the various statistical analyses we conduct when performing quantitative item analysis, in Exercise 11.2, you will review research questions and then identify the most appropriate statistical analyses.

**YOUR TASK**

1. **Choosing the right statistic.** Review the "Conducting Quantitative Item Analysis" section of Chapter 11 of your textbook to learn more about the statistical analyses we conduct with quantitative item analysis. Review the research questions listed in the table below. For each question, determine which one or more statistical analyses best answer the research question. Document your answer in the table below.

| Research Question | Appropriate Statistical Analysis(es) |
|---|---|
| 1. Does this item measure the same construct as other items? | |
| 2. Is this item easier for men than for women? | |
| 3. Does this item provide information that helps predict a criterion? | |
| 4. How difficult is this item? | |
| 5. If I drop this item from the test, will it increase or decrease internal reliability? | |
| 6. How did the people who did well on this test do on this item? | |
| 7. Is this item of sufficient difficulty, and does it discriminate between high and low performers on the test? | |
| 8. Is this test biased against a minority group? | |
| 9. How well does the answer on this item correlate with the individual's overall test score? | |

# Exercise 11.3: What Constitutes an Insensitive or Unfair Test Item?

**OBJECTIVE**

Identify potentially insensitive or unfair test items.

**BACKGROUND**

In addition to conducting quantitative item analysis to determine the psychometric quality of the items, those who develop tests often conduct qualitative item analysis using questionnaires. Qualitative item analysis typically is useful in determining perceptions of a test and to determine potential sources of error or bias, and usually involves having test takers or expert panels review and answer questions about test items. For example, test developers might have test takers review test items and comment on whether any of the items are discriminatory in nature or may be unfair to certain groups of test takers. Or, test developers may have expert panels review items looking for content that may offend or insult a test taker. To increase your understanding of what types of questions may offend or insult test takers, in Exercise 11.3 you will research fairness guidelines when writing test items and then evaluate a sample of test items for potential insensitive or unfair content.

**YOUR TASK**

1. **Review guidelines for fairness reviews.** After reviewing the "Conducting Qualitative Item Analysis" section in Chapter 11 of the textbook, search the Internet to find fairness guidelines that major test developers use to write and review items. Use search terms such as, "ETS Guidelines for Fairness Review of Assessments," "ETS Standards for Quality and Fairness," "ETS International Principles for Fairness Reviews of Assessments," and "ACT Fairness Report." Document 10 things you would see in a test item that might indicate the item contains potentially insensitive or unfair content. Document your findings in the table below.

|    | Source | Indicator of Potential Insensitivity or Unfairness |
|----|--------|----------------------------------------------------|
| 1. |        |                                                    |
| 2. |        |                                                    |
| 3. |        |                                                    |
| 4. |        |                                                    |
| 5. |        |                                                    |

*(Continued)*

(Continued)

|   | Source | Indicator of Potential Insensitivity or Unfairness |
|---|--------|----------------------------------------------------|
| 6. |  |  |
| 7. |  |  |
| 8. |  |  |
| 9. |  |  |
| 10. |  |  |

2. **Identify potentially insensitive or unfair content.** Review the test items below. Based on your learning from the above activity, identify any potentially insensitive or unfair content in the items below. For each item, indicate what the potentially insensitive or unfair content is and why, and propose how the question could be rewritten. Then, write five of your own test items that are examples of five of the 10 indicators you identified above. Document your responses in the table below.

| Test Items | Insensitive/Unfair Content | New Question |
|------------|----------------------------|--------------|
| 1. Frankie, a male nurse, ordered 0.125 mg pills. How many pills should Frankie give to the patient if the required dosage is 0.25 mg? |  |  |
| 2. At her high school basketball game, Ebony made 5 free throws, 5 baskets, and 2 three-pointers. How many total points did she score? |  |  |
| 3. If an average of 3.5 people per square mile were seriously injured or killed in a hurricane, approximately how many people were injured in a city of 75 square miles? |  |  |

| Test Items | Insensitive/Unfair Content | New Question |
|---|---|---|
| 4. If each borough has 75 gas stations, and there are five boroughs in the city, how many gas stations are in the city? | | |
| 5. In America, each state has two senators. How many senators are there in total? | | |
| 6. | | |
| 7. | | |
| 8. | | |
| 9. | | |
| 10. | | |

## Exercise 11.4: What Is Computerized Adaptive Testing?

**OBJECTIVE**

Identify answers to frequently asked questions about computerized adaptive testing.

**BACKGROUND**

With computerized adaptive testing (CAT), while all test takers begin with the same test items, the test items subsequently change based on whether the test takers answer items correctly or incorrectly. The difficulty of each item on the test has been previously estimated by a statistical procedure called item response theory (IRT). Typically, test takers begin with a few moderately difficult questions and then the questions presented differ based on a particular test taker's skill level, which is determined by a test taker's responses to previous questions. CAT is used for many important tests, including the National Council Licensure Exam for Nurses (NCLEX), the GRE, the Armed Services Vocational Aptitude Battery (ASVAB), and various other achievement tests. To increase your understanding of computer adaptive testing, in Exercise 11.4, you will develop a resource to answer 10–15 questions about CAT.

**YOUR TASK**

1. **Read the information below.**

    Several important tests are administered using the CAT technology. One of these tests is the NCLEX. Imagine you are a nursing instructor for a class of graduating students who have all fulfilled their academic requirements to apply and take the NCLEX to become registered nurses. The students have several questions about the NCLEX and are unfamiliar with CAT. To assist with providing them, and future students, answers to their questions about CAT, you decide to develop a resource containing important information about CAT.

2. **Develop a resource to answer frequently asked questions about CAT.** After reviewing For Your Information Boxes 11.1 and 11.2 in Chapter 11 of the textbook, conduct an Internet search to learn more about computer adaptive testing and the NCLEX. Identify 10–15 questions graduating students who are preparing to take a test using CAT might have. When creating your questions, consider what CAT is, the history of CAT, how CAT works, what it means for test takers, and how CAT is scored. Document your questions below. Then, develop a resource (such as a pamphlet, brochure, or tips and tricks handout) that contains answers to these questions.

|    | Question |
|----|----------|
| 1. |          |
| 2. |          |

|  | **Question** |
|---|---|
| 3. | |
| 4. | |
| 5. | |
| 6. | |
| 7. | |
| 8. | |
| 9. | |
| 10. | |

# Exercise 11.5: Can you Differentiate Between Validation and Cross-Validation?

**OBJECTIVE**

Differentiate between validation and cross-validation.

**BACKGROUND**

After finalizing test items based on a pilot study (consisting of a quantitative and/or qualitative item analysis), test developers often conduct another round of data collection, often referred to as the validation study. The purpose of the validation study is to gather evidence of validity beyond validity based on test content (which is carried out as the test is developed) and gather evidence of reliability/precision. Based on the validation study results, test developers may make minor changes to the test and then proceed with one or more rounds of final data collection—replication and/or cross-validation. To increase your understanding of the differences between validation and cross-validation, in Exercise 11.5, you will answer various questions to distinguish between a validation study and a cross-validation study, calculate a predicted evaluation score for a cross-validation, and then answer some questions.

**YOUR TASK**

1. **Distinguish between a validation study and a cross-validation study.** Read the "Validation and Cross-Validation" sections of Chapter 11 of your textbook. Answer the questions below, documenting your answers in the table.

| Study | What is the overall objective? | What type of evidence is collected? | What are standards for setting up the study? | Who are the test takers? | What types of decisions may be made based on the results? |
|---|---|---|---|---|---|
| Validation | | | | | |
| Cross-Validation | | | | | |

2. **Calculate the Predicted Evaluation Score.** Review In Greater Depth Box 11.1 in Chapter 11 of your textbook to see an example of how we would cross-validate a regression used to provide predictive evidence of validity for an employee selection test. In that section, we calculated the predicted evaluation score of the first three test takers. The regression equation that was developed on the screening sample and used to make the calculation was:

Predicted score = 3.387 + (.033 × Test Score)

Using the same equation, calculate the predicted evaluation scores for the next five test takers in the validation sample.

| Test Taker ID | Test Score | Calculation | Predicted Performance Evaluation Score |
|---|---|---|---|
| 4 | 97 | | |
| 5 | 76 | | |
| 6 | 88 | | |
| 7 | 90 | | |
| 8 | 84 | | |

3. **Answer the questions below.**

What would the next step be in the cross-validation process?

_____
_____
_____
_____
_____
_____
_____

In a cross-validation, the amount of variance that a predictor accounts for in the criterion in the screening sample is almost always less than the amount of variance accounted for when the same equation is used to predict the criterion in the validation sample. What is the name given to this phenomenon?

What is a major potential problem that test developers may encounter when using a cross-validation strategy to gather predictive evidence of validity of a test?

What other alternative could a test developer use to gather the same evidence without this potential problem?

# Exercise 11.6: Reflect on Your Learning

**OBJECTIVE**

Describe key takeaways and confusing concepts from Chapter 11.

**BACKGROUND**

In Chapter 11 of the textbook, you were introduced to assessing the psychometric quality of a test. You read about how to conduct quantitative and qualitative item analyses. You were introduced to how to determine item difficulty, item discrimination, interitem correlations, item–criterion correlations, item bias, and item characteristic curves. You were also introduced to computerized adaptive testing. Lastly, you learned about the criteria for retaining and dropping a test time, the process of validation and cross-validation, the concepts of validity and unfair test discrimination, measurement bias, and cut scores. For Exercise 11.6, you will reflect on your learning from Chapter 11 of the textbook and identify key takeaways from the chapter.

**YOUR TASK**

1. **Identify your "Aha!" moments from Chapter 11**.
   - Identify 3 to 4 new insights or realizations you had after reading Chapter 11, referred to as "Aha!" moments.
   - Consider things that made you look at a concept, your life, or an issue in a completely different way than you had in the past.
   - Document your insights and realizations below, providing details of your learning.

2. **Identify some muddy moment discussion questions.**
   - Identify 2 to 3 concepts that are still "muddy" for you from the chapter.
   - Consider concepts you still don't understand, concepts you need clarified, and/or questions you want to ask.
   - Develop 1 to 3 questions to initiate a discussion in class to further your understanding of the concepts and get your questions answered.

| **Insights and Realizations** | 1. _____<br>2. _____<br>3. _____<br>4. _____ |
|---|---|
| **Muddy Moments Discussion Questions** | 1. _____<br>2. _____<br>3. _____ |

# Chapter-Level Projects

## Project 1

**BACKGROUND**

Piloting and then revising a test is a major part of the test-development process. Test developers often write many more test items than necessary because the results of the pilot test may result in eliminating items that do not perform well. To determine which items do and do not perform well, test developers review item-level results, including item–total correlations, item–criterion correlations, item difficulty, item discrimination, and item bias. Test developers often display these item-level results in an item statistics matrix.

**YOUR TASK**

1. **Review the information below.**

    Imagine you were in the process of developing a 10-item test to measure two mathematical constructs: knowledge of calculus and knowledge of geometry. You wrote 20 items, and then conducted a pilot test to assess the test item's ability to discriminate high- and low-scoring individuals, test item difficulty, and item bias. You also correlated item responses with a criterion measure to calculate item–criterion correlations. You assembled the pilot results into an item statistics matrix.

2. **Review item statistics for your test of mathematical knowledge.**
    Review the "Revising the Test" section of Chapter 11 of your textbook. Review your item statistics matrix below. Interpret the performance of each test item and select the 10 best items to include in your final test. Remember that each item must be judged as acceptable on several criteria to be chosen for the inclusion in the test. Circle the 10 items you would keep.

| Item Number | Content Construct* | Item–Total Correlation | Item–Criterion Correlation | Difficulty ($p$) | Discrimination ($D$) | Bias |
|---|---|---|---|---|---|---|
| 1 | Calculus | .25 | .01 | .50 | 15 | Yes |
| 2 | Calculus | .56 | .25 | .49 | 30 | No |
| 3 | Calculus | −.20 | .00 | .50 | −.10 | No |
| 4 | Calculus | .40 | .08 | .60 | 36 | No |
| 5 | Calculus | .03 | −.05 | .90 | −.20 | Yes |
| 6 | Calculus | .84 | .20 | .70 | 48 | No |
| 7 | Calculus | .35 | .00 | .20 | 35 | No |

| Item Number | Content Construct* | Item–Total Correlation | Item–Criterion Correlation | Difficulty (p) | Discrimination (D) | Bias |
|---|---|---|---|---|---|---|
| 8 | Calculus | −.05 | −.02 | .50 | −.35 | No |
| 9 | Calculus | .80 | .12 | .65 | 40 | No |
| 10 | Calculus | .50 | .20 | .90 | .30 | No |
| 11 | Geometry | −.05 | −.02 | .40 | −.35 | No |
| 12 | Geometry | .60 | .25 | .49 | 40 | No |
| 13 | Geometry | .25 | .01 | .50 | 15 | No |
| 14 | Geometry | −.05 | −.02 | .40 | −.35 | No |
| 15 | Geometry | .40 | .08 | .60 | 36 | Yes |
| 16 | Geometry | .40 | .25 | .70 | 60 | Yes |
| 17 | Geometry | .30 | .30 | .10 | .50 | No |
| 18 | Geometry | .84 | .20 | .70 | 48 | No |
| 19 | Geometry | −.20 | .10 | .50 | −.10 | No |
| 20 | Geometry | .84 | .20 | .70 | 48 | No |

3. **Prepare a PPT or Prezi report.** Prepare a PPT or Prezi report that could serve as professional documentation of your pilot study process and results. Include the following in your report:

   - The purpose of the test
   - The step-by-step process used to pilot the test (include more information than provided above)
   - A description of each statistic calculated, including your rationale for each statistic
   - Your item statistics matrix
   - The items you eliminated and kept, with rationale for each decision

# Project 2

**BACKGROUND**

Test developers conduct quantitative item analysis to examine the performance of each item to identify items that perform well, revise those that could perform better, and to eliminate items that do not yield the desired information. This item analysis is completed through several statistical analyses of the individual items.

**YOUR TASK**

1. **Enter the data into the table below.** Ask your professor if he or she could provide you with the full results of a classroom test that has been given in the past (with the names of the students removed). It would be best if the test has at least 10 questions and was given to 20–30 students. You will need the actual answers (correct vs. incorrect) for each student on each question of the test. Enter the data into the table below or the statistical software program of your choosing. For each item, enter a "1" if the student answered the question correctly; enter a "0" if the student answered the question incorrectly. Complete the table for all students (adjust the table for a different number of items or students).

| Student | Item 1 | Item 2 | Item 3 | Item 4 | Item 5 | Item 6 | Item 7 | Item 8 | Item 9 | Item 10 | Score |
|---|---|---|---|---|---|---|---|---|---|---|---|
| 1 | | | | | | | | | | | |
| 2 | | | | | | | | | | | |
| 3 | | | | | | | | | | | |
| 4 | | | | | | | | | | | |
| 5 | | | | | | | | | | | |
| 6 | | | | | | | | | | | |
| 7 | | | | | | | | | | | |
| 8 | | | | | | | | | | | |
| 9 | | | | | | | | | | | |
| 10 | | | | | | | | | | | |
| 11 | | | | | | | | | | | |
| 12 | | | | | | | | | | | |
| 13 | | | | | | | | | | | |
| 14 | | | | | | | | | | | |
| 15 | | | | | | | | | | | |
| 16 | | | | | | | | | | | |
| 17 | | | | | | | | | | | |

| Student | Item 1 | Item 2 | Item 3 | Item 4 | Item 5 | Item 6 | Item 7 | Item 8 | Item 9 | Item 10 | Score |
|---|---|---|---|---|---|---|---|---|---|---|---|
| 18 | | | | | | | | | | | |
| 19 | | | | | | | | | | | |
| 20 | | | | | | | | | | | |

2. **Conduct a quantitative item analysis and present your results.** Use the data to conduct a quantitative item analysis on the test. For each item, calculate the item difficulty ($p$ value), and the discrimination index ($D$). Then review the results and make a recommendation of whether the item should be kept in the test or removed and provide the reason for your recommendation. Present the results in a PPT or Prezi report along with your conclusion about the overall psychometric quality of the test.

# Project 3

**BACKGROUND**

Imagine you were in graduate school serving as the teaching assistant for a psychology instructor. Because some of the students in the course are struggling with the concepts in Chapter 11, the instructor has asked you to spend 1 hour with these students to help increase their understanding of the Chapter 11 material. In addition to meeting with the students, the instructor requested that you create a visual learning aid you can use not only as an instructional tool when meeting with the students, but that students can take with them and use as a study tool for future exams.

**YOUR TASK**

1. **Search the Internet to learn more about visual learning aids.** Conduct a search of the Internet to learn more about the value of visual learning aids and the different types of learning aids. When searching, consider using key terms such as *visual learning aids, graphic organizer, concept maps, cognitive organizer, concept diagrams,* and *story maps.*

2. **Create a visual learning aid of Chapter 11 material.** Review the learning objectives at the beginning of Chapter 11. Create a well-thought-out visual learning aid to enhance student understanding of the important concepts associated with each learning objective. Your visual learning aid should be professional-looking and include visual symbols and words to express Chapter 11 concepts, as well as the connections between them. Creativity is encouraged.

# Practice Questions

## Multiple Choice

1. When Isaac conducted an item analysis of the data from his pilot study, he first calculated for each item the percentage of test takers who got the item right. In this analysis, what was he measuring?
   a. Item difficulty
   b. Item discrimination
   c. Item reliability
   d. Item bias

2. Items for which the $p$ value falls in the range between .90 and 1.00 are usually considered
   a. too difficult.
   b. about right.
   c. too easy.
   d. too biased.

3. When analyzing the data from her pilot study, Lucretia compared the performance on each item of those who achieved very high test scores with the performance on each item of those who achieved very low test scores. What was she calculating?
   a. Item difficulty
   b. Item discrimination
   c. Item reliability
   d. Item bias

4. Which one of the following is TRUE about items for which the D value is around 0.00?
   a. They do not discriminate well among test takers.
   b. They are too easy for test takers.
   c. They are too difficult for test takers.
   d. They are biased against low performers.

5. The interitem correlation matrix provides important information for identifying what?
   a. Items that are too easy
   b. Items that are too difficult
   c. Items that do not discriminate among test takers
   d. The test's internal consistency

6. Which one of the following contrasts the probability of answering an item correctly with the level of ability on the construct being measured?
   a. The $p$ value
   b. The $D$ value
   c. The item characteristic curve
   d. The interitem correlation matrix

7. What is the preferred method for determining item bias?
   a. Item discrimination index
   b. Item characteristic curve
   c. Item difficulty level
   d. Interitem correlation matrix

8. Who would be the most appropriate person to put on an expert panel for conducting a qualitative analysis of a school test?
   a. A parent of a child who was tested in the pilot study
   b. A member of the school board
   c. An expert on the constructs being measured
   d. An outside objective party who has no knowledge of the test

9. Which one of the following items would be best to drop from a test?
   a. $p = .4, D = 90$
   b. $p = .5, D = 70$
   c. $p = .6, D = 50$
   d. $p = .9, D = -1$

10. Which one of the following does NOT need to be included in the test manual?

a. The test itself

b. Evidence of reliability

c. Evidence of validity

d. A description of the target audience

11. Which one of the following correctly describes the most likely relationship between a validity coefficient found in an initial validation study and the validity coefficient that will be found when the study is cross-validated?

   a. The cross-validated validity coefficient will be lower than the coefficient found in the original study.

   b. The cross-validated validity coefficient will be the same as the coefficient found in the original study.

   c. The cross-validated validity coefficient will be higher than the coefficient found in the original study.

   d. The cross-validated validity coefficient will be unrelated to the coefficient found in the original study.

12. When Erica conducted the validation study for her test, she found that the validity coefficient for "men only" was not statistically significant; however, the validity coefficient for "women only" was statistically significant. These results suggest that the test has evidence of what type of validity?

   a. Discriminant evidence of validity

   b. Single-group validity

   c. Multiple-group validity

   d. No evidence of validity

13. What are the statistics that describe subgroups of the target audience called?

   a. Norms

   b. Subgroup norms

   c. Differential norms

   d. In-group norms

14. When we use tests for making selection decisions, which one of the following is the score at which the decision changes from hire to do not hire?

   a. The normative score

   b. The standard error of measurement

   c. The cut score

   d. The maximum score

15. Which one of the following coefficients is the result of correlating two dichotomous (having only two values) variables?

   a. Validity coefficient

   b. Reliability coefficient

   c. Phi coefficient

   d. Correlation matrix

16. The strength and direction of the relationship between the way test takers responded to an item and the way they responded to all of the items on a test as a whole is described by what coefficient?

   a. Item–total correlation coefficient

   b. Phi coefficient

   c. Item–criterion correlation coefficient

   d. Reliability coefficient

17. According to your textbook, what did researchers Rojdev, Nelson, Hart, and Fercho (1994) conclude about the Minnesota Multiphasic Personality Inventory-1 (MMPI-1) and MMPI-2?

   a. They measure different constructs.

   b. They have significantly different validity coefficients.

   c. They have significantly different reliability estimates.

   d. They are equivalent.

18. An analysis shows that differential validity exists for a test. The regression equation for male students is $Y' = 4.50 + .024x$, and the regression equation for female students is $Y' = 4.50 + .155x$. What type of bias exists?

   a. Slope bias

   b. Intercept bias

c. Differential item functioning

   d. Fairness bias

19. Which one of the following concepts is associated with social issues rather than statistical or scientific issues?

   a. Slope bias

   b. Differential validity

   c. Measurement bias

   d. Test fairness

20. When using test scores for decision making, the test user is ethically and morally responsible for ascertaining that the test shows acceptable evidence of what?

   a. Predictive and concurrent evidence of validity

   b. Face validity and test taker acceptance

   c. Reliability and validity

   d. Reliability and face validity

21. Who has the responsibility for preventing test misuse by making test manuals and validity information available before purchase?

   a. Test users

   b. Test takers

   c. Test publishers

   d. Test developers

## Short Answer

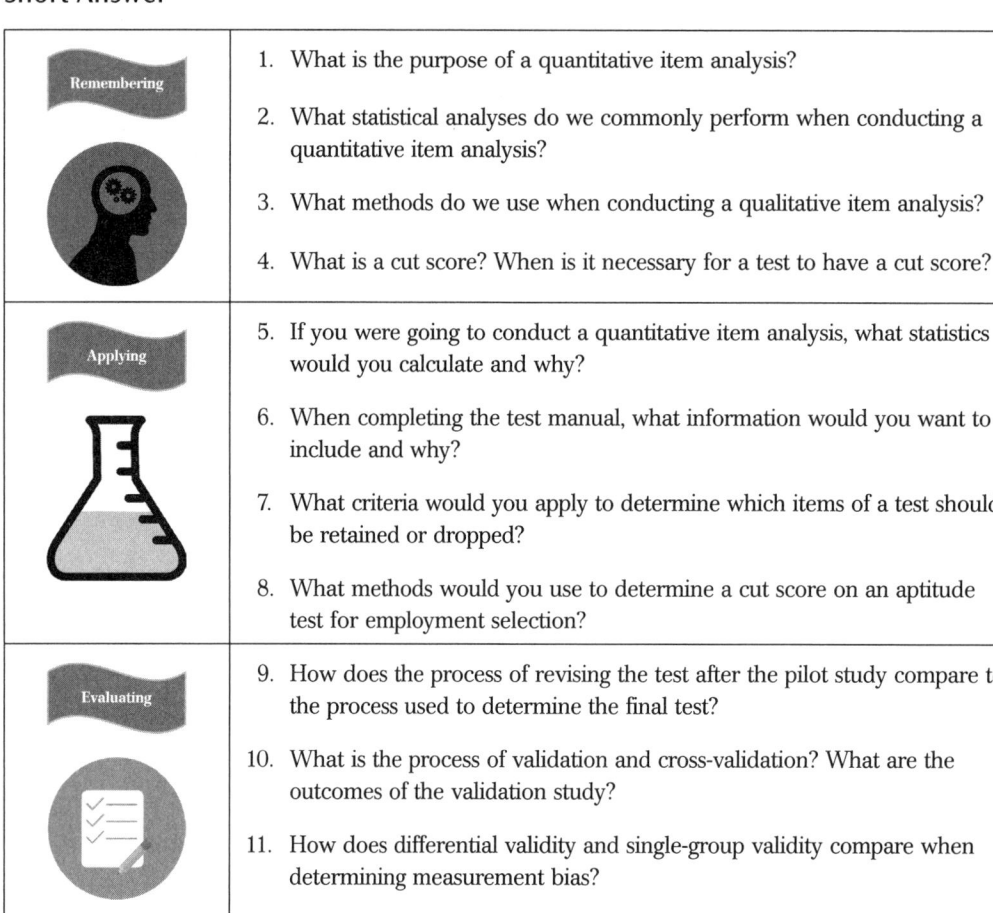

**Remembering**
1. What is the purpose of a quantitative item analysis?
2. What statistical analyses do we commonly perform when conducting a quantitative item analysis?
3. What methods do we use when conducting a qualitative item analysis?
4. What is a cut score? When is it necessary for a test to have a cut score?

**Applying**
5. If you were going to conduct a quantitative item analysis, what statistics would you calculate and why?
6. When completing the test manual, what information would you want to include and why?
7. What criteria would you apply to determine which items of a test should be retained or dropped?
8. What methods would you use to determine a cut score on an aptitude test for employment selection?

**Evaluating**
9. How does the process of revising the test after the pilot study compare to the process used to determine the final test?
10. What is the process of validation and cross-validation? What are the outcomes of the validation study?
11. How does differential validity and single-group validity compare when determining measurement bias?
12. Compare the benefits and drawbacks of Computerized Adaptive Testing for standardized tests.

# Multiple-Choice and Short-Answer Practice Question Answer Key

## Multiple Choice

| Question | Answer | Textbook Page | Explanation |
|---|---|---|---|
| 1. | a | 311 | Item difficulty is defined as the percentage of test takers who respond correctly to a test item. An item's difficulty is calculated by dividing the number of people who answered the question correctly by the total number of people who answered the question. Typically, the resulting value is not multiplied by 100 as is done when calculating a percentage; thus the value ranges from 0.00 to 1.00. In a sense, it is really a measure of the item's easiness because higher values indicate more people got the item right, and it is therefore easier. |
| 2. | c | 312 | Based on how item difficulty is calculated, higher values mean more people responded correctly. Therefore, a value of .90 would mean that 90% of the people who answered the question did so correctly, and a value of 1.00 would mean that everyone who answered the question got it right. Thus, questions with item difficulties in this range would be considered easy. |
| 3. | b | 312 | Item discrimination compares the item performance of individuals who achieved high scores on the test with the item performance of those who achieved low scores on the test. Typically test developers will take the top one-third of test scorers and the bottom one-third of test scorers and use the formula shown below. $$U = \frac{\text{Number in Upper Group who responded correctly}}{\text{Total number in Upper Group}} \times 100$$ $$L = \frac{\text{Number in Lower Group who responded correctly}}{\text{Total number in Lower Group}} \times 100$$ $$D = U - L$$ Test developers look for items that have high positive $D$ values. In contrast, negative numbers indicate that those who scored low on the test overall responded to the item correctly and that those who scored high on the test responded incorrectly. Low positive numbers suggest that nearly as many people who had low scores responded correctly as did those who had high scores. Each of these situations indicates that the item is not discriminating between high scorers and low scorers. |

*(Continued)*

(Continued)

| Question | Answer | Textbook Page | Explanation |
|---|---|---|---|
| 4. | a | 313 | Using the formula shown above in Question 4, it is clear that when an item has a D value of 0.00, the same percentage of test takers in the lower scoring group answered the item correctly as those in the higher scoring group. Therefore, there is no difference between high and low scorers on the item, and the item does not discriminate between the two groups. |
| 5. | d | 314 | The interitem correlation matrix provides important information about the test's internal consistency. Each item that measures the same construct should be correlated with other items that measure the same construct. Conversely, items that measure different constructs should not be correlated with each other. Typically, items that are not correlated with other items as expected are removed from the test, which increases the test's internal consistency. |
| 6. | c | 315 | The item characteristic curve or ICC is derived from a complex statistical procedure called item response theory (IRT). An ICC describes the relationship between a test taker's ability and the probability of answering a test item correctly. ICCs provide rich information to the test developer concerning an item's difficulty and discrimination. |
| 7. | b | 319 | Although there are a variety of methods for detecting item bias, which is defined as occurring when an item is easier for one group than another group, the ICC is the preferred approach. This is because when ICCs are used, the test developer can easily compare the probability of answering the question correctly when both group membership and ability level are considered. The problem with the simple measure of item difficulty that has been used in the past is that it does not consider possible group differences in the ability level. |
| 8. | c | 324 | While parents and school board members may have a large interest in a test's quality, they are not likely to know much about measurement or about the intended test construct. Therefore, experts on the construct being measured are most likely to provide useful information about improving the test. |
| 9. | d | 325 | A negative discrimination (D) value indicates that lower scoring individuals were more likely to answer the question correctly than high-scoring individuals. In addition, a difficulty value (p) of .9 means that 90% of the test takers correctly answered the question, which shows it was extremely easy. Thus, of the answer options provided, answer d is the worst performing question. |
| 10. | a | 325 | Evidence of reliability, validity, and of the target audience are key pieces of information that would allow a test user to make an informed judgment about administering a test. Test users and administrators do not need to have prior knowledge of every test item. Providing widespread and easy access to the test would compromise test security. |

| Question | Answer | Textbook Page | Explanation |
|---|---|---|---|
| 11. | a | 327 | Cross-validation is a method for providing evidence of validity by applying a regression equation calculated on one sample of test takers to a second sample of test takers. The key to answering this question correctly is understanding the concept of shrinkage in regression. Statistically, applying a regression equation derived on one group of people to predict the performance of a different group of people will usually result in a lower validity coefficient than was obtained in the original group. It is typical that when the regression weights obtained from one sample are applied to another sample, the R2 value will become smaller. |
| 12. | b | 328 | Single group validity occurs when the test is valid for one group of test takers, but not for other groups of test takers. In this case, it was valid for men, but not for women. This is an indication of measurement bias. |
| 13. | b | 341 | Norms are used to compare test scores of similar test takers and aid in test score interpretation. When tests are given to large groups of individuals, it is often possible to calculate norms that describe very specific subgroups based on characteristics such as race, sex, and age. These group specific norms are called subgroup norms. |
| 14. | c | 341 | A cut score is a specific score where a decision changes based on test results. For example, an organization may decide that those who score 65 and above on a job knowledge test pass, and those who score less than 65 fail. Setting valid and legally defensible cut scores can be a challenging task for the test developer. |
| 15. | c | 314 | Phi coefficients are a statistic that indicates the relationship (correlation) of two dichotomous variables, which are variables that are scored using only two options such as correct (1) and incorrect (0). They are interpreted identically to the well-known Pearson product–moment correlation. |
| 16. | a | 313 | An item–total correlation correlates the relationship between answering a question correctly/incorrectly and the total test score obtained. Item–total correlations are expected to be greater than 0.00, as this indicates that higher scoring individuals tended to answer the item correctly more than lower scoring individuals. If a question has an item–total correlation of less than 0.00, then this means that lower-scoring individuals tended to perform better on the item than higher-scoring individuals, which is an indication of a problem with the item. |

*(Continued)*

(Continued)

| Question | Answer | Textbook Page | Explanation |
|---|---|---|---|
| 17. | d | 315 | Rojdev et al. (1994) compared evidence of validity based on relationships with other external variables of the MMPI-1 and MMPI-2. It is important to conduct such studies when updating or revising a test because test users need to know if different forms of a test are comparable in terms of validity. |
| 18. | a | 332 | Differential validity occurs when two regression equations describe the test results better than a single overall regression equation. In this case, the question states that the test exhibited differential validity and two equations are given. The type of bias can be determined by examining the regression equations. Because both equations have the same $y$-intercept (4.50) and different slopes (.024 for males and .155 for females), the test shows slope bias. |
| 19. | d | 337 | The issue of test fairness often comes up when the test validity issue is discussed. It is important to understand that fairness is based on societal values rather than statistics. |
| 20. | c | 340 | Decisions based on tests can have far-reaching consequences, and therefore test users must make sure that the test is both reliable and valid, which is key to ensuring that decisions are fair and unbiased. In contrast, face validity is only the appearance that the test measures what it is supposed to and does not have anything to do with the test's accuracy. Face validity does, however, lead to test taker acceptance. In addition, predictive and concurrent studies are specific types of validity evidence, but the answer option "a" does not include the key feature of reliability. |
| 21. | c | 340 | Test publishers are ethically responsible for ensuring that tests are not misused. One way to contribute to this goal is to provide test manuals that contain information about the test's reliability and validity, test users' qualifications, administration instructions, norming information, and so on. |

## Short Answer

| Question | Explanation |
|---|---|
| 1. | Qualitative item analyses provide rich and useful information concerning test items that might be missed only using quantitative analyses. For example, a qualitative interview can explore how test takers react emotionally to questions, can illustrate cognitive strategies that test takers use to answer test questions, or determine if test takers understand the administration instructions. To collect qualitative information, test developers can interview and conduct focus groups with test takers or with subject matter experts. |
| 2. | The quantitative item analysis includes measures of item difficulty, item discrimination, interitem correlations, item–criterion correlations, item bias, and item characteristic curve. |
| 3. | There are three methods test developers use to conduct qualitative item analysis. The first is conducted by asking the test takers to complete a questionnaire about how they viewed the test itself and how they answered the test items. The second method test developers may use is individual or group discussions with test takers for understanding how test takers perceived the test and how changes in the test items or instructions may improve the accuracy of test results. Lastly, test developers may also ask a panel of experts about the test's content or about testing in general to get their opinions on possible sources of error or bias. |
| 4. | A cut score is a decision point. At or above a cut score, one decision would be made, and below the cut score, a different decision would be made. Most commonly, the decision on a test is pass/fail. Thus, for a certification test, individuals at or above the cut score would pass and become certified, and those below the score would fail. It is important to have a cut score when a test user must make a dichotomous decision such as pass/fail, hire/don't hire, pathological/not pathological, and so on. Identifying cut scores can be a difficult task, but there are well-accepted approaches. One approach is to use a panel of judges to estimate the number of items that a minimally qualified person is likely to answer correctly. A second approach is to use an external criterion such as job performance. A regression model would be developed using test score to predict job performance. The point at which job performance became unacceptable would be identified, and then whatever test score corresponded to this value on the regression line would be taken as the cut score. |
| 5. | There are several important quantitative statistics to examine during a pilot test. The item difficulty is the percentage of test takers who answer a question correctly. This statistic can help weed out overly easy or overly hard test questions. Item discrimination is another important statistic. This statistic indicates the relationship between success on the test overall and success on a test question. A question with a 0.00 discrimination means that there is no relationship between test score and success on the question. In other words, the question does not help in discriminating high from low performers. Positive values indicate that better performing individuals perform better on the question. Negative values indicate that there is a problem with the test question because low performers are more likely to get the question correct than are high performers. Interitem correlations show how the test questions interrelate and provide important construct related validity evidence allowing test developers to remove items that do not contribute to the measurement of the intended construct(s). Item–total correlations provide additional information on the questions' discrimination. Item–criterion correlations show whether each test question contributes to the prediction of an external criterion, allowing the test developer to use only items that prove to be valuable in the prediction of important outcomes. Item characteristics curves (ICC) from item response theory are useful to examine the difficulty, discrimination, and bias of test questions. Finally, item bias is an important consideration. While there are a lot of statistics that examine item bias, the ICC is the preferred method. |

*(Continued)*

(Continued)

| Question | Explanation |
|---|---|
| 6. | A test manual is a critical component of the test development process. This document gives test users the ability to evaluate the test in terms of reliability, validity, and potential usefulness for their particular application. What is included in the test manual depends on the development process, but some common and important elements include reliability evidence, validity evidence, norms, and information on interpreting test scores. Basically, the manual should document the validation and test development process in detail and in its entirety. |
| 7. | The reason test developers begin writing more items than are needed is so they can eliminate items when necessary. Test developers use the quantitative and qualitative analyses of the test to choose the items that together provide the most information about the construct being measured. The test developers need to weigh each item's evidence of validity, item difficulty and discrimination, interitem correlation, and bias. Issues such as test length and face validity are also considered. |
| 8. | Cut scores may be determined by either the test developer or the test user. Setting a cut score is difficult and should be done objectively and carefully. There are generally two approaches used to set cut scores. One approach used for employment tests involves a panel of expert judges who provide an opinion or rating about the number of test items that a minimally qualified person is likely to answer correctly. The other approach is more empirical and uses the correlation between the test and an outside criterion to predict the test score that a person who performs at a minimum level of acceptability is likely to make. |
| 9. | Using quantitative and qualitative information collected during a pilot test to revise a test is a major part of the development process. Because test developers nearly always develop more items than needed, they can use the pilot test results to weed out poorly performing items, thereby improving the overall functioning of the test. Or they may choose to revise and rewrite poorly performing items. However, this can be dangerous because the item is unlikely to be pilot tested again, and there is no guarantee that the item will work as intended. In addition, test developers may need to revise the administration instructions, so there is no confusion. This helps to ensure the test measures the desired construct and not the ability to understand test instructions. |
| 10. | Because the pilot test is a single administration, the test may predict differently when administered and used in a different setting. Cross-validation helps to evaluate this potential. Typically, the data obtained in a pilot test are divided into two data sets. Using one data set, called the screening sample, a statistical regression model is developed. Then this model is applied to the second data set, called the validation sample, and is used to predict values on the criterion. These predicted values are then compared to the actual criterion values obtained in the validation sample. Finally, the predicted and actual criterion scores are correlated to tell you how closely the scores align. |
| 11. | The Standards clearly state that mean group differences in test scores are not an indication of test or measurement bias. This is because in some cases, different groups do have different group means on the construct being measured. Although there are different models of bias, the most common model used is predictive bias. This occurs when separate regression lines for each group would predict better than a single overall regression line. This is an indication that the test predicts differently for the groups. |

| Question | Explanation |
|---|---|
| 12. | Student responses will vary. While answers should include a brief description of what CAT is and how the scoring is conducted, answers should also include details of the student's critique of CAT for standardized tests. The student should include the benefits and drawbacks of such a testing method, with examples supporting their position on the use of CAT. |

# Exercise 12.1: What Decisions Do Educators Make Based on Test Results?

**OBJECTIVE**

Investigate the types of decisions educators make by reviewing test results.

**BACKGROUND**

Educational professionals at the elementary school, middle school, high school, college, and state level make many different types of decisions based on psychological test results. Some of these educational professionals include administrators, classroom teachers, school psychologists, and school counselors. Some of the types of decisions include placement decisions, instructional decisions, counseling decisions, grading decisions, and diagnostic decisions. To increase your understanding of how professionals in educational settings use test results, for Exercise 12.1, you will interview three educational professionals to learn more about the tests they use and the decisions they make.

**YOUR TASK**

1. **Identify three educational professionals**. Review Chapter 12 of your textbook to learn more about the different types of professionals who use psychological tests in educational settings. Find three different types of educational professionals who use psychological tests who agree to be interviewed.

2. **Interview three professionals**. Interview the three professionals, asking the two questions below, as well as two other questions provided by your instructor or that you'd like answered. Document the name and job title of each professional and answers to the questions in the chart provided below. Probe to uncover as much information as you can about the tests they use and the types of decisions made.

|  | Professionals | | |
| --- | --- | --- | --- |
| **Questions** | Name:<br>Job Title: | Name:<br>Job Title: | Name:<br>Job Title: |
| I'm currently enrolled in a college course where we are learning about the types of tests professionals in educational settings use. What types of tests do you use? | | | |
| How do you use the test results? That is, what types of decisions do you and/or the test takers make based on the test results? | | | |
| | | | |
| | | | |

3. **Answer the questions below.**

What surprised you the most while you conducted your interview?

_____
_____
_____
_____
_____

If you were to offer any advice to educational institutions, what would you offer after conducting your interview?

_____
_____
_____
_____
_____

What additional question(s) do you have now that you collected and analyzed your data?

_____
_____
_____
_____
_____

# Exercise 12.2: What Tests Are Used to Make Counseling and Guidance Decisions?

**OBJECTIVE**

Evaluate tests used to make counseling and guidance decisions.

**BACKGROUND**

In educational settings, tests are often used to make counseling and guidance decisions. For example, there are a variety of psychological tests available that can help students understand their interests, strengths, abilities, and preferences. Career counselors often use the results of these tests to provide career guidance to students. To increase your understanding of the types of tests career counselors use to make counseling and guidance decisions and the value of such tests, for Exercise 12.2, you will conduct research on commonly used tests and then visit your career services office to experience the process.

**YOUR TASK**

1. **Learn about tests used by career counselors.** Below is a list of six tests commonly used by career counselors. Conduct an Internet search to learn as much as you can about each test. Identify two additional tests that career counselors might use. The test publisher's website is typically the best place to gather in-depth information about a test.

    - Campbell Interest and Skill Survey
    - Career Assessment Inventory
    - Jackson Vocational Interest Survey
    - Self-Directed Search
    - SIGI3
    - Strong Interest Inventory

2. **Document your learnings.** For each test, document the answers to the following questions.

| Test | What does the test measure? | How can the results of the test help you with career decisions? | Where/how can you take the test? |
|---|---|---|---|
| 1. Campbell Interest and Skill Survey | | | |
| 2. Career Assessment Inventory | | | |

*(Continued)*

(Continued)

| Test | What does the test measure? | How can the results of the test help you with career decisions? | Where/how can you take the test? |
|---|---|---|---|
| 3. Jackson Vocational Interest Survey | | | |
| 4. Self-Directed Search | | | |
| 5. SIGI3 | | | |
| 6. Strong Interest Inventory | | | |
| | | | |
| | | | |

3. **Experience the process.** Go to your career services office and find out what tests they use to help provide students with career guidance. Arrange to take one or more tests and to sit with a career counselor to learn about your results. Write a 2-page paper explaining the test(s) you took, what they measure, and what insights you gained from the process.

# Exercise 12.3: Why Should Educators Follow Professional Practice Standards?

**OBJECTIVE**

Identify and describe the consequences of educators not following professional practice standards.

**BACKGROUND**

Professionals in educational settings make many different types of important decisions using psychological test results. For example, teachers might use test results in the classroom to determine how much learning occurred and to assign grades. School boards might use test scores to determine how to enhance educational instruction in a classroom or determine what training teachers need to enhance the learning process. In educational settings, for more formal, standardized tests, test users are expected to abide by professional practice standards, such as the Standards for Educational and Psychological Testing (AERA, APA, & NCME, 2014). To increase your understanding of professional practice standards, in Exercise 12.3, you will identify potential violations of standards and describe the consequences.

**YOUR TASK**

1. **Read the scenario below.**

   Imagine you are a high school teacher, and the school is preparing to administer the yearly standardized test to students. The yearly test is administered in various testing sessions and is proctored by the school's teachers. The administrative staff assigned teachers their proctoring roles and provided them the training they needed to be effective test proctors. You missed the training due to a previous commitment, but the vice principal decided that you would not need to go through another training since you had proctored the prior year. You planned to review the testing material during breakfast the day of the standardized testing, but you slept through your alarm clock and had to rush to work. You went to your assigned classroom as a testing proctor, took roll, and waited for an administrative staff member to direct you when to begin testing. However, the intercom system in the classroom did not work. You decide to get the students started on testing because you knew they had limited time to complete the first portion of the test, and you did not want students to be jeopardized. To speed things up, you put the directions to the side and quickly advised students on what to do based on the training you received the year before. You did not read the directions verbatim as provided in the testing administrator's guidebook for the new testing year. Students completed the first testing session, and you dismissed them when they finished.

2. **Identify issues and consequences of professional practice standards.** Review the "Educational Professionals as Test Users" and the "Standards Specific to Educational Professionals as Test Users" sections of Chapter 12 of the textbook. Identify four issues/problems with the scenario above. For each issue/problem, identify what part of the *Standards for Educational and Psychological Testing* (AERA et al., 2014) was not followed, and the consequence of not following the standard. Document your work in the table below.

| Issue/Problem | Standard Not Followed | Consequence |
|---|---|---|
|  |  |  |
|  |  |  |
|  |  |  |
|  |  |  |

# Exercise 12.4: How Are Assessments Used in Educational Settings?

**OBJECTIVE**

Identify types of assessments and decisions made in educational settings.

**BACKGROUND**

Professionals use various types of assessments in educational settings. For example, they use placement, formative, diagnostic, and summative assessments. They also use different types of assessments to make different types of decisions. These decisions include instructional, grading, diagnostic, selection, placements, counseling and guidance, program and curriculum, and administrative policy decisions. To increase your understanding of how assessments are used in educational settings, for Exercise 12.4, after reading examples of tests used in educational settings, you will then identify both the type of assessment used and the type of decision made.

**YOUR TASK**

1. **Review how assessments are used in educational settings.** Review the "Types of Decisions Made in Educational Settings" and the "Specific Uses of Psychological Tests in Educational Settings" sections of Chapter 12 of your textbook.

2. **Identify how tests are being used and the types of decisions being made.** Read each of the testing examples in the table below. For each example, identify how the test is being used; that is, is the test being used as a placement assessment, formative assessment, diagnostic assessment, or summative assessment? For each example, also identify the type of decision made: instructional, grading, diagnostic, selection, placements, counseling and guidance, program and curriculum, or administrative policy. Document your findings in the table below.

| Testing Example | How Test Is Being Used | Type of Decision Made |
|---|---|---|
| A test is given to determine if a systemwide math program should be continued. | | |
| A student is given a test to help her decide what career she may want to pursue. | | |

*(Continued)*

(Continued)

| Testing Example | How Test Is Being Used | Type of Decision Made |
|---|---|---|
| A student takes a test to determine what major he should pursue in college. | | |
| A teacher administers a classroom test to determine students' final grade. | | |
| A student is given a test to determine if he should be placed in a remedial writing class. | | |
| A college professor administers a test at the beginning of the semester to determine how much students know so she can plan the semester curriculum. | | |
| A school psychologist administers a test to a student who is having difficulty in math class. | | |

3. **Create your own testing examples.** Create eight testing examples of professionals in educational settings using psychological test results to make decisions. The testing examples should not be any of those described above. Indicate if the test in each example is being used as a placement assessment, formative assessment, diagnostic assessment, or summative assessment. For each example, also identify the type of decision made: instructional, grading, diagnostic, selection, placements, counseling and guidance, program and curriculum, or administrative policy. Document your findings in the table below.

| Testing Example | How Test Is Being Used | Type of Decision Made |
|---|---|---|
| | | |
| | | |
| | | |
| | | |
| | | |
| | | |
| | | |
| | | |

# Exercise 12.5: How Do I Differentiate Between Norm- and Criterion-Referenced Tests?

**OBJECTIVE**

Differentiate between norm- and criterion-referenced tests.

**BACKGROUND**

Tests used in educational settings can be classified as either norm-referenced or criterion-referenced tests. Professionals in educational settings use norm-referenced and criterion-referenced tests to make many different important instructional, grading, diagnostic, selection, placement, counseling and guidance, program and curriculum, and administrative policy decisions. To increase your understanding of the difference between norm-referenced and criterion-referenced tests, in Exercise 12.5, you will research individual tests, identifying if each is norm-referenced or criterion-referenced, identifying the types of decisions made using each test, and determining who uses each test. You will also answer some questions.

**YOUR TASK**

1. **Define norm- and criterion-referenced tests.** Review the "Norm-Referenced, Criterion-Referenced, and Authentic Assessment of Achievement" section in Chapter 12 of your textbook. In your own words, write a definition of a norm-referenced test and a criterion-referenced test. Identify an example of when each type of test would be appropriate to use. Document your work in the table below.

|  | **Definition** | **When to Use** |
|---|---|---|
| Norm-referenced test | | |
| Criterion-referenced test | | |

Chapter 12 ■ How Are Tests Used in Educational Settings?   323

2. **Research norm-referenced and criterion-referenced tests.** After conducting research on each test shown in the table below, indicate if the test is a norm-referenced test or a criterion-referenced test, the type of decisions that might be made from the results, and who might make the decisions. Document your findings in the table below.

| Test | Norm-Referenced or Criterion-Referenced? | Type of Decision | Who Makes the Decision |
|---|---|---|---|
| 1. SAT | | | |
| 2. Praxis Teacher Certification Tests | | | |
| 3. ACT | | | |
| 4. Georgia High School Graduation Tests | | | |
| 5. Stanford Achievement Test | | | |
| 6. California High School Exit Examination | | | |

3. **Answer the questions below.**

What are the benefits of developing a norm-referenced test? What are the consequences?

What are the benefits of developing a criterion-referenced test? What are the consequences?

What can you conclude about norm-referenced and criterion-referenced tests?

## Exercise 12.6: Reflect on Your Learning

**OBJECTIVE**

Describe key takeaways and confusing concepts from Chapter 12.

**BACKGROUND**

In Chapter 12 of the textbook, you were introduced to how tests are used in educational settings. You read about what type of decisions are made with tests in educational settings. You were introduced to why test users should obtain training on the proper administration of tests. You were also introduced to information on the decision educators make after review of test results. Last, you learned about the differences between norm- and criterion-referenced tests. For Exercise 12.6, you will reflect on your learning from Chapter 12 of the textbook and identify key takeaways from the chapter.

**YOUR TASK**

1. **Identify your "Aha!" moments from Chapter 12**.
   - Identify 3 to 4 new insights or realizations you had after reading Chapter 12, referred to as "Aha!" moments.
   - Consider things that made you look at a concept, your life, or an issue in a completely different way than you had in the past.
   - Document your insights and realizations below, providing details of your learning.

2. **Identify some muddy moment discussion questions.**
   - Identify 2 to 3 concepts that are still "muddy" for you from the chapter.
   - Consider concepts you still don't understand, concepts you need clarified, and/or questions you want to ask.
   - Develop 1 to 3 questions to initiate a discussion in class to further your understanding of the concepts and get your questions answered.

| | |
|---|---|
| **Insights and Realizations** | 1. _____ <br> 2. _____ <br> 3. _____ <br> 4. _____ |
| **Muddy Moments Discussion Questions** | 1. _____ <br> 2. _____ <br> 3. _____ |

## Chapter-Level Projects

### Project 1

**BACKGROUND**

Critics of standardized testing often point out that test prep and coaching are huge industries, with costs often running into the thousands for students and parents. Furthermore, critics argue that there is unequal access to test prep and coaching, with the poorest students being at a disadvantage. Proponents of standardized testing argue that despite the claims of test-prep companies, gains in scores attributable to the test prep and coaching is minimal (Powers & Rock, 1999).[1] Furthermore, most reported gains can be attributed to practice and familiarization, neither of which require an expensive training class, as many standardized tests, such as the ACT and SAT, have information and practice tests freely available from the test publishers. Additionally, proponents contend that well-designed programs, which are extensive and exhaustive, do result in student learning. Therefore, well-designed test prep and coaching programs should result in slight score increases.

In 2014, the College Board announced that it would redesign the SAT for 2016. The Board also announced a partnership with the well-known educational website, the Khan Academy. College Board President David Coleman said in an interview, "The College Board cannot stand by while some test-prep providers intimidate parents at all levels of income into the belief that the only way to secure their child's success is to pay for costly test preparation and coaching" (Herold, 2014, para. 4).[2] The president indicated that the arrangement would not involve any exchange of money between the two organizations. The Khan Academy, a not-for-profit organization, stated on their website that they are "For free. For everyone, Forever. No ads, no subscriptions. We are a not-for-profit because we believe in a free, world-class education for anyone, anywhere" (Khan Academy, 2014, para. 6).[3]

**YOUR TASK**

1. **Conduct research on the SAT and the Khan Academy.** Conduct Internet research to learn as much as you can about Khan Academy's free-for-all SAT prep program. Seek to learn as much as you can about the SAT study resources offered by the Khan Academy (e.g., lessons, practice tests) available at www.khanacademy.org/test-prep. Seek to identify materials available for individuals at different educational levels. Ask yourself if you would use this material for yourself, a child, a parent, a sibling, or other situation.

---

[1] Powers, D. E., & Rock, D. A. (1999). Effects of coaching on SAT I: Reasoning test scores. *Journal of Educational Measurement, 36*, 93–118. Retrieved from http://onlinelibrary.wiley.com/journal/10.1111/%28ISSN%291745-3984

[2] Herold, B. (March 12, 2014). College board enlists Khan Academy for SAT prep. *Education Week*. Retrieved from http://www.edweek.org/ew/articles/2014/03/12/24satside.h33.html

[3] Khan Academy. (2014). About. Retrieved from https://www.khanacademy.org/about

2. **Review and identify five to seven concepts found in Chapter 12.** Review Chapter 12 and identify five to seven concepts that would be helpful for evaluating the effectiveness of a test-preparation program, such as the one offered by the Khan Academy, or a different test-preparation program applicable to an educational setting. For example, one concept in Chapter 12 is the administration, scoring, and reporting of educational assessment results found in Figure 12.1 Testing of Standards Specific to Educational Testing and Assessment. You could use this concept to evaluate the test-preparation program by how the test-preparation program provides recommendations for instructional interventions or information the test taker should study prior to sitting to take the test.

3. **Create a checklist.** After you identify five to seven concepts presented in Chapter 12 that would help you evaluate the effectiveness of a test-preparation program, create a checklist. The checklist should be styled in a format that a high school student and their parents can use to help them choose between different test-preparation programs.

# Project 2

## BACKGROUND

One common criticism of standardized testing in educational settings is that it relies too heavily on multiple-choice tests, emphasizing recall and recognition rather than higher-order thinking skills. As a result, other test formats are at times suggested, such as short answer and essay. These other formats are called *constructed response tests* because the test taker must construct a response rather than selecting an answer from a set of predetermined response options. However, these types of tests come with their own set of challenges. Constructed responses must be graded in a way that is much different from multiple-choice questions. Grading these types of questions requires more time and, sometimes, money. And, it is not an easy task to consistently and fairly score hundreds, thousands, or in the case of the SAT and ACT, millions of constructed responses.

## YOUR TASK

1. **Read the information below.**

   Consider Todd Farley, who has worked for 15 years developing and grading constructed responses for major standardized testing efforts. In 2009, he wrote an exposé book describing his experiences. His first grading task involved a situation where a state Department of Education decided to have 10-year-olds draw a bike safety poster rather than having them answer multiple-choice questions to demonstrate their knowledge of bike safety. Mr. Farley sat through the rater training on how to apply the scoring rubric, which was pretty simple. The scoring rule was that if the poster clearly demonstrated a bike safety rule, one of which was wearing a helmet, then the drawing would receive full credit. If it did not, then it would receive no credit. The training had the raters practice scoring individually and then discuss their ratings to ensure consistency and a common understanding. Then, off he went to score his assigned posters. His very first poster showed a young cyclist, a helmet tightly attached to his head, flying his bike in a fantastic parabola up and over a canal filled with flaming oil, his two arms waving wildly in the air, a gleeful grin plastered on his mug. A caption below the drawing screamed, "Remember to Wear Your Helmet!"

   His initial response was, "Huh?" The poster clearly demonstrated the bike safety rule of wearing a helmet, but nothing about the poster indicated safe bike riding. After calling over the team leader and discussing the poster with her, he gave the poster full credit because of the helmet.

2. **Review Chapter 12**. Review Chapter 12 for information on how educational professionals use tests in educational settings, why educational professionals are considered test users, and the professional practice standards specific to educational professionals as test users. Think about the rubric used to grade the poster and the criteria used to determine if the student would receive full credit for the assignment. Also, think about the limitations of the rubric as applied to this situation. In the example above, the student clearly understood a helmet is necessary to ride a bike, but it does not include a description of what not to represent in the picture, such as a risky behavior.

3. **Identify five new scoring guidelines.** Reflect on the issue Todd Farley experienced, including the challenge and implications incorporating this type of assessment in an educational setting. Identify five new scoring guidelines you could incorporate that would help Todd grade the poster. Consider professional practice standards to use when developing a new rubric. Reflect on the design and implementation of the assessment, such as why this assignment is necessary; the importance of interpreting scores, the skills assessed, and any associated evidence; and scoring, training, measurement, and the recommendations that can be made from this assignment.

4. **Create a statement in support of the new scoring guidelines.** Assume you are Todd's mentor and that he came to you for advice on what to do in this situation. You told Todd that you would seek out the advice of other expert teachers and would respond in an email with advice. In your email, provide Todd with five new scoring guidelines and a detailed rationale to support your suggestions. Describe how Todd would include the new guidelines in his scoring rubric and describe how he would incorporate professional practice standards in his evaluation of the poster.

# Project 3

**BACKGROUND**

Imagine you were in graduate school serving as the teaching assistant for a psychology instructor. Because some of the students in the course are struggling with the concepts in Chapter 12, the instructor has asked you to spend 1 hour with these students to help increase their understanding of the Chapter 12 material. In addition to meeting with the students, the instructor requested that you create a visual learning aid you can use not only as an instructional tool when meeting with the students, but that students can take with them and use as a study tool for future exams.

**YOUR TASK**

1. **Search the Internet to learn more about visual learning aids.** Conduct a search of the Internet to learn more about the value of visual learning aids and the different types of learning aids. When searching, consider using key terms such as *visual learning aids, graphic organizer, concept maps, cognitive organizer, concept diagrams,* and *story maps*.

2. **Create a visual learning aid of Chapter 12 material.** Review the learning objectives at the beginning of Chapter 12. Create a well-thought-out visual learning aid to enhance student understanding of the important concepts associated with each learning objective. Your visual learning aid should be professional-looking and include visual symbols and words to express Chapter 12 concepts, as well as the connections between them. Creativity is encouraged.

# Practice Questions

## Multiple Choice

1. Which one of the following types of decisions is frequently made by teachers using teacher-made tests?
   a. Placement
   b. Diagnostic
   c. Counseling
   d. Curriculum

2. If teachers use psychological tests to determine whether students have the knowledge necessary to learn new material, they are using the tests as what type of assessment?
   a. Diagnostic
   b. Formative
   c. Placement
   d. Summative

3. Teachers use what type of assessment to answer the question, "On which learning tasks are the students progressing satisfactorily?"
   a. Diagnostic
   b. Formative
   c. Placement
   d. Summative

4. Teachers use what type of assessment to answer the question, "Which students have mastered the learning tasks to such a degree that they should proceed to the next course or unit of instruction?"
   a. Diagnostic
   b. Formative
   c. Placement
   d. Summative

5. What was the first vocational test developed in 1927?
   a. Graduate Record Examination (GRE)
   b. Kuder Preference Record (KPR)
   c. Strong Vocational Interest Blank (SVIB)
   d. Jackson Vocational Interest Survey (JVIS)

6. Periodically throughout a school year, teachers may use psychological tests as what type of assessment?
   a. Summative
   b. Formative
   c. Placement
   d. Diagnostic

7. If a teacher suspects a student may be having learning difficulties, the teacher may suggest that the student's learning abilities be evaluated using what type of assessment?
   a. Summative
   b. Formative
   c. Placement
   d. Diagnostic

8. Which one of the following is FALSE about the SAT?
   a. The SAT consists of four sections.
   b. The SAT has a guessing penalty.
   c. The SAT is an achievement test.
   d. Math makes up 50% of the score.

9. Which one of the following is TRUE about the ACT?
   a. The ACT has questions on trigonometry.
   b. The ACT measures science reasoning.
   c. The ACT is an achievement test.
   d. Math questions make up 50% of the test.

10. What tests involve comparing an individual's test score with an objectively stated standard of achievement?

a. Authentic assessments
b. Standardized tests
c. Norm referenced tests
d. Criterion referenced tests

11. If you had to provide three examples of a norm-referenced test, which one of the following would you NOT provide?
    a. ACT
    b. SAT
    c. Stanford Achievement Test
    d. Authentic assessment

12. Which one of the following is TRUE about authentic assessment?
    a. Authentic assessment is most valuable for measuring application of learning.
    b. Authentic assessment is a norm-referenced test.
    c. Authentic assessment is more reliable than criterion-referenced and norm-referenced tests.
    d. Authentic assessment often includes more than one measure of performance.

## Short Answer

**Remembering**

1. What types of decisions do educators make based on the results of psychological tests?
2. What are norm-referenced and criterion-referenced tests?
3. How would you describe and distinguish formative assessment and summative assessment?
4. What are placement tests, and when are they used?

**Applying**

5. How do educators use test scores to make curriculum and administrative policy decisions? Provide examples.
6. How do teachers use psychological tests in the classroom before, during, and after instruction? Give examples of each.
7. What are the similarities and differences between the ACT and the SAT? If you have well-developed math skills and an extensive vocabulary, on which test (the ACT or the SAT) might you perform better? Why?
8. What are the similarities and differences between norm-referenced and criterion-referenced tests? Provide an example of each.

**Evaluating**

9. Why would someone want to or choose to use authentic assessment?
10. How would you justify why educational institutions use tests to make selection and placement decisions? Include a discussion of some of the most common tests used for selection.
11. How would you defend why educators are test users and why they need to follow professional practice guidelines?
12. What are some examples of how psychological tests can benefit student motivation, retention and transfer of learning, self-assessment, and instructional effectiveness?

# Multiple-Choice and Short-Answer Practice Question Answer Key

## Multiple Choice

| Question | Answer | Textbook Page | Explanation |
|---|---|---|---|
| 1. | b | 378 | Teachers use tests to understand a student's strengths and difficulties. In addition, it is important to note that these tests tend to be teacher-made and are not constructed by professional test developers. In contrast, the other answer options are used by a specialist. |
| 2. | c | 378 | Teachers will often use psychological tests as placement assessments that determine the extent to which students possess the knowledge, skills, and abilities necessary to understand new material and how much of the material to be taught that students already know. |
| 3. | b | 378 | Throughout the school year, teachers may administer tests as formative assessments. Formative assessments help teachers determine what information students are and are not learning during the instructional process. Formative assessments allow teachers to identify areas that students need help with and decide whether it is appropriate to move to the next unit of instruction. These assessments are not used to assign grades; instead, teachers use formative assessments to make immediate adjustments to their own curriculum and teaching methods. That is, teachers can use the results of formative assessments to adjust the pace of their teaching and the material they are covering. Formative assessments are different from diagnostic assessments, in that teachers use tests to determine what information students are and are not learning. In contrast, teachers use diagnostic assessment tests to assess students' learning abilities. |
| 4. | d | 378 | Teachers use summative assessments at the end of instruction to determine what students do and do not know and to assign grades. For example, teachers use midterms and final exams to assess the students' level of knowledge and learning and then assign grades using the results. Sometimes students confuse formative and summative assessment, but there are differences. When an assessment is formative, the results are used to direct future instruction. In contrast, when an assessment is used as a summative assessment, the test is often used as a final evaluation to determine grades. |

| Question | Answer | Textbook Page | Explanation |
|---|---|---|---|
| 5. | c | 371 | E. K. Strong developed the first vocational test in 1927, called the Strong Vocational Interest Blank. Updated versions are still used today under the name Strong Interest Inventory. |
| 6. | b | 361 | During the course of instruction, teachers my use formative assessments to determine what information students are and are not learning. The assessments provide information allowing teachers to gauge student learning. They can then adjust their teaching as needed. |
| 7. | d | 361 | When students have problems with learning, teachers may suggest evaluating the student's learning abilities using a more focused diagnostic assessment. Diagnostic tests are generally quite long, but they do allow for more accurate evaluation of learning difficulties. |
| 8. | c | 368 | The SAT is an *aptitude* test that measures skills students have learned in school. In contrast, the ACT is a content-based *achievement* test that measures what students have learned in school. |
| 9. | c | 368 | The math portion of the ACT makes up 25% of the total score. In contrast, the math portion of the SAT makes up 50% of the total score for that college admission test. |
| 10. | d | 373 | All of the tests described in Chapter 12 can be considered either norm-referenced or criterion-referenced tests. Norm-referenced tests are standardized tests in which a test taker's score is compared with the scores of a group of test takers who previously took the test. Criterion-referenced tests, on the other hand, are tests that compare a test taker's scores with an objectively stated standard of achievement, such as the learning objectives for this chapter. With criterion-referenced tests, an individual's performance is based on how well he or she has learned a specific body of knowledge or skills or on how well the individual performs compared with some predetermined standard of performance. |
| 11. | d | 373 | The ACT, SAT, and Stanford Achievement Test are all norm-referenced tests because scores are interpreted in comparison to other test takers. In contrast, the focus of authentic assessment is on assessing a student's ability to perform real-world tasks by applying the knowledge and skills he or she has learned. |

*(Continued)*

(Continued)

| Question | Answer | Textbook Page | Explanation |
|---|---|---|---|
| 12. | a | 373 | Authentic assessment is very valuable for measuring the application of learning. This is because the focus of authentic assessment is on assessing a student's ability to perform real-world tasks. It requires that students apply the knowledge and skills they have learned. Authentic assessment relies on more than one measure of performance, is criterion-referenced, and relies on human judgment. |

## Short Answer

| Question | Explanation |
|---|---|
| 1. | *Instructional decisions*: Decisions made by classroom teachers based on tests typically constructed by teachers themselves. The decisions determine instructional strategies such as the pace of the course.<br><br>*Grading decisions*: Decisions made by classroom teachers based on tests typically constructed by teachers themselves. As the title describes, these decisions are used to determine grades and assessments using quizzes, midterms, and so on.<br><br>*Diagnostic decisions*: Decisions made by classroom teachers based on tests typically constructed by teachers themselves. The assessment information is used to understand the student's strengths and weakness. For example, does the student know single digit multiplication?<br><br>*Selection decisions*: Decisions made by a specialist or administrator based on standardized tests. Assessments are used to make group, program, or institutional decisions such as selection into a gifted program.<br><br>*Placement decisions*: Decisions made by a specialist or administrator based on standardized tests. These decisions use assessment to determine the placement of individuals such as if the student should be placed in a remedial, standard, or advancement mathematics course.<br><br>*Counseling and guidance decisions*: Decisions made by a specialist or administrator based on standardized tests. These types of decisions occur when students are given assistance and help in selecting things such as a career or program of study.<br><br>*Program and curriculum decisions*: Decisions made by a specialist or administrator based on standardized tests. These types of decisions are made when specialists or administrators use test scores to make broad program or curricular decisions such as adding or dropping an educational program.<br><br>*Administrative policy decisions*: High-level decisions made at the district, state, or national level by a specialist or administrator based on standardized tests. The decisions often involve aspects of education such as budgets or program implementation at a broad level. |
| 2. | Norm-referenced tests are tests that determine how well an individual's achievement compares with the achievement of others and that distinguish between high and low achievers. They are standardized tests that have been given to a large representative group of test takers from which scores have been used to create norms. Criterion-referenced tests are tests designed to measure a student's knowledge against objectively stated standards of achievement or criteria (for example, what they are expected to be able to do or to know). |
| 3. | Formative assessments help teachers determine what information students are and are not learning during the instructional process. Teachers use formative assessments to identify where students need help and decide whether it is appropriate to move to the next unit of instruction. On the other hand, summative assessments help students determine what students do and do not know. Teachers use summative assessments to gauge student learning and to assign grades. While formative assessments help teachers guide learning, summative assessments help teachers evaluate what has been learned. |

*(Continued)*

(Continued)

| Question | Explanation |
|---|---|
| 4. | Placement assessments are often used by teachers at the beginning of a course or unit of instruction to determine whether students have the skills or knowledge necessary to understand new material and to determine how much information students already know about the new material. This information is then used as a guide to determine which courses to enroll. |
| 5. | Administrators are responsible for making broad systemwide improvements and their decisions, which are often informed by test and assessment information, have policy, curricular, and budgetary implications. For example, recently many school districts have implemented pay-for-performance programs for teachers that at least partially link teacher pay to student performance on standardized tests. Administrators may also use test information to assess curriculum at the end of the year to decide if programs need to be added, dropped, or modified. |
| 6. | Teachers make a variety of decisions before, during, and after instruction. At each stage, they may ask slightly different questions and make different decisions, but the goal is always to make accurate decisions. For example, during instruction, the teacher may ask what skills and knowledge the students possess and then make placement decisions. During instruction, the teacher may ask what the students are learning and where students need help. Thus, they are making formative and diagnostic decisions at this point. After instruction, the teacher may ask what the students have learned and what grade they should receive, and as a result, they are making summative assessments. |
| 7. | Teachers make a variety of decisions before, during, and after instruction. At each stage, they may ask slightly different questions and make different decisions, but the goal is always to make accurate decisions. For example, during instruction, the teacher may ask what skills and knowledge the students possess and then make placement decisions. During instruction, the teacher may ask what the students are learning and where students need help. Thus, they are making formative and diagnostic decisions at this point. After instruction, the teacher may ask what the students have learned and what grade they should receive, and as a result, they are making summative assessments. |
| 8. | Both norm-referenced and criterion-referenced tests can be used as an input into educational decisions. In a norm-referenced test, test takers' scores are compared to the other test takers, and the scores are interpreted based on their relationship to the other scores. In contrast, a criterion-referenced test compares scores to an objectively defined standard of achievement, and there is no comparison to other test takers. Examples of norm-referenced tests are the ACT and SAT. If you scored 500 on the SAT math test, then you scored better than 50% of the test takers. On the other hand, most certification and licensing tests are criterion-referenced tests, and passing is based on passing a specific score, which indicates that the test taker possesses the requisite knowledge and skills to be successful. |
| 9. | Authentic assessment is a form of assessment where students are asked to perform tasks that are real world in nature and demonstrate the application of specific knowledge and skills. Proponents of authentic assessment believe students acquire their knowledge to perform a task or produce a product, and therefore, assessment should focus on the capability to actually perform the task or produce the product. Thus, authentic assessment is a good choice when there is a need to demonstrate a skill rather than just knowing about it. For example, being able to successfully draw blood rather than just knowing the steps. |

| Question | Explanation |
|---|---|
| 10. | Educational institutions are faced with making many selection and placement decisions. For example, colleges and universities may receive many more student applications than they can admit. Thus, they need a fair and objective method to screen out individuals who are not likely to succeed and admit those who are likely to perform well. At the undergraduate level, the two most common tests used for selection are the ACT and SAT. However, there have been recent efforts to rely less on a single test for admission. Student portfolios of work have been used as an alternative to standardized tests, but these can be difficult to implement and hard to ensure that they adhere to testing standards. Once students are accepted, colleges and universities often use tests to make decisions regarding placement of students into classes. For example, it is common to give incoming freshmen writing and math tests to determine placement into an appropriate level class. |
| 11. | Teachers are test users because they use test information as input to decisions. Any time decisions are made on the basis of test scores, the users should adhere to the testing standards described in Chapter 3. It would be irresponsible and unethical to make important decisions using tests for which the reliability and validity were unknown or unsubstantiated. |
| 12. | Tests can aid in the instructional process in several ways. First, tests can influence student motivation by increasing the desire to study and by providing feedback on what the student did correctly and incorrectly on the test. Second, tests can increase retention and transfer of learning to real situations. Test questions can be written in such a way that requires students to apply what they have learned to different situations, and repeated exposure to test questions can help in recall and memorization. Third, tests can promote student self-assessment and self-awareness by providing students objective and accurate information that they can then act on for improvement. Fourth, test can be used to determine instructional effectiveness, thus allowing teachers to improve their methods or tailor teaching strategies to the students' needs. |

# 13 How Are Tests Used in Clinical and Counseling Settings?

## Overview

In Chapter 13 of the textbook, you were introduced to how clinical and counseling psychologists and other mental health counselors use tests. Hopefully, after reading the chapter you have a clearer understanding of the type of work clinical and counseling professionals perform, how they use psychological tests, the practice of evidence-based assessment, the differences between *The Diagnostic and Statistical Manual of Mental Disorders*, fifth edition (DSM-V) and *International Classification of Diseases* (ICD), how dishonesty affects testing results, and how projective tests are used in clinical settings. While Chapter 13 of the textbook included information on how tests are used in clinical and counseling settings, Chapter 13 of the workbook provides you with the opportunity to demonstrate your understanding of material presented in the textbook and apply your learning by completing some practical and critical-thinking exercises linked with specific learning objectives. Chapter 13 of the workbook will also allow you to complete chapter-level projects to demonstrate your understanding of multiple topics within the chapter. Chapter 13 of the workbook ends with some multiple-choice and short-answer questions you can use to self-assess your understanding of the material.

## Practical and Critical-Thinking Exercises

### Purpose

This section contains five exercises you can complete to demonstrate your understanding and apply your learning (Exercises 13.1–13.5) and one exercise you can complete to reflect on your learning (Exercise 13.6). The exercises, linked to learning objectives, are displayed below.

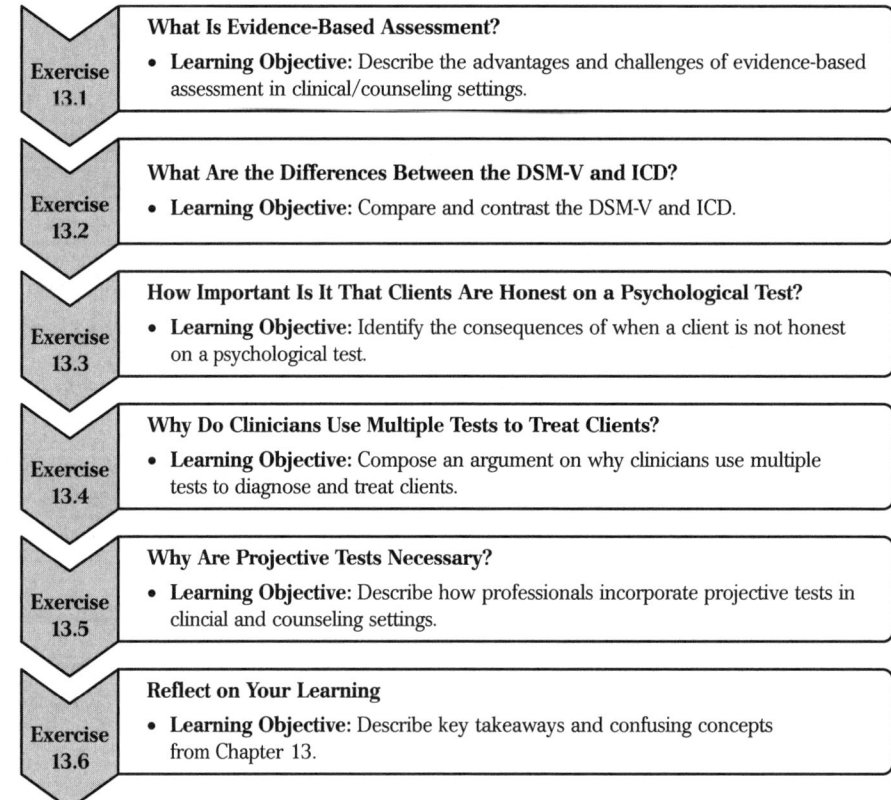

**Exercise 13.1**
**What Is Evidence-Based Assessment?**
- **Learning Objective:** Describe the advantages and challenges of evidence-based assessment in clinical/counseling settings.

**Exercise 13.2**
**What Are the Differences Between the DSM-V and ICD?**
- **Learning Objective:** Compare and contrast the DSM-V and ICD.

**Exercise 13.3**
**How Important Is It That Clients Are Honest on a Psychological Test?**
- **Learning Objective:** Identify the consequences of when a client is not honest on a psychological test.

**Exercise 13.4**
**Why Do Clinicians Use Multiple Tests to Treat Clients?**
- **Learning Objective:** Compose an argument on why clinicians use multiple tests to diagnose and treat clients.

**Exercise 13.5**
**Why Are Projective Tests Necessary?**
- **Learning Objective:** Describe how professionals incorporate projective tests in clincial and counseling settings.

**Exercise 13.6**
**Reflect on Your Learning**
- **Learning Objective:** Describe key takeaways and confusing concepts from Chapter 13.

# Exercise 13.1: What Is Evidence-Based Assessment?

**OBJECTIVE**

Describe the advantages and challenges of evidence-based assessment in clinical/counseling settings.

**BACKGROUND**

Psychologists and other mental health counselors who practice in clinical and counseling settings often use evidence-based assessments to help them diagnose mental health problems, plan treatment programs, monitor client progress, and assess treatment outcomes. For Exercise 13.1, you will review four articles to identify the advantages and challenges of evidence-based assessment and then write a brief speech.

**YOUR TASK**

1. **Identify the advantages and challenges of evidence-based assessment.** Review the "The Work of Clinical and Counseling Psychologists" and "Evidence-Based Assessment" sections in Chapter 13 of the textbook. In your own words, write two or three sentences describing what we mean by evidence-based treatment methods and evidence-based assessment. Locate four articles where the authors discuss the advantages and challenges associated with evidence-based assessment. The articles may be general qualitative or quantitative research articles, systematic case studies, public health research, or intervention studies. Document the complete reference for each article, including the advantages and challenges in the table below.

| Article | Advantages | Challenges |
|---|---|---|
| | | |
| | | |
| | | |
| | | |

2. **Prepare a brief speech.** Imagine you were in graduate school earning a PhD in clinical psychology. You were asked to make a presentation to a group of fellow clinical psychology students. Prepare a brief speech where you summarize the advantages and challenges. Include discussion of the likelihood you would use evidence-based assessment in your practice, explaining your rationale.

## Exercise 13.2: What Are the Differences Between the DSM-V and ICD?

**OBJECTIVE**

Compare and contrast the DSM-V and ICD.

**BACKGROUND**

Clinical psychologists, counseling psychologists, and mental health counselors administer tests and use the results to make decisions, such as to diagnose mental health problems of their clients. These mental health professionals use the DSM-V, published by the American Psychiatric Association, and the ICD, published by the World Health Organization, to help make evidence-based diagnostic decisions. When mental health professionals make a diagnosis, it is important they make the correct diagnosis, so they can help the client by planning and implementing an appropriate treatment plan. If a client is misdiagnosed, the mental health professional may suggest an inappropriate treatment plan, such as drug therapy when no medication is necessary, which could become life-threatening for the patient. For Exercise 13.2, you will conduct research on the DSM-V and ICD to identify the similarities, differences, and limitations of each.

**YOUR TASK**

1. **Research the similarities and differences between the DSM-V and ICD.** Conduct a search of the Internet to learn more about the DSM-V and ICD. When searching, explore numerous websites to find themes related to the purpose and intended use of each, how information is presented in each, and the type of information contained in each. Take notes in the chart below, including any other observations you believe are important.

|  | DSM-V | ICD |
|---|---|---|
| **Purpose and intended use** | | |
| **How information is presented** | | |

*(Continued)*

(Continued)

|  | DSM-V | ICD |
|---|---|---|
| **Type of information** | | |
| **Other observations** | | |

2. **Identify similarities, differences, and limitations of the DSM-V and ICD.** Review your notes above. Identify three factors that make the DSM-V and ICD similar and three factors that make them different. Identify one limitation of each. Choose either the DSM-V or ICD to further explore and discuss how the identified limitation might affect the client's diagnosis. Document your findings in the table below.

|  | DSM-V | ICD |
|---|---|---|
| **Three Similarities** | 1. <br> 2. <br> 3. | |
| **Three Differences** | 1. <br> 2. <br> 3. | 1. <br> 2. <br> 3. |
| **Limitation** | | |
| **Effect of Limitation** | DSM-V or ICD: _____ <br><br> Effect: | |

## Exercise 13.3: How Important Is It That Clients Are Honest on a Psychological Test?

**OBJECTIVE**

Identify the consequences of when a client is not honest on a psychological test.

**BACKGROUND**

The first step to receiving service in a clinical or counseling setting often involves collecting data. Part of the data collection is a self-report questionnaire that is used during the intake process. The intake process is where the client meets with a professional and, based on responses to the self-report questionnaire, the clinician will ask standardized questions along with clarifying questions. But as you can imagine, not everyone is honest or open to the process. People might be timid, ashamed, or may be shy, and not providing accurate and honest responses could delay treatment. For example, a person may not provide accurate information on the frequency of suicidal thoughts in fear of hospitalization or inappropriate sexual urges in fear of judgment. For Exercise 13.3, you will identify three clinical intake forms and associated consequences if the client is not honest during the structured interview process.

**YOUR TASK**

1. **Research three clinical intake forms.** Search the Internet to locate three different clinical intake forms a mental health professional/clinician/counselor may use during the intake process in a professional setting. Compare the intake forms. Identify a minimum of 10 similarities/commonalities between the three forms. Document your findings in the table below.

| Name of the Clinical Intake Form (if available) | Where did you find each form? (i.e., the URL or website name) |
|---|---|
|  |  |
|  |  |
|  |  |
| **Identify a minimum of 10 similarities/commonalities between all three forms.** ||
| 1. ||
| 2. ||
| 3. ||
| 4. ||
| 5. ||
| 6. ||
| 7. ||
| 8. ||
| 9. ||
| 10. ||

2. **Identify how omitted information may interfere with the development of a treatment plan.** Identify three ways clients may omit (intentional or not) information on the intake form or during the structured interview (intake interview) that could interfere with a counselor's interpretation of an individual's situation and, therefore, the ability to develop an effective treatment plan. For instance, if a client leaves out pertinent information on the intake form, such as the use of alcohol or drugs, the counselor may not be able to determine the cause of the issue the individual is seeking help for.

3. **Identify a relevant example.** Identify an example of when you or someone you know was reluctant to share information with someone, such as in a therapeutic situation. If you do not have an example, think of an example you might have seen on TV or from a story you read in a book. Using information from Task 2 above, identify how the reluctance to share information may have interfered with the treatment plan.

# Exercise 13.4: Why Do Clinicians Use Multiple Tests to Treat Clients?

**OBJECTIVE**

Compose an argument on why clinicians use multiple tests to diagnose and treat clients.

**BACKGROUND**

The use of multiple tests to diagnose and treat clients may be controversial, especially when there is a question of whether using additional tests would provide incremental validity over and above that of a single test. But clinicians and psychological professionals may need to use multimethod assessment techniques to identify additional characteristics or traits required to make a correct diagnosis for their client. The argument is whether evidence-based assessment is more beneficial than the use of multiple assessments designed to measure differences in human functioning. Vocational counselors explore client career options by using multiple assessments. Each assessment is designed to identify different factors of the person, such as interests, skills, personality, etc., to understand the ecological perspective of a client. For Exercise 13.4, you will make a case for why the use of multimethod assessments is important and how clinicians identify the ecological perspective to help them determine the correct tests to use.

**YOUR TASK**

1. **Describe multimethod and evidence-based assessment.** Research a clinical or counseling profession where the clinician may use multiple tests to identify services, counseling, or diagnosis for a client, such as a vocational counselor or a therapist. Research the ecological perspective the professional will explore to help them diagnose and treat their clients and locate factors the professional might test for their client. You will not identify specific tests; instead, your task is to determine the human factors professionals are interested in finding and the rationale for the use in their practice. We will assume any test they might use to measure human factors is reliable and demonstrates evidence of validity. Document your findings in the table below.

| Clinical or Counseling Profession | Ecological Perspective to Support the Use of Multimethod Assessment |
|---|---|
| | |

*(Continued)*

(Continued)

| Identify three pros and three cons for the use of multimethod assessment as compared to evidence-based assessment. ||
|---|---|
| **Pros** | **Cons** |
| 1 | 1 |
| 2 | 2 |
| 3 | 3 |

2. **Create an argument that does or does not support the inclusion of multimethod assessment.** Create an argument that does or does not support the use of multiple assessments. Be sure to include the perspective of evidence-based assessment in your argument. Clearly articulate which side of the argument you support based on your review of tests clinicians and mental health professionals use in their practice.

_____
_____
_____
_____
_____
_____
_____
_____
_____
_____
_____
_____
_____
_____
_____
_____

# Exercise 13.5: Why Are Projective Tests Necessary?

**OBJECTIVE**

Describe how professionals incorporate projective tests in clinical and counseling settings.

**BACKGROUND**

Some tests provide a lot of value but are considered controversial because they lack reliability/precision and/or evidence of validity. Projective tests are an example, but they do offer clinicians value in designing treatment plans. Remember, tests are important to help professionals make a decision, and if the test demonstrates both reliability/precision and evidence of validity, the decision made is considered more dependable. In the case of projective tests, the dependability of the test is determined by the standardized administration of the test and is considered supplemental when developing a treatment plan. On their own, projective tests are not a reliable diagnostic tool for mental health professionals. For Exercise 13.5, you will determine why projective tests are necessary by exploring the standardization of two projective tests, and you will describe how professionals use the Exner Comprehensive system.

**YOUR TASK**

1. **Identify differences between the two types of projective tests.** Compare the Rorschach psychodiagnostic technique to the Thematic Apperception Test (TAT). Both are projective tests; however, the application of these tests varies depending on the needs of the clinician. What are those differences, and why is it important? Document your findings in the table below.

|  | **Differences** | **Importance for Clinicians** |
|---|---|---|
| Rorschach | | |
| TAT | | |

2. **Describe three ways professionals incorporate projective test results.** Choose to explore either the Rorschach or TAT for this question. Discuss three ways clinicians use test results to help them develop a treatment plan for their client.

3. **Identify the accuracy of results from projective tests.** Now, identify three ways the results are inaccurate when a professional does not incorporate tests that demonstrate evidence of validity and are reliable/precise.

4. **Describe the Exner Comprehensive System.** Describe how professionals rate clients when they administer the Rorschach based on the Exner Comprehensive System. Refer to the reponses you provided in your review of projective tests for Exercise 13.5. Review Chapter 13 in Miller and Lovler's textbook for additional information to help you with this activity.

## Exercise 13.6: Reflect on Your Learning

**OBJECTIVE**

Describe key takeaways and confusing concepts from Chapter 13.

**BACKGROUND**

In Chapter 13 of the textbook, you were introduced to how tests are used in clinical and counseling settings. You read about the type of work clinical professionals perform. You were introduced to how they use psychological tests to diagnose mental health problems. You were also introduced to how they use psychological tests to monitor client progress and assess treatment outcomes. Last, you learned about the final products of psychological testing and how clinicians and practitioners use them in their practice. For Exercise 13.6, you will reflect on your learning from Chapter 13 of the textbook and identify key takeaways from the chapter.

**YOUR TASK**

1. **Identify your "Aha!" moments from Chapter 13.**
   - Identify 3 to 4 new insights or realizations you had after reading Chapter 13, referred to as "Aha!" moments.
   - Consider things that made you look at a concept, your life, or an issue in a completely different way than you had in the past.
   - Document your insights and realizations below, providing details of your learning.

2. **Identify some muddy moment discussion questions.**
   - Identify 2 to 3 concepts that are still "muddy" for you from the chapter.
   - Consider concepts you still don't understand, concepts you need clarified, and/or questions you want to ask.
   - Develop 1 to 3 questions to initiate a discussion in class to further your understanding of the concepts and get your questions answered.

| | |
|---|---|
| **Insights and Realizations** | 1. _____<br>2. _____<br>3. _____<br>4. _____ |
| **Muddy Moments Discussion Questions** | 1. _____<br>2. _____<br>3. _____ |

# Chapter-Level Projects

## Project 1

**BACKGROUND**

While it is easy to find tests online, all of them may not be "good" tests. Some are psychometrically sound, and some are not. For example, if you search the Internet for "WellMD Test Yourself," you will find links to a number of online tests Stanford Medicine offers as a part of the Stanford Health and Lifestyle Assessment offered as a part of their BeWell@Stanford Employee Incentive Program. In addition to others, there are tests to measure anxiety/posttraumatic stress disorder (PTSD), burnout, depression, and relationship trust. Another example is the self-tests offered on the *Psychology Today* website. If you search the Internet for Psychology Today tests, you will find links to a wide variety of tests, including those that claim to measure depression, self-esteem, and attention span. There are even some apparently fun tests such as the "Adventurousness Test" and the "Exercise Savvy" test.

**YOUR TASK**

1. **Read the information below.**

   There is probably little potential for damage with online tests that are presented in a fun way and do not assess clinical constructs (such as the Adventurousness Test). However, even if psychometrically sound, there are potential problems with tests that measure clinical constructs, such as depression or PTSD. For example, there can be potentially serious effects when people receive distressing feedback without proper interpretation, appropriate follow-up, and guidance. Interestingly, a post by Srini Pillay, MD at *Psychology Today*, warns about self-diagnosis with such online tests (Pillay, 2010).[1] For example, people can easily miss subtleties that a trained individual could easily identify. In addition, there are common cognitive biases that can prevent a person from seeing themselves accurately and disorders such as delusional disorder that can cause people to misrepresent themselves. Pillay stated that one of the greatest dangers of self-diagnosis of psychological problems is that a medical disease may be missed. (If you believe you have a problem or are having symptoms causing distress, you should see a professional for diagnosis and treatment. Self-education can be beneficial, but self-diagnosis can be dangerous.)

---

[1] Pillay, S. (2010). The dangers of self diagnosis. *Psychology Today*. Retrieved from https://www.psychologytoday.com/blog/debunking-myths-the-mind/201005/the-dangers-self-diagnosis

2. **Locate and take two online psychological tests**. Locate and take two psychological tests, one from each of the online sites described in the background above. Take one test that measures a clinical construct and one that does not.

3. **Review your online test results.** After you take the test, review information on how you should interpret the results according to the material presented in Chapter 13 of the Miller and Lovler textbook. Describe your test results according to 10–15 important considerations provided in Chapter 13 of the textbook. Consider how mental health practitioners may use the results from the tests you took to develop a treatment plan, monitor your progress, or assess your treatment outcomes. Explore how the results from the two tests you took qualify as an evidence-based assessment and/or a multimethod assessment.

4. **Create a public statement on the risks and possible benefits of making online tests available to the public.** Review Chapter 13. Create a public statement (an official speech or letter that you could deliver through the press) where you explain (a) the risks and possible benefits of making test available online, and (b) ethical issues that a publisher might face by putting a psychological test online with open access.

## Project 2

### BACKGROUND

Interest in forensic psychology has surged in the last few years. This may be partially attributable to popular television shows that portray criminal profiling, but often these shows provide an erroneous view of forensic psychology (Ward, 2013).[2] In reality, forensic psychology is the application of clinical psychology in legal settings. The most frequent activity for forensic psychologists is the psychological assessment of individuals who are involved with the legal system. After performing assessments, forensic psychologists write reports and may give testimony in court. Thus, the forensic psychologist must have a strong background in both testing and assessment and in the legal system. To become a forensic psychologist, you must obtain a PhD or PsyD from an American Psychological Association–accredited school and have 2 years of supervised professional experience. Licensing varies from state to state, and there is most likely a licensing examination as well.

### YOUR TASK

1. **Read the information below.**
   Because testing is a major component of the job, forensic psychologists must know and use many different types of assessments. Archer, Buffington-Vollum, Stredny, and Handel (2006)[3] looked at what tests are most likely to be used by surveying forensic psychologists. For example, they found that the most commonly used multiscale inventory was the Minnesota Multiphasic Personality Inventory, which was used at least once by 129 of the 131 responding forensic psychologists.

2. **Identify what type of information the legal system needs from psychological tests.** Identify the type of information the legal system requires from psychological tests to be used as evidence. Identify the main concerns of tests used in the legal system and the reason(s) they are needed. Focus on the needs specific to the court and not on whether a test is psychometrically sound.

3. **Evaluate three tests according to material found in Chapter 13.** Locate at least three tests that are used in the legal system and evaluate these tests according to material presented in Chapter 13 of the textbook. Determine the kind of information you need to collect for them to be admissible in court based on the material presented in Chapter 13. You may not have access to the tests, the questions, validation material, etc. Instead, focus on identifying 10–15 concepts presented in Chapter 13 on how professionals provide support for any legal decision requiring someone with professional experience from a clinical or counseling setting.

4. **Create an educational pamphlet.** Create an educational pamphlet that you would present to professionals who work in counseling centers to educate them on the proper use of tests in clinical and counseling settings.

---

[2]Ward, J. T. (September, 2013). What is forensic psychology? *American Psychological Association.* Retrieved from http://www.apa.org/ed/precollege/psn/2013/09/forensic-psychology.aspx

[3]Archer, R. P., Buffington-Vollum, J. K., Stredny, R. V., & Handel, R. W. (2006). A survey of psychological test use patterns among forensic psychologists. *Journal of Personality Assessment, 87*(1), 84–94. doi: 10.1207/s15327752jpa8701_07

# Project 3

**BACKGROUND**

Imagine you were in graduate school serving as the teaching assistant for a psychology instructor. Because some of the students in the course are struggling with the concepts in Chapter 13, the instructor has asked you to spend 1 hour with these students to help increase their understanding of the Chapter 13 material. In addition to meeting with the students, the instructor requested that you create a visual learning aid you can use not only as an instructional tool when meeting with the students, but that students can take with them and use as a study tool for future exams.

**YOUR TASK**

1. **Search the Internet to learn more about visual learning aids.** Conduct a search of the Internet to learn more about the value of visual learning aids and the different types of learning aids. When searching, consider using key terms such as *visual learning aids, graphic organizer, concept maps, cognitive organizer, concept diagrams,* and *story maps.*

2. **Create a visual learning aid of Chapter 13 material.** Review the learning objectives at the beginning of Chapter 13. Create a well-thought-out visual learning aid to enhance student understanding of the important concepts associated with each learning objective. Your visual learning aid should be professional-looking and include visual symbols and words to express Chapter 13 concepts, as well as the connections between them. Creativity is encouraged.

## Practice Questions

### Multiple Choice

1. Which one of the following mental health jobs requires a medical degree?
   a. Clinical psychologist
   b. Counseling psychologist
   c. Social worker
   d. Psychiatrist

2. What is it called when clinical psychologists use treatment methods based on documented research evidence that are effective for solving the problems being addressed?
   a. Psychotherapy
   b. Evidence-based treatment
   c. Behavioral-based therapy
   d. Clinical assessment and treatment

3. What is the most current edition of the *Diagnostic and Statistical Manual of Mental Disorders*?
   a. Second edition
   b. Third edition
   c. Fourth edition
   d. Fifth edition

4. Which one of the following is an example of a semistructured interview?
   a. Millon Clinical Multiaxial Inventory
   b. Minnesota Multiphasic Personality Inventory 2
   c. Yale-Brown Compulsive Scale
   d. The Posttraumatic Stress Disorder Checklist–Civilian

5. Which one of the following typically requires an informant, usually a parent or teacher, to rate a client regarding very specific behaviors?
   a. Rating scales
   b. Semistructured interviews
   c. Symptom checklists
   d. Minnesota Multiphasic Personality Inventory 2

6. What test was originally published in the 1940s and is still widely used in clinical settings?
   a. Personality Assessment Inventory
   b. Millon Clinical Multiaxial Inventory
   c. Minnesota Multiphasic Personality Inventory
   d. Clinical Assessment Tool

7. What type of mental health worker focuses on the relationship between brain functioning and behavior?
   a. Clinical psychologist
   b. Psychiatric nurse
   c. Forensic psychologist
   d. Neuropsychologist

8. Which one of the following is a screening tool clinicians often use for autism?
   a. Ages and Stages Questionnaire
   b. Bayley Scales of Infant and Toddler Development
   c. Millon Clinical Multiaxial Inventory
   d. Autism Spectrum Screener

9. Which one of the following conditions is a progressive illness associated with a gradual loss of memory, thinking, and speaking skills and often has behavioral and emotional symptoms, such as anxiety, agitation, and depression?
   a. Parkinson's Disease
   b. Alzheimer's Disease
   c. Stroke
   d. Dementia

10. What term is used when two mental conditions co-occur at the same time?
    a. Combined diagnoses
    b. Dissimulation
    c. Comorbid
    d. Dual diagnoses

## Short Answer

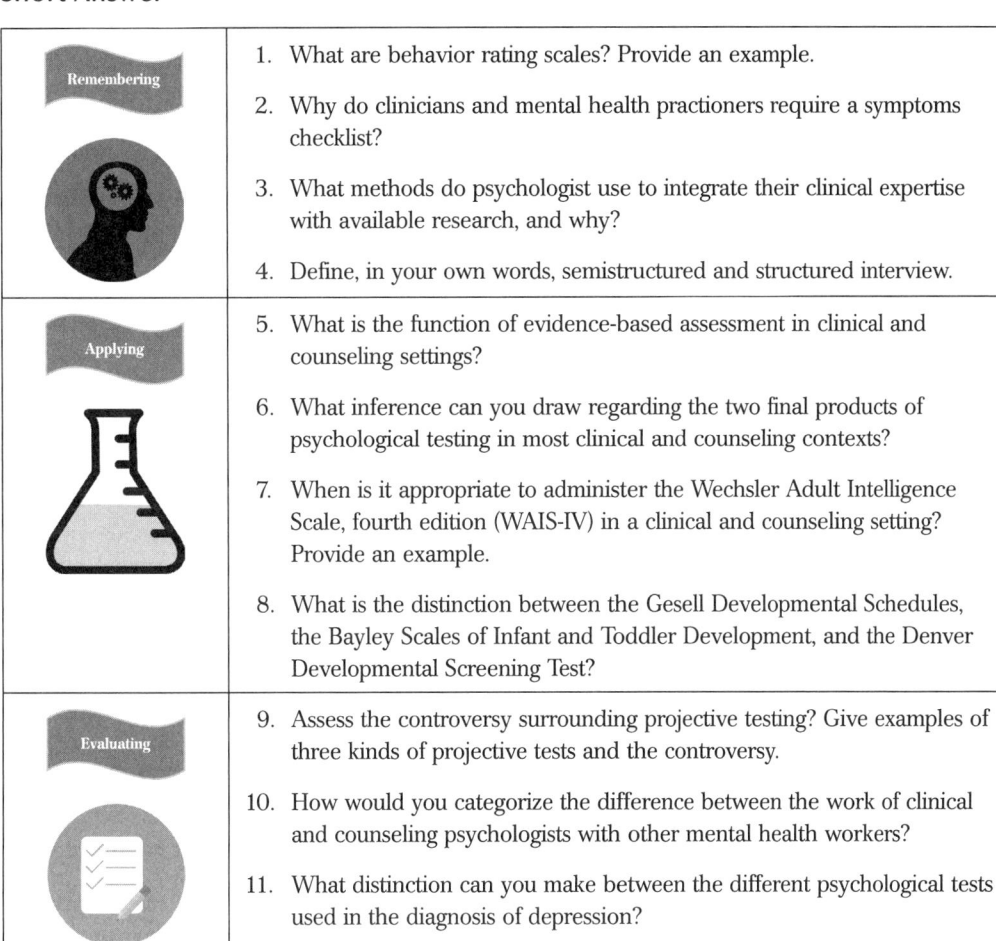

**Remembering**

1. What are behavior rating scales? Provide an example.
2. Why do clinicians and mental health practioners require a symptoms checklist?
3. What methods do psychologist use to integrate their clinical expertise with available research, and why?
4. Define, in your own words, semistructured and structured interview.

**Applying**

5. What is the function of evidence-based assessment in clinical and counseling settings?
6. What inference can you draw regarding the two final products of psychological testing in most clinical and counseling contexts?
7. When is it appropriate to administer the Wechsler Adult Intelligence Scale, fourth edition (WAIS-IV) in a clinical and counseling setting? Provide an example.
8. What is the distinction between the Gesell Developmental Schedules, the Bayley Scales of Infant and Toddler Development, and the Denver Developmental Screening Test?

**Evaluating**

9. Assess the controversy surrounding projective testing? Give examples of three kinds of projective tests and the controversy.
10. How would you categorize the difference between the work of clinical and counseling psychologists with other mental health workers?
11. What distinction can you make between the different psychological tests used in the diagnosis of depression?
12. Justify the DSM-V as an evidence-based treatment method and tool clinical counseling professionals use in their practice.

## Multiple-Choice and Short-Answer Practice Question Answer Key

### Multiple Choice

| Question | Answer | Textbook Page | Explanation |
|---|---|---|---|
| 1. | d | 383 | Psychiatrists are medical doctors who have a medical degree, and who completed a 4-year residency with at least a minimum of 3 years working with patients with mental disorders. The other occupations do not require a medical degree. |
| 2. | b | 383 | Mental health professionals use varied approaches to treatment, depending on their training, preferences, the client populations they serve, and the setting they work in. Most use evidence-based treatment methods—treatment methods with documented research evidence that the method is effective for solving the problems being addressed. However, evidence-based methods are not available for every client in every situation. |
| 3. | d | 383 | The DSM, a handbook published by the American Psychiatric Association and now in its fifth edition, contains descriptions, symptoms, and criteria for diagnosing over 300 mental disorders. The DSM-5 is the authoritative book professionals use to diagnose mental health problems. Medical and mental health professionals and all other parties involved in the diagnosis and treatment of mental health conditions use the DSM to help them diagnose mental disorders. |
| 4. | c | 386 | The Yale–Brown Compulsive Scale is known as the gold standard measure of obsessive compulsive disorder. The clinician is guided to ask the client a range of detailed questions about specific obsessive thoughts and compulsive behaviors, notes the current and past presence of each, and rates the severity of the symptoms based on specific criteria. Clinician ratings rely on the patient's report, observations, and reports of others. |
| 5. | a | 387 | Rating scales typically require an informant, usually a parent or teacher, to rate a client regarding very specific behaviors. In contrast, checklists are most often self-report tests that clients complete themselves. |
| 6. | c | 388 | The MMPI was first published in the 1940s and was revised (MMPI-2) in 1989. The PAI was first published in 1991, and the MCMI-III was first developed in the late 1970s. The Clinical Assessment Tool is a made-up assessment that does not exist. |

Chapter 13 ■ How Are Tests Used in Clinical and Counseling Settings?

| Question | Answer | Textbook Page | Explanation |
|---|---|---|---|
| 7. | d | 393 | Neuropsychologists are specially trained clinicians who focus on the relationship between brain functioning and behavior. They use a very wide range of specialized tests to assess different aspects of brain functioning, such as spatial perception, motor performance, and speed of information processing. |
| 8. | a | 397 | The Ages and Stages Questionnaire is used to screen for autism. The questionnaire assesses development and social-emotional functioning from early infancy through the age of 5 and is half-based on parent responses to a questionnaire. If concerns about an autism spectrum disorder are identified through screening, the child is typically referred for a multidisciplinary comprehensive evaluation. |
| 9. | b | 399 | Individuals with Alzheimer's disease suffer a gradual loss of memory, thinking, and speaking skills, and often have behavioral and emotional symptoms such as anxiety, agitation, and depression. At this point, Alzheimer's disease cannot be definitively diagnosed until after a patient dies through pathology studies of the brain. |
| 10. | c | 399 | Comorbidity is when one or more disorders co-occur with the primary disorder or disease. For example, alcoholism often co-occurs with depression. This can create challenges in psychological testing. |

## Short Answer

| Question | Explanation |
|---|---|
| 1. | Behavior rating scales require input from the client or some informant that can provide detailed information on their behaviors. The CBCL is an example of a behavior rating scale where some informant indicates some level of the behavioral occurrence for a child. Another example is when an informant is required for the diagnosis of attention-deficit/hyperactivity disorder, such as the NICHQ Vanderbilt Assessment Scale completed by a parent, teacher, or individual who spends a significant amount of time with the child. |
| 2. | Clinicians include a checklist, either administered by the practitioner or as a self-report, to help identify key elements to help with the diagnosis, treatment plan, or evaluation of progress. The information on the checklist includes feelings, thoughts, or behaviors that relate to the psychiatric disorder. These types of assessments are not to be used on their own, but in conjunction with other tests. |
| 3. | Psychologists integrate evidence-based methods to help solve client problems and treat the patients presenting symptoms. The clinician will review any material available, provide clients with the opportunity to take an assessment, and include information from other factors to treat patients. Evidence-based treatment methods are grounded on documented research evidence that demonstrates effective treatment for solving problems. |
| 4. | A semistructured interview includes predetermined questions, but the format also allows the assessor to ask some open-ended questions and follow-up questions to clarify the interviewee's responses. A structured interview has a predetermined set of questions in which the assessor assigns numbers or scores to the answers based on their content. |
| 5. | APA advocates that psychologists should use evidence-based practice, which is defined as "the integration of the best available research with clinical expertise in the context of patient characteristics, culture, and preferences" (APA, 2014, para. 2). Evidence-based assessment means that psychologists select tests and assessments based on clinical research findings showing that they accurately diagnose mental health conditions and are useful for planning treatment. The evidence-based approach minimizes theory, personal preferences, case studies, and qualitative evidence and instead focuses on high-quality quantitative studies to guide assessment decisions. |
| 6. | Feedback and a written report are generally the two final parts of the psychological testing process. Providing feedback to the client is an ethical obligation under the APA Standards. In addition, receiving feedback can be a therapeutic experience for the client. The purpose of the feedback session is to provide the client with information about test findings and conclusions and make recommendations for treatment or intervention if it is needed. The second product testing is generally a written report. The report will commonly be sent to the individual who referred the patient for testing and the report also might become part of a legal, educational, or medical record. Because of this, the report needs to be carefully and accurately prepared. It is important to write reports that are easy to read, answer referral questions, include recommendations, and are appropriate for the audience of the report. |

| Question | Explanation |
|---|---|
| 7. | The WAIS-IV is appropriate when the need to assess the intellectual ability of an adult emerges. The test is designed to measure verbal and nonverbal skills in a series of subtests based on four domains of intelligence: verbal comprehension, perceptual reasoning, working memory, and processing speed. Examples will vary, but the example should indicate if a person is able to comprehend the questions on the test, is between the ages of 16–90, the example includes a need to assess cognitive ability, and the scenario/example must be used as a neuropsychological or cognitive neuroscience assessment. |
| 8. | The Gesell Developmental Schedules, Bayley Scales of Infant and Toddler Development, and Denver Developmental Screening Test are tests professionals use to identify developmental or behavior problems in early childhood, but they are used for different situations. The Gesell Developmental Schedules are used to help parents or caregivers observe and record a child's behavior to determine neurological deficits or behavior abnormalities. The Bayley Scales of Infant and Toddler Development is a self-report completed by a child's caregiver designed to assess a child's developmental status and not predict ability levels. The Denver Developmental Screen Test is a norm-referenced test battery designed to identify developmental or behavioral problems. Each test is designed to measure childhood development completed by the clinician or caregiver, and each provides a different perspective on childhood development. |
| 9. | Projective testing is the most controversial type of psychological testing. The controversy surrounds the lack of research evidence to support their reliability and validity and, thus, their use. Proponents of projective testing, however, contend that with proper standardized administration and scoring, the tests can still be useful for treatment planning and developing a broad understanding of the client's functioning and needs. The Rorschach inkblot test is perhaps the most well-known projective technique. This test involves showing 10 inkblots to the client, one at a time, and the client is asked what each one might be. In the more recent versions of the test, the client is also asked to elaborate on what made the inkblot look like the image they described. Although various scoring systems have been developed to improve the reliability and validity of the Rorschach, there still remains much controversy over its use, but there does seem to be consensus that it can be useful for assessing thought disorders, such as schizophrenia. The Thematic Apperception Test (TAT) is another commonly used projective test. The TAT was developed in the 1930s and still uses the same set of stimuli. It consists of 31 black-and-white drawings, each one on a different card. The clinician administers a subset of the 31 cards, asking the client to make up a story for each one and to include specific details in the story. Like the Rorschach, scoring rules have been developed, but reliability and validity remain worrisome. A third type of projective test is the Draw-A-Person test, which is often used by clinicians who work with child victims of emotional and sexual violence. The child is given a blank piece of paper and asked to draw a person. After a person is drawn, the clinician asks the child to draw another person who is of the opposite sex. Again, there have been attempts to develop standardized scoring systems, and there is some evidence that it is possible to distinguish between sexually abused and non-abused children. |

*(Continued)*

(Continued)

| Question | Explanation |
|---|---|
| 10. | Clinical and counseling psychologists are similar to other mental health professionals in that they work with clients and treat illnesses that range from less serious (such as career indecision) to serious mental illness (such as schizophrenia). They also all work in a variety of settings and with a variety of people of all ages. The difference between clinical and counseling psychologists is that clinical psychologists tend to treat more serious problems, and counseling psychologists tend to treat more everyday problems. There is, however, a great deal of overlap. Both clinical and counseling psychologists are usually licensed by the same state public health or education authorities, and they work under the same license and regulations. In addition, clinical and counseling psychologists have either a PhD or a doctorate in psychology (PsyD). In contrast, other mental workers such as social workers, counselors, and psychiatric nurses normally have master's degrees. Psychiatrists, on the other hand, are medical doctors who have a medical degree, and they complete a 4-year residency, with a minimum of 3 years working with patients with mental disorders. |
| 11. | Depression is common and present throughout the world and affects people of all ages. In fact, in 2010, the Centers for Disease Control found that approximately 9% of the population in the United States met the criteria for a depressive disorder. Depression can be diagnosed in several different ways. The Structured Clinical Interview for DSM Disorders along with self-report tests can be used to provide evidence of a depressive disorder, but many psychologists believe it is too time consuming. The Beck Depression Inventory-II (BDI) is especially useful for screening large populations for depression and for monitoring the severity of depression during treatment. The BDI is a well-researched self-report test that is easily scored by the clinician. Tests with many scales such as the Minnesota Multiphasic Inventory-2 and the Personality Assessment Inventory both have depression scales and can be used as well. Assessing can be difficult if the client is non-cooperative or has low cognitive capabilities. In addition, the clinician must be aware of cultural differences and standards that can affect the diagnosis of depression. Finally, comorbid disorders can complicate diagnosis. For example, alcohol and drug dependency can co-occur with depression. |
| 12. | The DSM-V is a valuable tool that offers consistent evaluation tools and criteria for clinical professionals to make a diagnosis and develop an effective treatment program. The DSM-V is routinely updated after careful review of research to update criteria, the evaluation of symptoms, or the reorganization and classification of disorders. Although the DSM-V is readily used by professionals, a diagnosis is best supported with subsequent assessment. The DSM-V is also limited in the expression of intricate details of the symptoms. A person who specializes to work with clients diagnosed with a disorder will know the differences the untrained person would not be able to distinguish. For instance, there is a difference of someone who has a ritual to help keep their life organized compared to the behaviors a person who suffers from the symptoms of obsessive-compulsive disorder will experience. |

# 14 How Are Tests Used in Organizational Settings?

## Overview

In Chapter 14 of the textbook, you were introduced to how psychological tests are used in organizational settings. Hopefully, after reading the chapter you have a clearer understanding of the various types of tests employers use for hiring and evaluating employees, the legal constraints on employment testing, and how organizations use psychological assessment to evaluate employee performance. While Chapter 14 of the textbook included foundational information about how psychological tests are used in organizations, Chapter 14 of the workbook provides you with the opportunity to demonstrate your understanding of material presented in the textbook and apply your learnings by completing some practical and critical-thinking exercises linked to specific learning objectives. Chapter 14 of the workbook will also allow you to complete chapter-level projects to demonstrate your understanding of multiple topics within the chapter. Chapter 14 of the workbook ends with some multiple-choice and short-answer questions you can use to self-assess your understanding of the material.

# Practical and Critical-Thinking Exercises

## Purpose

This section contains five exercises you can complete to demonstrate your understanding and apply your learning (Exercises 14.1–14.5) and one exercise you can complete to reflect on your learning (Exercise 14.6). The exercises, linked to learning objectives, are displayed below.

**Exercise 14.1**
**What Is the Difference Between Traditional and Structured Interviews?**
- **Learning Objective:** Differentiate between traditional and structured interviews.

**Exercise 14.2**
**What Are the Different Types of Performance Tests?**
- **Learning Objective:** Identify different types of performance tests.

**Exercise 14.3**
**What Are the Concerns Surrounding the Use of Personality Inventories for Pre-employment Testing?**
- **Learning Objective:** Describe the controversies surrounding the use of personality inventories for pre-employment testing.

**Exercise 14.4**
**What Are the Three Strategies Organizations Use for Generalizing Evidence of Validity?**
- **Learning Objective:** Describe and differentiate the three strategies for generalizing evidence of validity.

**Exercise 14.5**
**What Are the Different Types of Performance Appraisals?**
- **Learning Objective:** Describe and compare different types of performance appraisals.

**Exercise 14.6**
**Reflect on Your Learning**
- **Learning Objective:** Describe key take aways and confusing concepts from Chapter 14.

# Exercise 14.1: What Is the Difference Between Traditional and Structured Interviews?

**OBJECTIVE**

Differentiate between traditional and structured interviews.

**BACKGROUND**

Many organizations use psychological assessments as the basis for hiring employees, with employee interviews being the most popular method of assessment used. Some organizations may also use other psychological tests to measure performance, skills, abilities, or personality characteristics. Furthermore, drug and integrity tests have also become acceptable methods for screening out candidates during the pre-employment testing process. To increase your understanding of interviews, in Exercise 14.1, you will differentiate between traditional and structured interviews and compare best and worst interview experiences.

**YOUR TASK**

1. **Differentiate between traditional and structured interviews.** Read the "Employment Interview" section of Chapter 14 of your textbook. Define what we mean by traditional interview and structured interview. Identify the similarities and differences between the traditional and structured interview. Document your answers in the space provided below.

|  | Definition | Similarities | Differences |
|---|---|---|---|
| **Traditional Interview** |  |  |  |
| **Structured Interview** |  |  |  |

2. **Describe your BEST and WORST interview experiences.** Think about the best employment or other interview experience you had in the past as well as the worst. If you haven't had personal experiences with employment interviews, think of what you imagine the best and worst experience would be like, or discuss with others who have had employment interview experiences what their experience was like. Provide a brief description for each experience below.

**BEST interview experience**

_____
_____
_____
_____
_____

**WORST interview experience**

_____
_____
_____
_____
_____

3. **Answer the questions below.**

   What specifically made the worst interview experience bad?

   _____
   _____
   _____
   _____
   _____

   What specifically made the best interview experience good?

   _____
   _____
   _____
   _____

   If you could provide feedback to the interviewer who conducted your worst interview experience to make it better, what would you say?

   _____
   _____
   _____
   _____
   _____

# Exercise 14.2: What Are the Different Types of Performance Tests?

**OBJECTIVE**

Identify different types of performance tests.

**BACKGROUND**

Performance tests include a broad range of assessments that require a test taker to perform one or more job tasks. These performance tests can range from a large-scale simulation of the job, referred to as assessment centers, to smaller-scale assessments such as work samples. Psychologists often categorize these performance tests into one of two categories; high-fidelity or low-fidelity tests. To increase your understanding of different types of performance tests, in Exercise 14.2, you will identify the type of performance tests being used for given scenarios and then create your own scenarios.

**YOUR TASK**

1. **Identify the type of performance test used.** Review each of the scenarios below. Indicate the type of performance test described (assessment center, work sample, situational judgment test, or behavioral interview) and whether the test is a high- or low-fidelity test. Document your answer in the table below.

| Scenario | Type of Performance Test | High or Low Fidelity Test |
|---|---|---|
| A job candidate is asked to describe a time when he had to give a presentation to a group that was not receptive to the presentation's content or message. | | |
| A job candidate attends an all-day session where she must participate in a role-play exercise, give a presentation, take a personality test, and answer interview questions. | | |
| A job candidate sits in front of a computer and watches multiple video-based scenarios of a manager interacting with an employee. The candidate is asked to indicate how he would respond, from four different options, in each situation. | | |
| A job candidate for a truck-driving job is asked to back a truck up to a loading dock. | | |

2. **Create scenarios for each type of performance assessment.** Create your own unique examples of a testing scenario for each of the performance assessments below. Provide enough detail to demonstrate your understanding of each type of assessment. Document your answers in the space provided below.

| Performance Test | Testing Scenario 1 | Testing Scenario 2 |
|---|---|---|
| Assessment center | | |
| Work sample | | |
| Situational judgment test | | |
| Behavioral interview | | |

3. **Answer the following questions.**

   Why is it important to be able to distinguish between different types of performance tests used by organizations?

   Do you believe that there is any one "best" method of performance testing? Why or why not?

# Exercise 14.3: What Are the Concerns Surrounding the Use of Personality Inventories for Pre-employment Testing?

**OBJECTIVE**

Describe the controversies surrounding the use of personality inventories for pre-employment testing.

**BACKGROUND**

Organizations sometimes use personality inventories as part of their pre-employment testing process. Personality inventories measure the personality traits of individuals that may predispose people to behave in certain ways. Examples of these traits that are commonly measured are conscientiousness, extraversion, and agreeableness. However, use of personality inventories as part of the pre-employment testing process has been and continues to be controversial. To increase your understanding of the controversies surrounding use of personality inventories, in Exercise 14.3, you will conduct research to uncover the controversies and then participate in a debate involving use of personality inventories during the hiring process.

**YOUR TASK**

1. **Conduct research to understand existing controversies.** Review the "Personality Inventories" section of Chapter 14 of your textbook, including For Your Information Box 14.2, to learn more personality inventories and the five-factor theory of personality. Then, conduct an Internet research to find three credible resources where the authors are in favor of using personality inventories as part of the pre-employment process and three credible resources where the authors are not in favor of using personality inventories as part of the pre-employment process. Document your sources and each author's argument/rationale in the table below.

|  | Source | Argument/Rationale |
|---|---|---|
| **IN FAVOR of using personality inventories** | 1. |  |
|  | 2. |  |
|  | 3. |  |
| **NOT IN FAVOR of using personality inventories** | 1. |  |
|  | 2. |  |
|  | 3. |  |

2. **Partner with a classmate and choose a side to debate.** Partner with a classmate and discuss your findings from the task above. Assign each person a side to debate (either for or against use of personality inventories during the pre-employment process). Work cooperatively to create an organized argument of ideas where you discuss the use of personality inventories as part of the pre-employment testing process from both perspectives (for and against).

3. **Participate in a debate.** As directed by your instructor, participate in a mock-debate regarding the use of personality inventories as part of pre-employment selection. Be sure to include specifics that either support or argue the use of personality inventories as part of the pre-employment testing process. Be prepared to defend your stance.

# Exercise 14.4: What Are the Three Strategies Organizations Use for Generalizing Evidence of Validity?

**OBJECTIVE**

Describe and differentiate the three strategies for generalizing evidence of validity.

**BACKGROUND**

According to the *Uniform Guidelines* and federal case law, organizations should use tests for which there is evidence of validity for the scores. Therefore, organizations that wish to use a pre-employment test for selecting employees often must demonstrate the test is valid for use in that organization. One of the ways that organizations can do so is by using one of three commonly used strategies for generalizing existing validity evidence: meta-analysis, synthetic validity, and transportability. To increase your understanding of the strategies for generalizing evidence of validity, in Exercise 14.4, you will describe the three different strategies, provide examples when each may be used, and compare them in a Venn diagram.

**YOUR TASK**

1. **Define generalizing validity and the strategies used.** Review the "Generalizing Validity Evidence" section of Chapter 14 in your textbook. In your own words, define what we mean by generalizing evidence of validity and describe the three strategies used. Document your definition and descriptions in the table below.

|  | **Definition** |
| --- | --- |
| **Generalizing evidence of validity** |  |
| **Meta-analysis** |  |
| **Synthetic validity** |  |
| **Transportability** |  |

2. **Read each scenario and select the best strategy.** Below you will find several scenarios that could require the use of one of the three validity generalization strategies discussed in Chapter 14. Read each scenario and decide which strategy would be most appropriate to utilize. Then discuss why you think the strategy you have chosen would be appropriate to use. Where necessary, indicate if there is any other information that was not mentioned in the scenarios that you might have to investigate before your chosen strategy was implemented.

### Scenario 1

A researcher is interested in using a test designed to measure the tendency people have toward being politically correct. She is interested in discovering the effect that political correctness has on responses to public opinion polls. The researcher is using only college students for the study and is concerned that the tendency toward political correctness might be influenced by a person's age. After conducting a literature review, she discovers that many studies have looked at this relationship, but the results are often contradictory. Some studies suggest that age is a strong predictor of political correctness, some suggest that it is a weak predictor, while still others find that there is no relationship between age and political correctness. The researcher is concerned that if age is really a predictor of political correctness, her study on the effect that political correctness has on responses to public opinion polls won't generalize to populations other than college students, so she needs to determine what the true relationship is between age and political correctness.

### Scenario 2

A department manager wants to use a test battery to select employees for a very small, high-potential development program. The manager has identified four characteristics that are important for the people selected to possess for this special program: collaboration, resilience, attention to detail, and interpersonal sensitivity. The manager knows that in other parts of the organization, there are tests that are being used that measure some of these skills, but no test that measures all the skills. The manager is concerned that because his program is so small, there is no way that he will be able to conduct any type of local validity study, but he wants to be sure that he has evidence of validity for any tests that he decides to use for selection into the program.

### Scenario 3

A human resource (HR) professional has been asked to identify a selection tool that can be used to select sales managers for the company's retail consumer electronics division. This is a new business for the company that is just being started and is very small. In the past, the company has faced legal challenges due to apparent gender bias in favor of men being selected for management roles, so the HR manager is very concerned that any test he selects can demonstrate evidence of validity for success as a manger. He also knows that due to an immediate need to fill the openings, he will not have the time necessary to conduct a validation study. However, he also knows that the company has a very large commercial paint division that has been using selection tests for their business-to-business sales managers for years, which have been validated for that position.

| Strategy | Scenario # | Rationale for Use | Additional Considerations |
|---|---|---|---|
| Meta-analysis | | | |
| Synthetic validity | | | |
| Transportability | | | |

## Exercise 14.5: What Are the Different Types of Performance Appraisals?

**OBJECTIVE**

Describe and compare different types of performance appraisals.

**BACKGROUND**

Performance appraisals are formal evaluations organizations use to evaluate employee performance. Typically, an employee's manager completes the performance appraisal, which might involve assigning numerical values to quantitatively measure an employee's performance. There are various psychometric methods organizations use to measure employee performance, and each is subject to rating errors. In Exercise 14.5, you will compare different performance appraisal methods, identify the pros and cons of different appraisal methods, review scenarios to identify the type of rating error, and search for additional types of rating errors.

**YOUR TASK**

1.  **Compare the psychometric methods that underlie the performance appraisal process.** Review the "Performance Appraisals" section of Chapter 14 of your textbook. Describe the different ranking and rating methods and provide an example of each. Document your descriptions and examples in the table below.

| | | Description | Example |
|---|---|---|---|
| **Ranking Methods** | Forced ranking | | |
| | Forced distribution | | |
| **Rating Methods** | Behaviorally anchored rating scale | | |
| | Behavioral checklist | | |

2. **Research four performance appraisal systems and identify pros and cons.** Research each of the four performance appraisal systems on the Internet. Try to identify at least three pros and three cons of each system. Discuss which of the four systems you would prefer to be evaluated on if you were an employee. Document your answers in the table below.

|  |  | Pros | Cons |
|---|---|---|---|
| **Ranking Methods** | **Forced ranking** |  |  |
|  | **Forced distribution** |  |  |
| **Rating Methods** | **Behaviorally anchored rating scale** |  |  |
|  | **Behavioral checklist** |  |  |
| **Discuss Your Preference** | | | |

3. **Identify the type of rating error.** Read each of the job performance scenarios below. Indicate the rating error in each scenario (leniency, severity, central tendency, or halo effect). Document your answers in the table below.

| Scenario | Type of Error |
|---|---|
| A supervisor notices that an employee is very personable and, as a result, rates him high on all performance dimensions. | |
| A supervisor wants to avoid difficult performance conversations with employees, so he rates them higher than they deserve. | |
| A supervisor does not differentiate among employees, rating them all as average so that they will receive the same rewards based on their evaluations. | |
| A new supervisor wants to be viewed as tough by her employees, so she gives everyone low ratings. | |
| A supervisor is extremely impressed with an employee's recent sales performance, so during the performance appraisal process, he rates the employee high on all performance dimensions. | |
| When rating an employee's performance on six different skills, a supervisor rates the individual a "3" on all skills, using the scale below:<br>1 = Very Good, 2 = Good, 3 = Acceptable, 4 = Poor, 5 = Very Poor | |

4. **Research and identify less common rater errors.** While the textbook described the four most common rater errors, researchers have identified several other less common errors that raters can make. Search the Internet to identify four other errors that raters can make, define them, and provide an example of what each one would look like in practice using the table below.

| Type of Error | Definition of the Error | Example of the Error |
|---|---|---|
| | | |
| | | |
| | | |
| | | |

# Exercise 14.6: Reflect on Your Learning

**OBJECTIVE**

Describe key takeaways and confusing concepts from Chapter 14.

**BACKGROUND**

In Chapter 14 of the textbook, you were introduced to how psychological tests are used in the organizational setting. You read about what types of psychological tests are routinely used for pre-employment testing. You were introduced to two performance tests commonly used by organizations. You were also introduced to the five-factor model of personality and integrity tests. In addition, you read about three ways in which validity evidence can be generalized to new situations. Last, you learned about performance appraisal instruments and types of rating scales and rating errors. For Exercise 14.6, you will reflect on your learning from Chapter 14 of the textbook and identify key takeaways from the chapter.

**YOUR TASK**

1. **Identify your "Aha!" moments from Chapter 14.**
   - Identify 3 to 4 new insights or realizations you had after reading Chapter 14, referred to as "Aha!" moments.
   - Consider things that made you look at a concept, your life, or an issue in a completely different way than you had in the past.
   - Document your insights and realizations below, providing details of your learning.

2. **Identify some muddy moment discussion questions.**
   - Identify 2 to 3 concepts that are still "muddy" for you from the chapter.
   - Consider concepts you still don't understand, concepts you need clarified, and/or questions you want to ask.
   - Develop 1 to 3 questions to initiate a discussion in class to further your understanding of the concepts and get your questions answered.

| | |
|---|---|
| **Insights and Realizations** | 1. _____ <br> 2. _____ <br> 3. _____ <br> 4. _____ |
| **Muddy Moments Discussion Questions** | 1. _____ <br> 2. _____ <br> 3. _____ |

# Chapter-Level Projects

## Project 1

**BACKGROUND**

Organizations use a variety of psychological assessments during the pre-employment screening process. For example, they might use employment interviews, performance tests, and even integrity tests. While the assessments they use might differ, all organizations are subject to legal constraints when it comes to pre-employment testing. All organizations should abide by guidelines and case law to ensure all pre-employment assessments are job related and do not discriminate against minorities and women.

**YOUR TASK**

1. **With a partner, select a job description.** Identify a partner and collaboratively conduct an Internet search and find a job description for an entry-level position, such as a barista at Starbucks or a brand representative at Hollister.

2. **Identify potential pre-employment assessments.** Based on the job description you locate, work together to identify potential pre-employment assessments you might use as part of the pre-employment hiring process for the position.

3. **Develop interview questions.** Based on the job description you locate, work together to develop mock-interview questions.

4. **Develop an evaluation checklist.** Based on learnings from Chapter 14, create a list of criteria you could use to evaluate the appropriateness of the assessments being used by an organization as part of the pre-employment testing process for a specific job. Include criteria to evaluate the appropriateness of interview questions.

5. **Evaluate each team's work.** As directed by your instructor, share your proposed pre-employment assessments and mock-interview questions with the class. Evaluate each using each team's evaluation checklist.

## Project 2

**BACKGROUND**

As a part of their performance management process, most organizations have a performance appraisal process that involves periodically evaluating employee performance against pre-determined criteria. Typically, an individual's direct manager conducts the performance appraisal. For example, an organization's process might involve a manager and employee meeting every quarter, and then once at the end of the year, to complete the performance appraisal.

**YOUR TASK**

1. **Identify two individuals who conduct performance appraisals.** Locate two individuals, from different organizations, who are responsible for completing employee performance appraisals (i.e., a supervisor, a manager, an HR professional) and who agree to participate in an interview with you. Schedule a time for each interview. In advance of the interview, obtain a copy of the organization's performance appraisal process and forms.

2. **Develop a list of questions.** Review the "Performance Appraisal" section of Chapter 14 of the textbook, as well as the process and forms provided by your two interviewees. Develop a list of 5–10 insightful questions you will ask each individual during the interview process. Be sure the questions elicit information about their performance evaluation process, related to the material presented in your textbook and your review of their process and forms.

3. **Evaluate the process and forms.** Based on the responses you receive during your interviews and what you learned about performance appraisals, evaluate the process and forms received from your two interviewees. Consider what you thought was good or what could be improved and why.

4. **Record a video or podcast.** Record yourself in a 5- to 10-minute video or podcast where you discuss the current process and forms used by your two interviewees, what you thought was good or what could be improved, linking your insights to best practices outlined in Chapter 14 of your textbook.

## Project 3

### BACKGROUND

Imagine you were in graduate school serving as the teaching assistant for a psychology instructor. Because some of the students in the course are struggling with the concepts in Chapter 14, the instructor has asked you to spend 1 hour with these students to help increase their understanding of the Chapter 14 material. In addition to meeting with the students, the instructor requested that you create a visual learning aid you can use not only as an instructional tool when meeting with the students, but that students can take with them and use as a study tool for future exams.

### YOUR TASK

1. **Search the Internet to learn more about visual learning aids.** Conduct a search of the Internet to learn more about the value of visual learning aids and the different types of learning aids. When searching, consider using key terms such as *visual learning aids, graphic organizer, concept maps, cognitive organizer, concept diagrams,* and *story maps.*

2. **Create a visual learning aid of Chapter 14 material.** Create a well-thought-out visual learning aid to enhance student understanding of subject matter included in Chapter 14. Your visual learning aid should be professional-looking and include visual symbols and words to express Chapter 14 concepts, as well as the connections between them. Creativity is encouraged.

## Practice Questions

### Multiple Choice

1. Which one of the following drew attention to issues of test validity and fairness during the latter half of the 20th century in the United States?
   a. The Psychological Corporation
   b. U.S. Army Alpha and Beta tests
   c. The civil rights movement
   d. Use of assessment centers during World War II

2. What is the MOST popular method for assessing job candidates?
   a. Assessment center
   b. Traditional employment interview
   c. Structured employment interview
   d. Performance appraisal

3. Which one of the following is the LEAST accurate method of predicting job performance?
   a. Traditional employment interview
   b. Structured interview
   c. Assessment center
   d. Work sample

4. The best prediction of job performance is obtained when interviews focus on an applicant's
   a. attitudes.
   b. opinions.
   c. beliefs.
   d. behaviors.

5. When designing a structured interview, developers use job analysis to establish evidence of validity based on
   a. relationships with other variables.
   b. reliability.
   c. constructs.
   d. content.

6. Which one of the following is an example of a high-fidelity test?
   a. Paper-and-pencil attitude survey
   b. Flight simulator
   c. Performance appraisal
   d. Traditional interview

7. Hunter and Hunter's (1984) meta-analysis suggests that personality tests are among the poorest predictors of job performance. Which one of the following has caused psychologists to look more favorably on personality tests?
   a. The traditional interview
   b. Integrity testing
   c. The five-factor model of personality
   d. Job analysis

8. The U.S. Congress has prohibited using which pre-employment test in most job settings?
   a. The polygraph
   b. Traditional interviews
   c. Assessment centers
   d. Personality tests

9. Which one of the following is most likely to make the "Othello error"—taking signs of distress as proof of unfaithfulness or dishonesty?
   a. Developers of integrity tests
   b. Employment interviewers
   c. Polygraph users
   d. Assessment center raters

10. Which one of the following is a concern of integrity test critics?
    a. Test publishers conducted many of the available studies.
    b. Integrity is too broad a concept to be useful in test development.
    c. Assessment centers are a better way of establishing honesty.
    d. The tests are based on the five-factor model of personality.

11. When Lilienfeld (1993) administered integrity tests to monks and nuns, college students, and incarcerated criminals, what did the test results show?

    a. Incarcerated criminals are the most dishonest.
    b. College students are the most dishonest.
    c. Monks and nuns are the most dishonest.
    d. All groups were equally dishonest.

12. Which one of the following is true about The Uniform Guidelines on Employee Selection Procedures the U.S. federal government published in 1978?

    a. They prohibit using polygraph tests for employment testing.
    b. They prohibit using integrity tests during the selection process.
    c. They consist of laws passed by Congress, which organizations must abide by.
    d. They include suggested procedures to follow when testing job candidates.

13. At the BKH Construction Company, supervisors are required to rank employees so that a certain number fall into each performance category. What is this method of performance appraisal known as?

    a. Forced distribution
    b. Forced choice
    c. Graphic rating
    d. 360° feedback

14. Naomi supervises several employees. When she rates their performance, however, she often lets her judgment of their conscientiousness influence her ratings of their decision-making and leadership ability. Which one of the following rating errors is Naomi making?

    a. Leniency error
    b. Severity error
    c. Halo effect
    d. Central tendency error

15. What test shows high validity for job performance criteria and even higher validity for predicting training criteria?

    a. Personality tests
    b. Cognitive tests
    c. Integrity tests
    d. Performance tests

16. In 2012, Van Iddekinge, Roth, Raymark, and Odle-Dusseau conducted a meta-analysis investigating the relationship between integrity tests and external criteria. What was their finding about the size of the validity coefficients?

    a. They depended on the statistical method used for the meta-analysis.
    b. They depended on the criterion measure used.
    c. They were much larger than those found in previous research.
    d. They were much smaller than those found in previous research.

17. What type of relationship has been found between conscientiousness and job performance by recent researchers using item response theory?

    a. Positive linear
    b. Negative linear
    c. Curvilinear
    d. No relationship

18. What term is used to describe a situation where test takers do not reply in an honest fashion to personality tests?

    a. Misrepresentation
    b. Test cheating
    c. Dishonesty
    d. Faking

## Short Answer

| | |
|---|---|
| **Remembering** | 1. List the major events in the history of pre-employment testing described in your textbook.<br><br>2. What are the differences between the traditional interview and the structured interview? Which do organizations use most often?<br><br>3. Describe how organizations evaluate employee performance.<br><br>4. What is the difference between a performance appraisal process that involves ranking employees and a process that involves rating employees? |
| **Applying** | 5. How might a small employer demonstrate evidence of validity for a test to select supervisors for his company that has only been validated for use in a different company?<br><br>6. What rating errors might individuals make when judging employee performance? What can be done to avoid the errors?<br><br>7. Compare and contrast Hogan Personality Inventory (HPI) and the Wonderlic Basic Skills Test (WBST). What do the tests have in common? What are their differences?<br><br>8. What approach would you use to evaluate employee performance? Why? |
| **Evaluating** | 9. Compare high- and low-fidelity tests. Provide three examples of each.<br><br>10. Are personality tests valid predictors of job performance? What is the role of the five-factor model in personality tests?<br><br>11. Discuss various ways to assess employee honesty. What does the research reveal about the utility of employee honesty tests?<br><br>12. How are the test validity generalization strategies of meta-analysis, synthetic validity, and transportability similar and different? |

# Multiple-Choice and Short-Answer Practice Question Answer Key

## Multiple Choice

| Question | Answer | Textbook Page | Explanation |
|---|---|---|---|
| 1. | c | 425 | The latter half of the 20th century saw a great increase in the use of psychological tests in the workplace. The civil rights movement drew attention to issues and fairness, reliability, and validity in the society in general and in the workplace. When Congress passed Title VII of the Civil Rights Act in 1964, it further stimulated governmental involvement in testing and led to the development of the Uniform Guidelines on Employee Selection Procedures (1978), which is an extremely important document for testing in the workplace. |
| 2. | b | 406 | Although the other methods listed may demonstrate higher validity, the most used method for assessing job candidates is the traditional employment interview, which is unstructured. |
| 3. | a | 406 | The traditional employment interview is the least accurate method of the answer options. For example, one meta-analysis discussed in the textbook found that it had a validity coefficient of .20. In comparison, the structured interview was found to have a validity coefficient of .57. Traditional unstructured interviews can still serve a useful purpose, however. For example, they can provide interviewees an opportunity to ask questions and develop a realistic view of the job. |
| 4. | d | 407 | Behavioral questions tend to have high evidence of validity based on content by drawing on real-life work situations that applicants are likely to face on the job. Also, they focus on behaviors rather than more subjective attributes such as attitudes and personality traits that can easily be faked and are harder to accurately assess. |
| 5. | d | 413 | Job analysis is a technique that identifies tasks, knowledge, skill, ability, and other characteristics (KSA&Os) that are required to successfully perform a job. From this information, interview questions that are related to the job can be developed. By first identifying the KSA&Os and then developing related interview questions, content-related evidence of validity can be established. |

*(Continued)*

(Continued)

| Question | Answer | Textbook Page | Explanation |
|---|---|---|---|
| 6. | b | 411 | High-fidelity tests replicate job settings as realistically as possible. Often test takers use the same equipment that is used on the job and complete actual job tasks. However, this is not always safe or practical. For instance, it would be unwise to evaluate a person to determine if they could fly a plane by putting them in an actual plane. Of course, the test would be highly valid, but it could lead to disastrous results for unqualified pilots. In such a case, a flight simulator would be a much better choice. |
| 7. | c | 416 | While there is still controversy over the use of personality tests for personnel selection, recent meta-analyses using the five-factor model of personality have shown that some factors can be good predictors of job performance. For example, conscientiousness has consistently been found to be a valid predictor of job performance for all jobs studied. |
| 8. | a | 423 | The Employee Polygraph Protection Act of 1988 outlawed the use of the polygraph in employment testing for most private organizations. However, the law has an exemption for security firms (armored car, alarm, and guard) and government agencies allowing those organizations to continue to use the polygraph in employment settings. |
| 9. | c | 422 | Lilienfeld (1993) concluded that there was no scientific evidence that a specific "lie response" exists. Instead physiological responses may occur for a variety of reasons, and thus polygraph users are making the "Othello error" or taking signs of distress as proof of dishonesty. |
| 10. | a | 423 | Ones, Viswesvaran, and Schmidt in 1993 published a meta-analysis of validation studies of integrity tests and found that the tests were valid across a variety of situations for thefts and counterproductive behaviors. However, others have criticized this meta-analysis because the studies they used were conducted by the test publishers and independent researchers. Such studies are likely to contain methodological flaws. |
| 11. | c | 423 | Lilienfeld's (1993) study showed that a well-known honesty test actually found that monks and nuns were more dishonest than college students and incarcerated criminals. |

| Question | Answer | Textbook Page | Explanation |
|---|---|---|---|
| 12. | d | 425 | The Uniform Guidelines on Employee Selection Procedures was published by several government agencies and not passed by Congress, so it is not law. However, the document has been given great deference by the courts as outlining the proper procedures that should be used when using tests in an employment setting. Interestingly, according to the Guidelines, nearly all tools used to make employment decisions could be considered a test. As a result, all such tools need to adhere to the requirements set forth in the Guidelines. |
| 13. | a | 430 | A forced distribution requires that a certain number of employees fall into each performance category, such as "poor," "average," and "outstanding." Many management consultants, however, advise against using forced distributions because the process may force supervisors to place an employee into a category that does not accurately describe his or her performance. |
| 14. | c | 434 | The halo effect is a common and well-known rating error. It occurs when raters allow one performance dimension to influence the judgments on other dimensions. In contrast, leniency errors result when raters give all employees better ratings than they deserve, severity errors result when raters give all employees worse ratings than they deserve, and central tendency errors result when raters use only the middle of the rating scale and ignore the highest and lowest scale categories. |
| 15. | b | 425 | A meta-analysis performed by Hunter and Hunter (1984) found that cognitive tests were among the most valid predictors of job performance. However, they are the most accurate for "thinking" jobs like manager and salesperson. In addition, while they are excellent predictors of job performance, they are even better predictors of training success. |
| 16. | b | 423 | Van Iddekinge and his colleagues (2012) found that some of the validity coefficients were below .2, and many approached .1, even when corrected for unreliability in the criterion. However, the authors also found higher validity coefficients when the tests were used to predict self-reported counterproductive work behavior (.26 uncorrected, and .32 corrected for unreliability). Like previous researchers, they found that the validity coefficients from studies conducted by the test publishers were higher (.27) than the coefficients from studies that were not conducted by the test publishers (.12). |

*(Continued)*

(Continued)

| Question | Answer | Textbook Page | Explanation |
|---|---|---|---|
| 17. | c | 421 | Carter, Dalal, Boyce, O'Connell, Kung, & Delgado (2014) investigated the nature of the relationship between conscientiousness and job performance. Using item response theory (IRT), they found a curvilinear relationship, meaning that job performance improved as conscientiousness scores increased, but only to a certain point. Once that point was reached, job performance began to decrease. |
| 18. | d | 418 | When a test taker does not respond to a test in an honest fashion, it is generically referred to as "faking." Usually, but not always, faking occurs when a person tries to respond to test questions in a way that he or she believes will present himself or herself in the most positive fashion. Presenting oneself in the most positive fashion is also called socially desirable responding (Edwards, 1957), and when this behavior is intentional, it is called impression management (Paulhaus, 1984). |

## Short Answer

| Question | Explanation |
|---|---|
| 1. | The textbook provides a short history of employment testing. It begins in 1915 when Walter Dill Scott published *The Scientific Selection of Salesmen*, which proposes that employers should use group tests for personnel selection. Scott was highly influential in the academic and military communities, but because of infighting among psychologists, he was not involved in the development of the U.S. Army's Alpha and Beta tests during World War I. The use of these tests set off concerns about the fairness of intelligence testing and the appropriate use of test scores that continues today. Following World War I, research continued on employment testing. Psychologists began studying methods for measuring job performance and placing workers in jobs based on their skills and qualifications. For example, the Strong–Campbell Interest Inventory, which is still in use today, originated from this work. Also during this time, two consulting firms that specialized in using tests in organizations were formed. One was founded by Walter Dill Scott, and the other, named the Psychological Corporation (now called Harcourt Assessment), was organized by J. McKeen Cattell. Psychologists and psychological testing became important again during World War II. Psychologist Walter Bingham oversaw the development of the Army General Classification Test used to place U.S. Army recruits. Also, the Office of Strategic Services (the forerunner to the Central Intelligence Agency) began to use assessment centers in their selection of spies and undercover agents. During the latter half of the 20th century, the use of tests by organizations greatly expanded. The civil rights movement and the passage of Title VII of the Civil Rights Act of 1964 set important standards for fair employment practices. Later, the federal government developed the Uniform Guidelines on Employee Selection Procedures (1978) to help ensure consistency and fairness in employment decisions. Today pre-employment testing is commonly used by both large and small organizations. Companies employ many different types of psychological tests to meet their business needs. |
| 2. | The employment interview is the most popular type of selection test used by organizations. There are two basic types of interviews: the traditional interview and the structured interview. Organizations tend to use the traditional interview more than structured interview even though research shows that structured interviews have greater reliability/precision and validity. Knowledge of the shortcomings of the traditional interview dates back to the initial development of employment testing when Scott in 1915 recognized and reported low agreement among hiring managers using traditional unstructured interviews. In contrast, structured interviews are standardized to ensure consistency. In a fully structured interview, all candidates are asked the same questions in the same order. The interviewer usually rates the candidates' answers using an anchored rating scale. Interviewers undergo training on question delivery, note taking, and rating. This training standardizes the candidates' experience during the interview and the process used to evaluate them. The result of the standardization is increased interrater reliability, internal consistency, and validity. |

*(Continued)*

(Continued)

| Question | Explanation |
|---|---|
| 3. | Because performance appraisals are used to make employment decisions, they are considered a test under the Uniform Guidelines on Employee Selection Procedures (1978). There are two basic approaches that organizations use when appraising employees. The first is ranking. Forced ranking is a method that requires raters place employees in the order of their performance, such as best employee, second best, and so on. A forced distribution is another ranking method. Here raters are required to place a specific number or percentage of employees into each performance category, such as "poor," "average," and "outstanding." Often, the percentage of employees in each category is set to approximate a normal distribution. Ranking approaches do have drawbacks. For example, consider the case when an organization has a large number of poor performers. With a forced ranking approach, there will still be a best employee even though he or she may not be performing adequately. The second approach is rating. This is the traditional approach where supervisors rate employees using various scales, such as behavioral anchored rating scales (BARS), graphical rating scales, and behavioral checklists. Using a rating approach, employees are evaluated using the written anchors provided on the rating scale and not by directly comparing one employee to another. |
| 4. | While ranking and rating may seem similar, they are in fact quite different. Organizations who use a forced ranking or forced distribution appraisal process require supervisors to either list their direct reports from "best" to "worst" employee or place a set number of staff into a performance category such as "poor," "below average," "average," "above average," or "outstanding." The ranking system is considered to be controversial and may lead to a supervisor placing an employee into a performance category that does not accurately reflect their performance.<br><br>Rating an employee based on a specified job dimension or job behaviors is a more commonly used performance assessment tool. An employee's behaviors are measured on a Likert-type scale and often are averaged to provide a single score. |
| 5. | It is often too time consuming and costly for a small employer to develop and validate a selection test. Also a small employer will not likely be able to obtain a large enough sample to be confident of any study results. Therefore, the company may try to generalize validity evidence found in a different setting to its own situation. There are three approaches that are endorsed by the Society for Industrial and Organizational Psychology. They are meta-analysis, synthetic validity, and transportability. Meta-analysis is a statistical technique that assembles and analyzes the results of many studies into a single result. Research has shown that much of the variation in validity coefficients obtained in different settings is the result of sampling error and statistical artifacts. Combining the results of multiple studies in a single larger analysis can remove these situational effects and provide the researcher with a better idea of the true relationship between the predictor and the criteria. Once this is done, if a relationship exists, then this provides evidence to "generalize" the relationship to other situations. The second approach, synthetic validity, also known as job component validity, is based on the idea that jobs are composed of various components. A validity coefficient can be "synthesized" by combining the known validities of a variety of different tests that have been validated on similar jobs so long as each test measures a necessary "component" of the job in question. This enables the employer to estimate the validity of tests for predicting performance in the employer's setting without having to conduct a new validity study. The third, and final, approach is transportability, which attempts to show that a valid test in one situation can be transported to another similar situation. For example, if a test has been shown to be a valid predictor of sales performance for car sales, clothing sales, insurance sales, and furniture sales, then it is likely to also be a valid predictor for other sales representative jobs such as flower sales or pharmaceutical sales as long as the sales skills required in each of the jobs are substantially the same. |

| Question | Explanation |
|---|---|
| 6. | Rating employees is a challenging task. Because it is a subjective process, there are a number of common errors that raters routinely make. Leniency errors result when raters give all employees better ratings than they deserve, and severity errors result when raters give all employees worse ratings than they deserve. Central tendency is another common error. These errors result when raters use only the middle of the rating scale and ignore the highest and lowest scale categories. A halo effect occurs when raters let their judgment on one dimension influence judgments on other dimensions. For example, if an employee is a good communicator, but does poorly on all other parts of the job, yet still receives excellent scores across the board, this could be a halo error. Organizations can provide rater training to try to improve the accuracy of the raters. However, research shows that rater training only has limited short-term effects. |
| 7. | The Hogan Personality Inventory (HPI) and the Wonderlic Basic Skills Test (WBST) share several common features. They are both professionally developed tests that can be used in an employment setting when making employment decisions. Because they have been professionally developed and perfected over many years, they both have good reliability/precision and validity for their intended uses. However, they measure completely different constructs. The HPI is a personality inventory consisting of the following seven primary scales: adjustment, ambition, sociality, interpersonal sensitivity, prudence, inquisitiveness, and learning approach. In contrast, the WBST is a short measure of adult language and math skills designed to measure job readiness of teenagers and adults. |
| 8. | Student answers will vary but should include a description of what performance appraisal system they would use and detail why they selected it. The student may select one specific approach or a combination of two or more. An example of a response may be a combination of a rating and ranking system. First the supervisor must rank employees from "best" to "worst" based on specific criteria (productivity, attendance, and teamwork). Next, the supervisor must rate each employee on specific behaviors that are critical to the job role. An end rating will be combined with the ranking and provide a more accurate reflection of the employee's performance from several aspects of the position. |
| 9. | Both high- and low-fidelity assessments are performance tests that mimic or inquire about work-related tasks and activities. Where they differ is in the degree of realism. High-fidelity tests replicate job settings and tasks as realistically as possible. Examples include a flight simulator for pilots and having instructors prepare and present a lecture. Using realistic simulations is often easier, safer, and cheaper than having test takers perform in a real-life situation. In contrast, a low-fidelity test is less realistic and simulates job-related tasks using written, verbal, or visual descriptions. Low-fidelity tests tend to be cheaper and easier to develop, safer to use, and simpler to administer than high-fidelity simulations. An example is a behavioral interview. For example, a pilot might be asked to describe landing procedures or discuss in detail how he or she responded to an emergency situation. Instructors could be asked about how they have or would go about developing and presenting a lecture or be asked to describe how they dealt with a situation when a student disrupted his or her lecture. |

*(Continued)*

(Continued)

| Question | Explanation |
|---|---|
| 10. | There are many different personality assessments that can be used in an organizational setting, and their use goes back to the 1940s with the publication of Cattell's 16 Personality Factor Questionnaire. Research has shown that the 16PF has a predictive relationship with absenteeism, turnover, tenure, safety, and job performance. More recent work has focused on the "Big Five" personality factors, a five-factor model of personality consisting of extroversion (sometimes referred to as surgency), emotional stability (sometimes called neuroticism), agreeableness, conscientiousness, and openness to experience (sometimes called intellect). Earlier work such as Hunter and Hunter's (1984) meta-analysis suggested that personality was a poor predictor of job performance. However, more recent work suggests otherwise. For example, Barrick and Mount (1991) found that conscientiousness is a valid predictor of job performance in all types of jobs and that extraversion and emotional stability are valid predictors of performance for some, but not all, jobs. Also, Ones, Dilchert, Viswesvaran, and Judge (2007) stated that the Big Five predict important organizational behaviors such as job performance, leadership, work attitudes, and motivation. With this said, however, there is still disagreement in the literature concerning the degree to which faking on personality measures can influence their validity. For example, Holden (2007) found that faking can substantially reduce the validity coefficient between test and criterion. However, Ones, Viswesvaran, and Reiss in a large-scale meta-analysis found that faking did not decrease the correlation between the Big Five personality dimensions and job performance. |
| 11. | Research shows that employee theft is quite costly for employers. For example, a survey by the University of Florida showed that employees are responsible for 48.5% of retail theft costing $15 billion annually (Horan, 2003). As a result, employers are very concerned with the integrity and honesty of the employees that they hire. One method that was previously used to test employee honesty is the polygraph. The idea behind the use of the polygraph is that when an individual gives an untruthful response, he or she exhibits increases in skin resistance, pulse or heart rate, and respiration, which the machine measures and records. The level of these physiological responses is compared to the level of physiological responses to "neutral" questions (such as "Is your name John?") to determine when the person is being deceptive. However, research suggests that there is no such "lie response," and that the test results in a high rate of false positives (identifying someone as dishonest when in fact they are honest). Because of these problems, the Employee Polygraph Protection Act of 1988 prohibited the use of the polygraph in most employment settings. There are some exemptions to the law allowed, such as for those companies that provide security services and government agencies. Paper-and-pencil integrity tests are another means used to test the honesty of employees or potential employees. There are two types: overt tests and personality-oriented tests. Overt tests ask test takers to provide information about their past behavior or to respond to how they would deal with hypothetical situations. Personality-oriented tests purport to measure characteristics that are predictive of honest behavior and positive organizational citizenship using items related to the Big Five personality factors. Research shows that both types of tests do have low-to-moderate predictive validities for predicting theft and counterproductive behaviors. Critics counter, however, that these research results come from the test publishers themselves and that the studies have methodological flaws. Interestingly, a study conducted by Lilienfeld (1993) found that the tests identified monks and nuns as more dishonest than college students and incarcerated criminals. In addition, Van Iddekinge et al. (2012) more recently conducted a meta-analysis of 104 studies that investigated the evidence of validity of integrity tests based on their relationship with external criteria. When the researchers looked specifically at the results of studies that met what they termed generally accepted professional standards for validity research, they found the validity coefficients to be modest. Most of the estimates were below .2, and many approached .1. |

| Question | Explanation |
|---|---|
| 12. | The three strategies used for validity generalization—meta-analysis, synthetic validity, and transportability—are used when traditional validation studies cannot be performed on pre-employment tests. The overarching purpose of all three strategies is to generalize evidence of validity across tests. Meta-analysis looks at the results of multiple studies of a similar construct and creates a single result. The rationale is that a combination score will more accurately reflect the predictor–criterion relationship than a single test would. Synthetic validity is used when comparing personal characteristics that predict performance within job families. The rationale is if a personal characteristic has been validated to predict performance in one job, it would stand to reason that the same personal characteristic would predict performance in another similar job sharing the same components. Transportability is the most commonly used strategy in organizational settings. Transportability, most similar to synthetic validity, is used when a given test has been validated for selection of employees for a job; therefore, the same test could be used to select employees for a different, but similar job. |